THE PERE-GRINA-TION of FERNÃO MENDES PINTO

This book is part of a series ASPECTS OF PORTUGAL.

So far published: *In the wake of the Portuguese Navigators* by Michael Teague • *Camões* translated by Keith Bosley; illustrated by Lima de Freitas • *The Grand Peregrination* by Maurice Collis • *They Went to Portugal Too* by Rose Macaulay • *Trade, Inquisition and the English Nation in Portugal 1650–1690* by L. M. E. Shaw • *The Portuguese Seaborne Empire 1415–1825* by C. R. Boxer • *The Book of Disquietude* by Fernando Pessoa; translated by Paul Zenith • *The Peregrination* by Fernão Mendes Pinto; translated by Michael Lowery • *Cousin Bazilio* by Eça de Queirós; translated by Roy Campbell •*The Illustrious House of Ramires* by Eça de Queirós; translated by Anne Stevens.

THE PEREGRINATION of FERNÃO MENDES PINTO

PINTO SOLDIER OF FORTUNE, TRADER, PIRATE, AGENT, AMBASSADOR, DURING TWENTY-ONE YEARS IN ETHIOPIA, PERSIA, MALAYA, INDIA, BURMA, SIAM, COCHIN-CHINA, EAST INDIES, CHINA, JAPAN. SAILING UNCHARTED ORIENTAL SEAS, HE WAS FIVE TIMES SHIPWRECKED, THIRTEEN TIMES CAPTURED, SIXTEEN TIMES EN-SLAVED. HE MET A SAINT, REPENTED HIS WAYS, RETURNED HOME AND WROTE HIS STORY FOR HIS CHILD-REN AND FOR POSTERITY ❧ *This tale has been abridged and translated by* MICHAEL LOWERY ❧ *Introduced by* DR LUÍS SOUSA REBELO *and furnished with illustrations*

CARCANET
in association with
THE CALOUSTE GULBENKIAN FOUNDATION
and THE DISCOVERIES COMMISSION, LISBON

Published in 1992 by Carcanet Press Limited
208–212 Corn Exchange Buildings, Manchester M4 3BQ

© Translation: Michael Lowery
© Introduction: Luís de Sousa Rebelo

Editorial design by L. C. Taylor
Cover and design by Kim Taylor. Cover based on a panel of 16th
Century Persian tiles at the Metropolitan Museum of Modern Art,
New York.

This book belongs to the series *Aspects of Portugal*, published in Great
Britain by Carcanet Press in association with the Calouste Gulbenkian
Foundation & with collaboration of the Anglo-Portuguese Foundation.

Series editors: Eugenio Lisboa, Michael Schmidt, L. C. Taylor.

A CIP catalogue record for this title is available from the British Library

ISBN 0 85635 9698 6

The publisher acknowledges financial assistance from the Arts Council
of Great Britain.

Printed and bound in England by SRP Ltd, Exeter

CONTENTS

Illustrations between pages 120 and 121

ACKNOWLEDGEMENTS

The translator wishes to thank:
Maire O'Hagan, who typed the manuscript. Dr Luis de Sousa
Rebelo and L. C. Taylor who edited and prepared the text for
publication. *And to dedicate* this translation, with love,
to MARTINA

The editor wishes to thank:
Dr. Vasco Graça Moura, Director of the Comissão Nacional para
as Comemorações dos Descombrimentos Portugueses, Lisboa,
for support for this publication. Dr. José Manuel Garcia, of the
above Commission, and Dra. Maria Emelia Oliviera Machado of
the Arquivo de Arte, Fundação Calouste Gulbenkian, Lisboa,
for their expert advice and generous help in assembling the
illustrations. Michael Eltenton for his kindness and assistance in
Lisbon, and for obtaining and having specially photographed
certain items from Portugal among the illustrations. The owners
of the copyrights in various illustrations (each identified on the
appropriate page) namely:
Museu Nacional de Arte Antiga, Lisboa
Biblioteca Nacional, Lisboa
Archivo Nacional da Torre de Tombo, Lisboa
Academia das Ciéncias, Lisboa
Santa Casa da Misericórdia de Lisboa – Museu São Roque
Museu – Biblioteca Conde Castro, Guimarães, Cascais
Biblioteca Pública e Arquivo Distrital, Évora
Museu Rainha D. Leonor, Beja
Museu do Caramulo, Caramulo (Fundação Abel Lacerda)
Kodasha International, Publishers, Tokyo
Dundee Art Galleries and Museums
Biblioteca Casanatense, Roma
Metropolitan Museum of Art, New York

Saskia Jackson, Andrée Mas and Lynne Cope for typing a
complex text.

The Trustee, Director and Staff of the Calouste Gulbenkian
Foundation's UK Branch, whose grant encouraged, and whose
frequent and cheerful practical help eased, the labours of
editing this book.

INTRODUCTION

FERNÃO MENDES PINTO (c. 1510–1583) was a traveller and
an adventurer whose life illustrated the experience of many Portuguese who sailed to the East in the sixteenth century determined to make a quick fortune.

New opportunities had been created by the voyage of Vasco
da Gama. He left Lisbon in July 1497, reached Calicut on the
20th May the following year, and arrived home again in August
1499. Thus was established that sea route to India which Europeans had sought since the century began. When Albuquerque
captured Goa in 1510, a regular sailing from Lisbon began, the
carreira da Índia, a year-long round trip. The subsequent conquest of such important entrepots as Malacca in 1511 and Ormuz
in 1515 and the use of Macao from 1557 gave the Portuguese the
bases they needed to secure their presence in the Far East. Nor
had they been idle in the West – on the fishing banks off New-
foundland, in Brazil, and along the Labrador coast. However, in
the first half of the sixteenth century the potential of the 'New'
World lay in the distant future: valued commercial contacts were
with the East, where trade in spices, gems, silk, porcelain and
other luxury goods offered handsome profits. In their pursuit,
the Portuguese, with extraordinary speed, established a network
of small possessions and settlements in West and East Africa, the
Persian Gulf, the Malabar coast of India, Ceylon, the Malay
archipelago and the Moluccas; and their trade soon extended still
further – to Indo-China, Indonesia, China and Japan.

The riches of India and the Orient had a powerful attraction
for many Portuguese. Those who were dissatisfied with their
position and prospects at home, and were sufficiently ambitious
and adventurous, dreamt of leaving for the East. Fernão Mendes
Pinto was one of them. His steps, though, are not easy to trace:
for other than some items from Jesuit sources and three surviving
letters, our information has to be derived from his own book, the

Peregrinaçam (Peregrination),[1] which, as we shall see, is not the straightforward memoir it first appears to be.

We need not doubt, however, the account Mendes Pinto gives in the *Peregrination* of his boyhood and of his reasons for leaving home. Born in Montemor-o-Velho, a town about ten miles to the north of Coimbra, Fernão Mendes Pinto was the son of poor parents who could not provide their family with adequate opportunities locally. He had two brothers, António and Álvaro, who both went to India, and he mentions in one of his letters that, in 1554, he has sisters and a brother in Lisbon[2]. His own chance came when an uncle decided to take him to Lisbon, where he arrived on Saint Lucy's Day (13th December) 1521. By then, he tells us, he has spent ten or twelve years in 'abject poverty' in his father's house, which places his birth somewhere between 1509 and 1511.[3]

Pinto's uncle found him a position in the household of a lady of noble lineage, who was expected to advance him in society. After eighteen months in her service, however, some incident occurred which put his life in such danger that he had to flee the house. Running like 'a man with Death snapping at his heels', he reached the Alfama district, where he took passage on a caravel bound for nearby Setúbal. On the way the ship was attacked by French pirates, and he and his companions were robbed of every possession and left naked on a beach. The people of Santiago de Cacém looked after them generously. When at last Mendes Pinto reached his destination, he was taken into the service of Francisco de Faria. As his luck would have it, this associated him throughout his active days with a very powerful family: another member of it, Fêro de Faria, captain of the fortress of Malacca, became Pinto's principal patron in the East. The former de Faria was a nobleman of the Order of Santiago and, after Mendes Pinto had been with him four years, he recommended him to the Master of the Order, Dom Jorge, Duke of Coimbra, illegitimate son of King John II. However, the allowances given Mendes Pinto were not enough to keep him fed and clothed to the standards of the prince's household and Pinto decided to try his luck in India. He set sail from Lisbon on 11th March 1537. So began those twenty-one years in the East which closed with his return home on 22nd September 1558, miraculously alive and even quite wealthy.

His was something of a success story, but a success painfully won by many sufferings, disasters, and abrupt reversals of fortune. Never was a traveller so accident- and adventure-prone. He would climb to riches and powerful prospects, only to be struck down by some disaster – shipwreck, embroilment in a conflict, seizure by pirates – and find himself left destitute in some desolate place, imprisoned, enslaved, in risk of death . . . then to be rescued and kindly treated by some unexpected saviour, released, ransomed and finally restored to fresh opportunities under some powerful patron. This pattern, repeated through widely differing circumstances and in various exotic locations, provides the structure of the *Peregrination*.

Only in the concluding chapters is there a distinct change, important to understanding the character of the book, and therefore meriting some examination in this Introduction. By chance these last three years of Pinto's life are also the subject of a long letter. During them the dominant figure was the saintly Francis Xavier. Born in Navarra in Spain in 1506, Xavier was a fellow-student of Ignatius Loyola in Paris and became imbued with the missionary fervour of the Society of Jesus. It was King John III who first invited the new Order to establish a mission in Lisbon for those eastern lands the Portuguese had opened to western activity. Xavier received his commission from the king and arrived in Goa in 1542. His impassioned zeal, his boundless energy, resulted in mass conversions.[4] After five years in India, Xavier decided to seek souls further east. In 1547 he arrived in Malacca where Mendes Pinto met him and became his fervent admirer. When Pinto made his third trading visit to Japan in 1550, Xavier was there. Pinto was able to help Xavier in his dealings with the Daimyo of Bungo (the local warlord or largely independent 'baron') and lent him money to build a church – the first Christian church in Japan.

Xavier and Pinto left Japan together but their paths then separated. By 1552 the indefatigable Xavier decided to carry his mission of conversion to China. He reached the island of Sanchuan, not far from Macao, and was trying to get permission to enter the empire when he fell ill and, on the third of December, died. There he was buried and a small chapel was built around his grave; but when news of his death reached Goa it was decided that his remains should be brought back for final interment. They arrived, by slow stages, in 1554.

At this time Mendes Pinto came to Goa; his fortune was made and he had decided to return to Lisbon. While waiting for the *carreira da India* to take him home, he visited the Jesuit mission, was recognized as a friend and helper of Xavier and told of his death. Indeed, a few days later, he was sharing recollections of Xavier with Father Belchior,[5] Principal of the Jesuit college, when a cutter arrived from Malacca with the remains of Xavier on board. Mendes Pinto was invited to join the group that went down to the harbour to bring the coffin ashore. They went aboard, the coffin was opened, the body revealed – incorrupt.

This seeming miracle moved Pinto deeply; and he was struck by the fervour of the populace as the coffin was taken in solemn procession for the interment at the cathedral. Just then he heard that the Daimyo of Bungo, with whom Xavier and Pinto had had dealings, had sent two letters to the viceroy asking that a full mission be sent to his fiefdom, the implication being that conversions would follow.

The coincidence of these events triggered off in Mendes Pinto a spiritual crisis that led to his conversion to the Society of Jesus: he was formally received as a Novice. He had been 'called', to a country where he had a special knowledge and connections, where he had once helped the living Xavier. He resolved to finance a large part of the cost of the new mission: here was a way in which a wealthy merchant such as he was, or had been, could serve his God. The viceroy proved willing to send Mendes Pinto as his representative, with the rank of ambassador, in the hope that diplomatic and mercantile developments could be advanced, as well as the conversion of souls. The Jesuits decided these opportunities should be seized even if it meant that Mendes Pinto, as ambassador, should not yet reveal his novitiate nor wear a habit. On the first of April 1555, with credentials from the viceroy and suitable support both civil and religious, Mendes Pinto and Father Belchior set sail for Japan.

The diplomatic mission was a success but the evangelical one (as we are told in the *Peregrination*) a failure. The endemic baronial strife in Japan had reached a critical stage for the Daimyo of Bungo, who also faced civil war. At such a moment support for the Christians would give his enemies a further rallying cause against him. After spending six months in Funai, Pinto and Father Belchior with their retinues set sail for Goa and arrived there on 17th February 1557.[6]

By then three years had passed since Pinto had become a Jesuit novice. The time had come when he was due to confirm his vows. But something had happened in Japan which made him doubt his vocation. Was it that he had come to see that the conversion of Japan was an illusion; worse, had he come to doubt the adequacy of the civilization and religion that the west aimed to bring to a country of such refinement? Such seems to be the implicit allegory of the comedy of the Wooden Hands, described in the *Peregrination* (ch 223).[7] We can only speculate on the nature of the discussion between Father Belchior and Mendes Pinto which led to his being released from his vows.

In any event, matters seem to have been resolved amicably, for Pinto's relations with the Jesuits remained friendly to the end of his life. For whatever reasons, Pinto seems to have decided that he remained incorrigibly the merchant he had always been, and that the time had come to revert to his earlier plan to return home – certainly poorer, perhaps wiser. He turned down the lucrative secular appointments the viceroy offered him as a reward for the success of the secular part of his Japanese mission; instead he took letters from the viceroy attesting his services to the Crown, hoping he would get his just reward back home. He set sail for Lisbon where he arrived on 22nd September 1558. There he presented his letters to Queen Dona Catarina, Regent for her three-year old grandson, Sebastian. She listened to Pinto's tales of hardship and adventure and passed his petition to one of her officers, promising satisfaction. Time passed; nothing happened. Fernão Mendes Pinto decided to retire on what was left of the fortune he had once had from his years in the East. He married Maria Correia de Brito and bought a small property at Pragal, near Almada, on the south bank of the Tagus, opposite Lisbon; and there he remained for the rest of his days.

In retirement he wrote the *Peregrination*. We don't know when he began the book, but a letter from one Jesuit father to another in 1569 says that the work was in progress and had generated great expectations.[8] For Pinto, contrary to what some scholars suppose, was well-known before his book appeared. It was Mendes Pinto who, in a long letter dated 5th December 1554 from Malacca, addressed to the Society of Jesus in Portugal, had officially reported the death of Francis Xavier. This letter was published by the Jesuits, and had been translated into Spanish, Italian and French.[9] Pinto's reputation as a first-hand authority in Eastern affairs was thereby established. Jesuit scholars came from afar to see him at Almada and João de Barros, the leading royal chronicler of the Orient, consulted him frequently. So his book was eagerly awaited, and it appears that by 1582 (that is, twenty-four years after his return from the East) he had reached the end of it. Yet Pinto held back from publication; perhaps he was correcting and polishing the text.[10] In April 1583 his services to the Crown were at last recognized: Philip II of Spain, who had become King of Portugal the previous year, granted him a pension, an allowance in kind. Three months later, on 8th July, Mendes Pinto died.

Following the instructions laid down in his last will, his daughters delivered his manuscript to the Casa Pia das Penitentes in Lisbon. The income arising from the sales of the book were to be paid into the coffers of that charitable institution for wayward women. Yet whatever the inducement to the Catholic hierarchy, the *Peregrination*, so long in the living and in the writing, was kept waiting another thirty-one years before it was authorized for publication. The long delay between completion and publication has given rise to many speculations. These were times of religious fanaticism; with the Counter-Reformation had come a more virulent form of Inquisition. Had Pinto himself held onto his manuscript lest some unintended transgression in it should lead to fearful consequence? And was the text, after his death, altered and expurgated? We cannot dismiss such suspicions. However, we should note that the editor of the text was the royal chronicler Francisco de Andrade, whose standing and general probity reduces the likelihood of such alteration occurring undeclared. Andrade's editorial work seems to have consisted mainly of imposing some sort of order on Pinto's sprawling manuscript, which was very long, without sectional divisions, and must have read like some inchoate dream. It was Andrade who put it into its present shape, who divided the whole into 226 chapters, providing each with a descriptive title. Other divisions have since been proposed, as a means of providing a framework that would better emphasize the rhythm and inherent structure of the book.[11] However, the form that was first imposed on the text has now acquired the integrity of a literary masterpiece. Launched with the required apparatus of printing licences and ecclesiastical approvals, the *Peregrination* finally appeared in 1614. It was an instant success.

The *Peregrination* has been the subject of that close analysis which scholars can be expected to give to any work that achieves the status of both an international bestseller and a classic. The *Peregrination* takes the form of an autobiography. To the many dramatic events it narrates in parts of the world then scarcely known to Europeans, and to the sights it describes in countries then fresh to European eyes, Mendes Pinto claims to have been an eye-witness. But can this be true?

Many readers doubted it from the first. By the time the earliest English translation appeared, (in 1653, forty years after the original publication), the translator admitted that Mendes Pinto might seem to be 'indued with a most rare, and extraordinary memory' and decided to include four pages of 'authentick Authors, that in their writings have confirmed the veracity of his Narrative'.[12] He concluded his 'Apologetical Defence of Fernand Mendes Pinto, His History' as follows:

> By all this now is my Author thoroughly vindicated from all aspersions of falsehood, that may be cast upon his Work, which, were it otherwise, and meerly devil'ed, yet it is so full of variety, and of such strange, both Comick and Tragick Events, as cannot chuse but delight far more than any Romance, or other of that kind. But being accompanyed with the truth, as I have sufficiently proved, it will no doubt give all the satisfaction and content, that can be desired of the Reader.

Dorothy Osborne, in her diary, was broadly inclined to agree, though she accepted that some passages might be a trifle over-coloured:

> Tis as diverting a book of the kind as ever I read and is handsomely written. You must allow him the privilege of a traveller, and he does not abuse it. His lies are pleasant harmless ones, as lies can be, and in no great number considering the scope he has for them. There is one in Dublin now, that ne'er saw much farther, has told twice as many (I dare swear) of Ireland'[13]

All the same, many readers – not least those who lived in settled places – read the *Peregrination* with incredulity. They would doubtless have agreed with Congreve's clownish Foresight in *Love for Love*: 'Ferdinand Mendes Pinto was but a type of thee, thou liar of the first magnitude'.

It is not difficult to catch Mendes Pinto out on various inconsistencies in his own text. For example (chapter 126) he gets involved in the Tartar invasion of north China and dates it 13th July 1544. After several months a Tartar captive, he is released, he says, on 9th May 1544, two months *before* his capture. There are several such inconsistencies – mere slips perhaps. More serious (if we choose to read the *Peregrination* as history) are what look like lies. For example (chapter 132) Pinto sets sail from the Chinese coast on 'the 12th of January' (no year given) on that fateful voyage which ended with the junk being blown onto the southern end of Japan. However, Pinto also claims subsequently to have been present at the fall of Prome in Burma (chapter 155) which we know to be in 1542. By implication, then, the Japanese landfall occurred earlier in 1542; but Japanese sources give the date as 23rd September 1543.[14] Pinto says he was one of those three Portuguese 'discoverers' and his claim has been vigorously defended[15], but 17th century Portuguese sources give the names of the three Portuguese, and Pinto's name is not among them.[16] That he was an early visitor to Japan is certain; that he was the first, unlikely. The 'discovery' of Japan is not the sort of event a person is likely to 'misremember'. From this, and other evidence, we can be certain the *Peregrination* is not – if it was ever meant to be – exact history.

The temptation to fib a bit must have been especially strong if a person is writing about distant events in remote places, and we need be no more censorious than was Dorothy Osborne if Mendes Pinto improves on the truth. In any case, autobiography as a literary form is always and inherently suspect. For memory is fallible and fickle (and Mendes Pinto was recalling 21 crowded years during 26 years of retirement); and memory is a cheat, since the author of an autobiography is a participant and lacks objectivity. Indeed, the very act of remembering the past leads to its re-construction – it is only in retrospect, in our anxiety to understand, that we perceive patterns of significance, so that the wisdom that comes after the event affects our recollection of it. In biography, it has been suggested, fact should be printed blue and fiction red; under any such convention, all autobiographies would have to be printed in varying hues of purple. We have a literary term for such mixtures of fact and fiction: 'faction'. Even sophisticated, cautious contemporary autobiographies are suspect as 'factional', but how much more so those written in the 16th century! Notions of probability, of the need for hard evidence to explain the unlikely, were then weak even in courts of law; printed books, still quite rare, combined prosaic fact with embellishments, marvels, rumours and wish-fulfilments which showed the persisting influence of oral tradition, with its familiar habit of 'improving' facts during the narration of them.

Of greater interest than whether the *Peregrination* is a reliable recital of the facts of his life, is whether Mendes Pinto ever intended it to be. If so, then some of its omissions are curious. Here was a successful merchant returned from the East, yet nowhere in his long account does he dwell, as retired merchants will, on his brilliant deals and far-sighted coups. They must have occupied a good deal of his time and effort, but describing them apparently lies outside his purpose. Then again, whereas Pinto tells us about the failure of the Jesuit mission to the Daimyo of Bungo, which he financed, he gives no details at all about the mercantile and diplomatic negotiations he conducted as ambassador, with such success that the viceroy offered him lucrative appointments. Whatever purpose Mendes Pinto had in writing an autobiography it was not 'laudator temporis acti' for he is remarkably reticent about the triumphs of the central character.

One major purpose he explicitly expresses at the start of his book. He had an inner call to write – as a witness:[17]

> (God) chose to preserve my life so that I could write this rough and ready narrative which I leave as an inheritance to my children – and it is for them alone that I write it – so that they can see for themselves the hardships and dangers I knew.[18]

Such belief in the active intervention of God in the daily life of an individual was as much the normal conviction of Christians then as the supposition is among Westerners now that the course of events is attributable variously to the workings of mundane cause and effect and to blind chance. Throughout the *Peregrination* Mendes Pinto and his companions face crises with impassioned pleas to Christ on their lips; disaster is portrayed as the punishment for sin and good fortune as God's mercy, so that the book becomes not a prosaic recital of unfolding events but the account of a life lived under divine surveillance. This explains Pinto's brutal frankness about his own and his Portuguese companions' misdoings. He seeks not to excuse but to expose them, even if at times, like St Augustine, he seems to take some pleasure in his confessions. In Portuguese, the word '*peregrinaçam*' means not only 'travels' or 'adventures', which is the usual translation into English, but 'pilgrimage' too. Thus, in his title, in his introductionary declaration, and thoughout his text, Mendes Pinto expresses his moral intent. The *Peregrination*, is not a straightforward personal history, but a work of conscious construction to a given purpose. To criticize it for its shortcomings as an accurate statement of fact is to miss the point.

And Mendes Pinto uses certain story-telling tricks which confirm that he is constructing his narrative deliberately. He may have had a good, even an exceptional memory, but it beggars belief that he should have observed and known, little less invariably have remembered, the type of every vessel he sailed on or saw, singly or in a flotilla, the dimensions of walls and buildings, the number of people captured, imprisoned, found in a boat or in a pirate hold, the value of cargoes, and so on. This sort of precision is a convention, a familiar device used by story-tellers to convince listeners or readers that the story-teller must actually have been there to see for himself, and such concrete detail enables us, by the use of imagination, to construct a vivid picture, exact at significant points, for ourselves. Then again, someone trying to lie, rather than artistically to construct, would not make such frequent use of direct speech: for example, no boy of thirteen ever spoke with such clarity and composure (and at such length) as the Chinese boy in chapter 55; and if he had, Mendes Pinto could scarcely have understood his Chinese words, not to mention those of assorted Malays, Cochins, Tartars, Burmese, Japanese and the rest. Again he was using a story-teller's convention, switching from narration to direct, acted-out speech, in order to bring variety, immediacy and verisimilitude to his tale. With such narrative devices Mendes Pinto induces in the mind of the reader a state of suspension of disbelief – the hallmark of successful artistic creation.

Mendes Pinto describes the splendours and barbarities of

various remote kingdoms, and gives us information about their administrative, religious and social practices, as well as regaling us with lively incidents in their history. No doubt he acquired his knowledge from numerous sources: from his own direct observation certainly, but also from the experience of his Portuguese colleagues, from natives in the countries concerned, from traders who trafficked up and down the coast and, particularly in the case of China, from books. To this vast assemblage of material he gives coherence and vitality by imposing on it the unifying structure of autobiography, of one man's experience. Maurice Collis, an orientalist, has pointed out that much of what used to be taken in the *Peregrination* to constitute a sort of remoter 'Arabian Nights' has proved, with increasing knowledge of eastern history, to be true.[19] But truth in substance and content is not the same as truth in the detail of how Mendes says he acquired his knowledge – almost always at first-hand. That he travelled widely and saw much is certain, but in and out of this framework of personal experience he weaves what he has heard and what he has learnt second-hand, stucturing the whole into an absorbing narrative and a moral story. It is a curious compliment to his consummate skill as an artist that readers, even scholars, should still contend whether his 'rough and ready narrative', is to be read as a literal account of his life.

What expectations would readers in the early years of the 17th century have had as they turned the pages of the *Peregrination*? We shall need to consider what literary *genres* were current at the time, among which readers would have sought to place it. In more recent times, critics have tried vainly to position the book in categories familiar to them, nominating this one or that as most appropriate, and seldom agreeing. One critic, defeated by the task, called the *Peregrination* 'a crazed, dreamy, fascinating, elliptical book'.[20] The very multiplicity of suggestions indicate that it spills out of any attempt at neat definition, and mixes *genres* in a daring way to achieve a subtle cocktail of effects.

The *Peregrination*, as we have seen above, takes the ostensible form of simple autobiography, however *faux naif*. We follow in the footsteps of an author on whom is weighed an exemplary burden of experience. In twenty-one years (1537–1558) he endures the most appalling misfortunes: 'five times shipwrecked, thirteen times imprisoned, sixteen times sold,' he tells us. He is marooned and commits cannibalism to survive; he risks dangerous journeys in jungles and up rivers; he is a soldier and a pirate. After a long succession of awful misdeeds, he meets a saintly Jesuit and at last realizes the meaning of Christian life and virtue.

This confessional narrative, at the personal level, has strong elements of the genre of pilgrim literature, the more so because Mendes Pinto extends his strictures beyond the personal to the general. In the *Peregrination* we witness extreme violence committed by pagans and, worse, by Pinto's Christian companions. António de Faria, Pinto's captain, has a ferocious hatred for Islam. He pursues a Moslem pirate (who has robbed him) and in the process becomes a pirate himself, so ruthless that he robs Chinese royal tombs. His end in a storm seems a just punishment from God. Yet, at Ningpo – the Portuguese enclave near Canton – de Faria had been given a royal welcome by other Christians. This episode is a parody of the celebrated Roman triumph enacted in Goa by the viceroy, Dom João de Castro, after his victory at Diu in 1546. 'He won as a Christian and celebrated as a heathen' was the comment of Queen Dona Catarina in Lisbon when she heard the news. Mendes Pinto is implacable in his exposure of the values and practices derived from Christian feudalism. Diogo Soares, who had become a mercenary general serving the King of Burma, tries to enforce on a pretty bride a sort of seigniorial right of *ius primae noctis*. António de Faria takes advantage of the mistake of a passing junk to seize a Chinese bride and her dowry. Mendes Pinto uses pagan speakers – an old woman, a young Chinese boy – to expound the behaviour and attitudes the Christian should have displayed. Any pretension to moral superiority, such as might have seemed to justify a Christian crusade among the heathen, is wholly dispelled by the *Peregrination*.

However, the gap between virtuous declaration and vicious action is not seen by Mendes Pinto as solely a Christian problem. The kings and commoners, the great and small in every walk of life and of every religion – all go through a journey of life so transitory that it compels consideration of the question of salvation. The multitude and variety of the people who appear in the pages of the *Peregrination* (treated with a notable equality of respect) are a reminder of a common plight. The book is not so much the story of one soul's pilgrim progress as the peregrination of all humankind through the labyrinth of the world towards death. The *Peregrination* often strikes a mediaeval tone, in the contrition and repentance of wrong-doers, in divine punishment, however delayed, for evil. We hear echoes of the troubadours' familiar theme: truant behaviour and recantation – followed all too soon by renewed surrender to the temptations of life. As in other examples of pilgrim literature, it is Man, not just a particular man, who is portrayed as plagued by a recurrent lust for evil.

The contrast between pious resolution and brutal reality is the stuff not only of pilgrim literature but, in a different mood, of comedy and the picaresque. It opens the way for satire and for other forms of irony. Pinto, the narrator, telling his adventures in a rough and ready style, is a typical anti-hero, an unscrupulous survivor, who invariably praises his master, António de Faria, despite de Faria's atrocious deeds. Such bizarre harmony in the relationship of master and servant is one of the main characteristics of picaresque literature. Pinto learns the ways of the world from António de Faria with a naivety and candid reverence which are those of a real-life *picaro*. Small wonder that in 17th century Spain, readers of Pinto's work in the Castilian version (1620), made by Francisco Maldonado, accepted it as a picaresque novel.

Recently Rebecca Catz has proposed a more comprehensive reading of the *Peregrination*. She detects in the narrator four different *personae*, each of whom speaks with a distinguishable voice. The voice of the *picaro* is one of these; second is the voice of the good man, the stoic who wins our confidence; third, the voice of the *ingénu* or naif, 'who wins our sympathy by presenting an image of himself as an innocent man'; and finally there is the voice of the hero, the defender of the faith, who bravely combats or exposes evil. All these voices join together to comprise a text which, she believes, is intended as a corrosive satire of the Portuguese empire and its ideals for the expansion of the faith.[21]

No one will dispute that the *Peregrination* gives a sharply critical account of the Portuguese administration in the East and of the greed of the people who ventured into those regions. With Mendes Pinto we descend into the dark shadows cast by the Portuguese discoveries, whose blaze was Camões' subject in his epic poem *The Lusiads* (1572). Certainly, Mendes Pinto reveals a sad state of affairs in the Portuguese possessions, but objections have to be raised to the idea that the whole complex work is satirical.[22] The formal and structural coherence of satire as a genre is not maintained in the text, which digresses into other modes, covers an immense variety of episodes, and is governed by religious and moral ideas that often submerge any ironical aspect in Pinto's writing.

It would be to miss the obvious not to see the *Peregrination* as a notable exemplar among books of travel and adventure – the first one to be set on the seaboard of the Orient, the first to introduce in Western literature stories of eastern pirates. Pinto knew what his readers were likely to look for in a work of this kind. The long European tradition of travel literature went back to the 13th century. The *Travels* of Marco Polo (who spent as many years in the East as did Mendes Pinto) were written probably in 1298/9. The Polos, father and son, had taken the Silk Road, which dated from the days of the Romans, to explore the secrets of China. In 1330, Fr. Odoric of Pardenone produced an account of his travels from 1316 to 1330. Odoric went through Iran to reach India, and thence travelled on to Ceylon and to Canton in China. By 1400 the *Travels of Sir John Mandeville* were available in every major European language.

Both Marco Polo and Mandeville provide information about China and speak of Prester John – the priest king of a perfect Christian state, situated no one knew quite where. Mandeville speculated upon an earthly paradise in some remote corner of the world beyond the empire of China, and Marco Polo had reported some advanced civilization there called 'Cipangu' – Japan. Mendes Pinto, in continuation, claims to have been one of three Portuguese who found this long-sought realm. Gradually the search for some generalized earthly paradise was replaced in travel literature by the search for the kingdom of Prester John. The Portuguese nurtured the idea that he might become an ally of the West in their ardent struggle against Islam. In the 16th century, they believed they had found Prester John in the person of the Emperor of (Christian) Ethiopia. Literature then returned to the search for a remoter utopia.

The *Peregrination*, indeed, in presenting China (and, to a less fulsome degree, Japan) as a society better than any known in the

West, or at the least capable of progress to a degree of perfection unattainable in the West, shared the aims of Thomas More's classic *Utopia* (1516), a book which had launched a literary genre.

We can trace four utopian characteristics in Pinto's work. The first requires the identification of the perfect place. Plato, to make his proposals for a better society more convincing, had invented the myth of Atlantis, where perfection had once existed. The island of Utopia, as described to Thomas More by the Portuguese sailor, Raphael Hythloday, was located somewhere in the southern hemisphere, but More carelessly forgot to ask exactly where. In choosing the real if remote country of China, Pinto rendered his utopia more substantial, sketching an existing society, its perfections humanly attainable, rather than some ideal in a drowned or lost space.

A second characteristic of the utopian genre is that the ideal society should be contrasted, directly or by implication, with a corrupt society – the Celestial City set against the Condemned City. In the *Peregrination* China is not simply a country of wonders and prodigies, as it was for Marco Polo, but a painful measure to set against the vicious character of the society created by merchants, soldiers, pirates and others in the East, under cover of their protestations of religious principle. The Chinese, says Pinto, represented the world upside down, to show that visible material things conceal what really matters, and distract the soul from the path of virtue. The wickedness of human beings is such that the Chinese excluded Incarnation from their idea of divinity, for divine nature had to be 'free from human miseries and indifferent to worldly treasures'.[23]

The third characteristic of a utopian narrative is the depiction of the economic, social and administrative organization of the model society. Pinto's certain knowledge of China did not extend beyond the islands off the Chinese coast and ports of the mainland – even his visit to Peking is disputed by scholars[24]; but he gives us detailed descriptions of villages, towns and cities throughout the empire. He tells us about the sweetness of the air and the richness of the soil, but most of the time he centres his attention on the works of man and the products of human intelligence. The plan of the cities, the order of the streets, the markets, the number of bridges and waterways, the size and number of walls that encircle the living area – all are minutely described. By means of cumulative detail and enumeration – devices used also by Plato in his description of Atlantis – Mendes Pinto creates the effect of magnitude and harmony in his imposing model. He remarks with pleasure that the government was keen on promoting simple labouring jobs, and compelled people to work. The obligation (a golden rule in More's *Utopia*) accounted, in Pinto's opinion, for the prosperity of China.

The organization of a just, a 'welfare' society is a fourth characteristic common to utopias. Mendes Pinto describes Chinese hostels for the poor and for prostitutes and various other elements of a 'welfare state'. As for justice, he portrays a Chinese court (in chapter 103), where the ideal quality of the justice dispensed was reflected in the ceremonies accompanying the trial. This court is a construct of Pinto's imagination. His description, though, has certain affinities with the cult of the Holy Ghost, introduced to Portugal by the Franciscans, and widespread at the time, especially in rural communities. A feature of this cult was the enthronement of a child as ruler of the world in its last days, a brief reign of messianic promise. In Pinto's Chinese court the proceedings are ceremonially regulated by two beautiful boys, one representing Justice, the other Mercy – the two virtues that should be used in governance over us through all the trials of our lives.[25]

In his descriptions of China Pinto drew upon the records of other Portuguese travellers, especially upon the *Tractado em que se cõtam por estẽso as cousas da China* (Évora, 1569–70) – without acknowledgement. Other travellers have also projected their hopes into the vision of a perfect society, whether in China or, later, in paradises described as existing in remote parts of South America. In reality, of course, Chinese prosperity was relative (to that of other Eastern societies), its social needs numerous, and justice under the Ming dynasty far from exemplary. The praise of Galeote Pereira, Gaspar da Cruz, Mendes Pinto and others is based on fragile understanding and reflects a purpose beyond mere reportage.[26]

The effective representation of societies remote and critically different from those of Europe presented technical problems. The new world had to be depicted through a repertoire of images and expectations familiar to readers in the old. Marco Polo had faced the same problem. When he described the palace of Kublai Khan, he used the literary devices and *topoi* common in mediaeval literature, creating a magnificence that tells us more about mediaeval visions of paradise than about the actual qualities of the building.[27] Similar literary strategies were used by Mendes Pinto in the *Peregrination*. When he wants to extol the fertility of Japanese soil, he speaks of the quality of the grapes growing there. In fact there were none: but what reader bred in a Mediterranean culture would consider a country fertile if vines were not abundant?

Mendes Pinto found among the Japanese, especially at the court of the Daimyo of Bungo, a receptiveness to the truths of Christianity, as well as a decorum, superior to that of born Christians.[28] The question then arose whether Christians were fit to convert them. Similar doubts had been expressed by Mandeville, who declared that Christians did not deserve to recover the Holy Land in view of their wickedness. Near the end of this book, in chapter 223, Mendes Pinto describes the little play of the Wooden Hands, extemporized by the Daimyo's daughter and her attendants at the court of Bungo. Maurice Collis sees this play as a representation of the inferiority of Christian civilization and culture by comparison with Japanese refinement; but Pinto's acute discomfiture during the performance suggests further meanings. The morality play served as a reminder of the gap between his own brute behaviour as a trader (and worse) and the Christians' pretensions as missionaries, between deed and creed. The play marks the end of that Christian mission.

For greed had perverted Christians in the East, and the Portuguese had entangled themselves in hopeless paradox and contradiction in their twin ambitions of 'the Faith and the Empire' (to use one of Camões ringing slogans in *The Lusiads*). The *Peregrination* revealed the reality – 'Catholic robbery and a religious free market' as a critic has put it.[29] Violence was endemic in the East. Pinto describes in horrifying detail the ferocious wars waged by Asian kings and their interminable, unforgiving quarrels that caused such suffering to ordinary people, and Pinto shows the Christians as no better than anyone else. They had simply compounded the region's confusions.

The tensions and contradictions arising in the Portuguese mind as a consequence of their presence in the East are poignantly exemplified in the actions of Francis Xavier. Here was a man of the highest personal virtue, of unflinching courage and principle – and yet, in a moment of crisis, he makes a curious compromise. He was in Malacca, in 1547, as Pinto was, when Malacca was under imminent threat from an Achin fleet. The mercenary Diogo Soares (whose villainy Pinto describes elsewhere) arrived with two ships in nearby waters. It was Xavier who negotiated with the Captain of Malacca to waive the normal customs duties on Soares' trading merchandise, in return for his military aid. The Achin were duly defeated. Ironically, some years later, the next Captain of Malacca refused to allow a similar customs exemption, despite the viceroy's letter of instruction, on a trading vessel on which Xavier was being taken to China. Xavier was delayed many months, had to sail with Chinese traders, was deposited on San-chuan island and died there, before he could enter the land he believed (as did Pinto) more suited than any other to hear the Christian message.

The death of Xavier deeply affected Mendes Pinto. This was a man like no other Pinto had ever met, least of all in the Babylon of the Portuguese in the East. Xavier was for him the embodiment of Christian virtue, surrounded by the aura of sainthood. Yet Xavier's hopes of saving Chinese souls had been denied. When Pinto met Xavier in Japan, he had been able to help him, being by then something of an expert on the country, and rich besides. Xavier made a promising start (though the depth of his listeners' understanding, given linguistic barriers, may be doubted: Christianity was first received in both Japan and China as a form of Buddhism).[30] Yet when Pinto attempted to have Xavier's work in Japan continued that attempt also failed. The Celestial City was certainly not to be achieved in this world. No wonder the *Peregrination* ended on a melancholy note, and no wonder a critical moral current runs strongly beneath the ceaseless flood of events.

Yet however central the elements of pilgrim literature and utopian literature in the *Peregrination*, the book also evokes echoes of older forms of narrative, made famous by Herodotus in his *Histories* and by the authors of the Byzantine novel. The description of unfamiliar customs and social practices, and of the myths, legends and religious ideas of the peoples visited by the narrator in his travels; the reporting of his conversations with priests, philosophers and wise men in alien lands; the story of wars and palace intrigues, set in a historical framework – all these are narrative features Pinto has in common with Herodotus. Ethnic and historical interests combine in both writers with acute observation and a critical mind that does not exclude the accounts given by others. They both show their inclination to digress and comment on the events reported.

On the other hand, the particular themes developed by Pinto in his Asian stories – incest, piracy, enslavement, love, betrayal and revenge – were those that had characterized the Byzantine novel. Reasonably well-known to the educated élite of Western Europe in the sixteenth century was the *Ethiopica* by Heliodorus.[31] In this prodigious work of fiction such themes are woven into narrative patterns which reveal remarkable similarities with those in the *Peregrination*. The plethora of events, and dramatic reversals of fortune, ruled whether by chance or by Providence, show that Pinto was well aware of the great tradition of the Byzantine novel. Pinto richly satisfied those appetites in readers that had once been fed, before printing, by the traditional, oral teller of tales.

Pinto's 'rough and ready' style serves admirably the different modes of his text. With it, he can engage the attention of his reader quickly and can work effectively on the emotions;[32] he can mingle the heroic with the ironic, move nimbly from the satirical to the devotional, or invent a form of speech that imitates or evokes the style of oriental languages (as they are perceived by the untutored western ear) and so can conjure up for his reader the flavour of remote cultures and exotic civilizations.

These literary qualities and their broad appeal to a wide public made the *Peregrination* a best-seller both at home and outside Portugal. The Spanish translation appeared in 1620 and was reprinted four times from 1627 to 1664. In the seventeenth century alone, according to Maurice Collis, the *Peregrination* ran to nineteen editions in six languages: two Portuguese editions, seven Spanish, three French, two Dutch, two German and three English. Most educated people in Europe had read it by 1700, and by then Pinto's name was as well-known as that of Cervantes.[33]

These early translations were either inaccurate or abridged

versions (or both) of the original. It was not until 1989 that the first complete and scholarly edition of the whole work appeared in English, the admirable achievement of Rebecca Catz.[34] Two years later Robert Viale similarly produced the first scholarly and complete translation into French.[35] These editions will remain the definitive texts in English and French. It is pleasant to record that the sales of both editions have been good – a tribute to the translators and to Mendes Pinto.

But the general reader may well be daunted by the dimensions of these new editions. Rebecca Catz runs to 663 pages – plus a 46 page introductory section – and these are large pages bearing twice the number of words as a page of the volume in hand. In sum, printed to the same dimensions, the Catz edition is four times as long as this one. Viale's edition has 808 pages. The *Peregrination* is a massive, discursive work, and the proper scholarly apparatus adds yet further to the weight of the text itself.

Not all readers will want to make the sort of investment these complete editions require. For this present edition Michael Lowery had made a skilful abridgement of the original, cutting some chapters, condensing others, reducing the original by a half. The chapter numbers of the original have been retained, so that readers can see where the main cuts occur, and connecting summaries have been inserted to bridge the gaps, so that the reader can journey continuously through the text. This Introduction, and the brief historical note following it, should help the reader put the *Peregrination* into context; beyond this, no explanatory material has been included. The intentions of the author are clear enough even if we are not told the exact value of a *cruzado* at this moment in our own currency, or the metric equivalent of a measurement given in palms, or the nature of the different sorts of vessels referred to, or numerous other matters of considerable interest, but chiefly to scholars. Michael Lowery has achieved an accurate version in an English style similar to Mendes Pinto's 'rough and ready' original. The result is a vividly readable text and an un-put-downable book. It may well whet the appetite of some readers for a closer, detailed examination of the *Peregrination* in full, and these have the new complete versions, fully annotated, to resort to.

The aim of this edition has been to make accessible to the general reader the classic creation of a writer who survived a bizarre life in regions then fresh to the West, a book that must surely rank among the most extraordinary tales of travel and adventure (and, as we have seen, of much more besides) that have ever been written.

Luís de Sousa Rebelo
King's College, London

NOTES

1. All the documentation on Fernão Mendes Pinto has been collected by Rebecca Catz, *Cartas de Fernão Mendes Pinto e outros documentos*, Lisbon: Biblioteca Nacional – Editorial Presença, 1983.
2. Rebecca Catz, *Cartas*, *p. 14*.
3. *Maurice Collis, The Grand Peregrination*. Manchester, Carcanet Press 1990 p. 294.
4. M. N. Pearson, *The New Cambridge History of India*, *The Portuguese in India*. Cambridge University Press, Cambridge, 1987, p. 118.
5. The name given throughout the *Peregrinaçam* by Fernão Mendes Pinto to the Provincial of the Jesuits in Goa is Father Belchior Nunes. But in all the documentation we possess, his name appears as Melchior Nunes Barreto – a point hitherto unnoticed by critics and commentators.
6. See Maurice Collis, *The Grand Peregrination*, p. 282.
7. Maurice Collis, *op. cit.*, p. 277.
8. Rebecca Catz, *Cartas*, p. 110.
9. Catz, *Cartas*, Document no. 6, pp. 39–45.
10. Rebecca Catz, *Cartas*, p. 123.
11. Review by Jonathan D. Spence, *The Travels of Fernão Mendes Pinto*, introduction and translation by Rebecca Catz, *The New York Review of Books*, April 12, 1990, pp. 38–40. Jonathan D. Spence suggests ten narrative blocks to accentuate the recurrent pattern of the narrative.
12. Henry Cogan, *The Voyage and Adventures of Fernand Mendes Pinto, Done into English by H. C. Gent* 1653. Facsimile edition by Dawsons of Pall Mall 1969.
13. Maurice Collis, *op. cit.*, p. 298.
14. ed. John Whitney Hall, *Cambridge History of Japan vol 4* C.U.P. 1991. See ch 7 by Jurgis Elisones, footnote p 302.
15. Notably by Professor Armando Cortesão, *Portugaliae Monumenta Cartographica* 5:171.

16. Such as Diogo do Couto 1597, António Galvão 1563, and João Rodrigues 1633. See Charles Ralph Boxer, *The Christian Century in Japan 1549–1650*, Univ. of California Press 1951.

17. Rebecca D. Catz, introduction, *The Travels of Mendes Pinto*, The University of Chicago Press, Chicago and London, 1989, p. xxv. See also Thomas R. Hart, 'Style and Substance in the *Peregrination*', *Portuguese Studies*. Ed. by Department of Portuguese, King's College, London, Modern Humanities Research Association, 2, 1986, p. 49.

18. Fernão Mendes Pinto, *Peregrination*, chapter I.

19. Maurice Collis, *op. cit.*, pp. 300–302.

20. Jonathan D. Spence in the review quoted in note 13. Erilde Mellilo Reali, 'Una "Peregrinação" inconclusa'. *Quaderni Portoghesi*, Pisa, 4 (Autumn 1978), pp. 101–133, considers the *Peregrination* to be outside any literary genre.

21. Rebecca Catz, introduction to *The Travels of Fernão Mendes Pinto*, Chicago and London, 1989, pp xxxix–xliv, *A Sátira social de Fernão Mendes Pinto*, Lisbon: Prelo Editora, 1978; *Fernão Mendes Pinto – Sátira e anti-cruzada na Peregrinação*, Lisbon: Biblioteca Breve, Icalpe, 1981.

22. Patrick O'Brian in his review of Rebecca Catz's *Travels of Fernão Mendes Pinto*: 'Prodigies', *London Review of Books*, 10 May 1990.

23. Fernão Mendes Pinto, *Peregrinação*, chapter 48.

24. Charles Ralph Boxer (editor) *South China in the Sixteenth Century*, London: Hakluyt Society, 1953.

25. Luís de Sousa Rebelo, 'The search for an ideal kingdom: Portuguese voyages in the sixteenth century', *PEN International. The Silk road: a Symposium on Travel Literature*, vol. xli, 1., 1991, pp. 56–60.

26. C. R. Boxer, *South China in the Sixteenth Century*, p. xxx.

27. Marco Polo, *Il Milione*, chapter lxix.

28. Charles Ralph Boxer, *The Christian Century in Japan, 1549–1650*.

29. Erilde Reali, '*Una "Peregrinação" inconclusa*', *Quaderni Portoghesi*, no. 4, 1978, p. 126.

30. ed. John Whitney Hall *op. cit.* pp. 307–308. Jurgis Elisones writes: 'Xavier's principal interpreter Yajirō gave a later account which reveals that the Trinity was equated with Mahavairocana, the central Buddha of the Shingo sect of

Buddhism (Dainichi in Japanese) shown in the iconography with other Buddhas surrounding him. The confusion was made easier by Xavier having come from India, the classical homeland of Buddhism'.

31. Tomas Hägg, *The Novel in Antiquity*, Oxford: Basil Blackwell, 1983, pp. 192–210.
32. Thomas R. Hart, 'Style and Substance in the *Peregrination*', *Portuguese Studies*. Ed. by Department of Portuguese, King's College, London, Modern Humanities Research Association, 2, 1986, pp. 49–55.
33. Rebecca Catz, 'A Note on Previous Translations of the *Peregrinação*,' *Portuguese Studies*. Ed. by the Department of Portuguese, King's College, London, Modern Humanities Research Association, 4, 1988, p. 71.
34. See note no. 17. See the review of Rebecca Catz's work by J. S. Cummins 'The Pirate and the Saint', *Times Literary Supplement*, March 9, 1990, p. 262.
35. Robert Viale, *Pérégrination de Fernão Mendes Pinto*, Editions de la Différence, Paris, 1991.

Title pages of first edition, 1614; and of first English edition, 1653

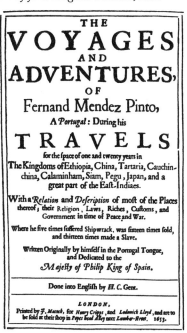

BACKGROUND NOTE AND MAPS

A surprising feature of the *Peregrination* is the unrelenting hostility displayed by Fernão Mendes Pinto towards Islam, (though not to all individual Muslims) for he usually showed curiosity and tolerance to the cultures and religions he encountered.

The three great monotheistic religions that arose in the 'Middle East' had intertwining roots: Christianity embraced the Jewish prophets as part of an 'Old Testament' revealed before the coming of Jesus; Islam recognized the insights of Jewish leaders and prophets, culminating in Jesus, as preparatory to the new revelation bestowed on Mohammed. Such accommodation did not prove endearing to those who adhered to an earlier faith as the ultimate revelation of the one and only God, and contention became conflict when the salvation of the benighted was held to justify the use of force.

For Christians, the threat from Islam achieved two periods of particular intensity: first, from the middle of the seventh to the middle of the eighth century; second, from early in the fifteenth to late in the seventeenth century. For Muslims, in turn, the Christian threat was acute if intermittent during the intervening period of the Crusades.

Portugal was involved with Islam with a directness not experienced by the countries of northern Europe in both periods of Muslim expansion. From the mid-seventh century, militant Arabs swept through the regions to the east of the Mediterranean, along the northern shores of Africa and through the whole Iberian peninsula to the Pyrennees. The small regions that were later to constitute 'Portugal' came under Islamic control for some five centuries. By their victories around the Mediterranean basin, the Muslims severed the tenuous overland routes (such as the Roman silk road to China) between the Christianized west of Europe and India, China and the Orient, and with the hinterland of Africa. Throughout those areas, Islamic penetration and conversion continued without Christian challenge, and earlier Christianity survived only in such fastnesses, remote to Europeans, as

Ethiopia and South India. The very existence of early Christian countries passed into myth, especially the myth of 'Prester John', the priest-king of a fabulously rich Christian kingdom who, when found, would help Christians in their battles with the Muslims. The Muslim barrier to India, China and Africa was occasionally penetrated by travellers, like Marco Polo and his son, but the overland trade was entirely monopolized by Muslims (and their chosen Christian intermediaries): from Asia in silk, jewels and spices; from Africa, in gold and slaves – in such small quantities as caravans to distant places could carry, and at prices which scarcity and monopoly maintained. Such trade was a source of riches and strength to the Muslim world.

The reconquest by the Christians of what became 'Portugal' took a century and a half, from the victory at Ourique in 1139 to the definitive recognition of Portuguese borders (the oldest in Europe) at the Treaty of Alcanices in 1297. A century later the Portuguese carried the war against the Moors into North Africa and in 1415 seized the important fortress of Ceuta. Intermittently they held Tangier, and began to explore the coastline further west and south, periodically raiding inland and taking pickings from a trade dominated by Muslim caravans. It was held by most contemporary cosmographers, following Ptolemy, that this coastline soon turned west again, and then north, enclosing the Atlantic like a lake. The Portuguese knew from Arab sources that the coast continued south for some distance, and they began to wonder whether, yet further south, the Atlantic and the Indian Oceans might meet. If that proved to be so, Christian ships should be able to sail to India, outflanking the Muslim blockade of the overland routes, and breaking the Muslim monopoly on trade and conversion. The Portuguese developed appropriate ships and navigational techniques, first to inch down the African coast, then to progress by great arcs until in 1487, Bartolomeu Dias reached what proved to be the last cape of the vast continent and, rounding it, called it 'Boa Esperança', for the Good Hope it offered of a sea-route to the East.

During the century of Portuguese nautical activity, the principal concern of Christian Spain remained the expulsion of the Moors. Not until 1492 was the Islamic kingdom of Granada at last defeated. In the same year, the Spanish queen was persuaded by the deluded Columbus that the eastern extremities of Asia

Sketch map illustrating the travels of FERNÃO MENDES PINTO

were not far off – the shortest route lay west. The Portuguese, who knew better, persisted with the African route, and six years later, in 1498, Vasco da Gama reached India itself. But by the time the Moors had at last been cleared from Iberia, and the Muslim barrier to the East had been outflanked by sea, a new champion of Islam had arisen – the Ottoman Turk. For three centuries the Christian west was again under threat, this time on its eastern borders. Already in the first half of the 15th century the Turks occupied the Balkans; in 1453 they captured Constantinople itself; soon, the whole of the once-great Christian empire of Byzantium was theirs. Nor was there any sign of their ambitions ending there.

With the arrival of the Portuguese in the East a new arena for the conflict between Islam and Christianity was opened. From

xxxvi

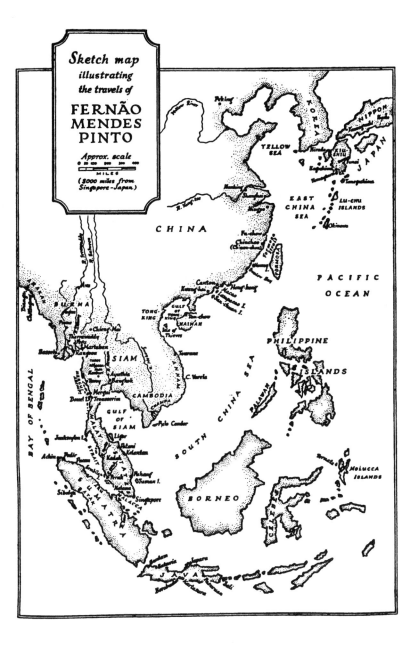

Sketch map
*illustrating
the travels of*
**FERNÃO
MENDES
PINTO**

Approx. scale

MILES
*(3000 miles from
Singapore–Japan.)*

1509 the Turks over-ran Arabia and Syria, occupied Persia (1514) and Egypt (1517) and threatened the fragile Portuguese trade. Led by Albuquerque, the Portuguese established fortified bases at Moçambique and then at Diu (1509), Goa (1510) and Malacca (1511) and Ormuz (1515), and from about 1513 they made effective contact with 'Prester John' in the lost kingdom of Ethiopia.

Albuquerque's last expedition pursued his ultimate aim – to capture Mecca and to ransom it for Jerusalem.

With their position in the Persian Gulf and west India relatively secure, the Portuguese rapidly established trading settlements throughout the Orient – in South India, Ceylon, Malaya, the Moluccas, and the East Indies; in the 1520s an unofficial trade was established with China, in 1543 with Japan. The Muslim trade monopoly was thoroughly broached. And wherever the Portuguese traded, the missionaries soon followed, especially after 1540 when the recently-formed Jesuit order was invited to establish a headquarters in Lisbon for a new mission overseas. Portuguese and Christian progress in the Orient was not repeated in Europe. The bitter struggles of Catholic and Protestant (in succession to the schism between Rome and Byzantium) weakened Christendom, and the Islamic cause prospered. By 1541 the Turks had over-run Hungary and occupied Buda. The young Portuguese king, Sebastian, led a crusade against the Moors in North Africa and was disastrously defeated at Alcacer-Quibir in 1578. During the next hundred years the Turks frequently invaded Poland, Russia and Austria, and in 1683 besieged Vienna itself.

To understand Mendes Pinto's hostility to Islam we need to place him in this historical context. If we focus on a period from twenty years before to twenty years after his birth (circa 1510) as being formative, then we should notice that, during that forty year period, the Moors ruled – as they had done for some 800 years – in neighbouring south Spain; the Portuguese had managed, after centuries of Muslim exclusion, to find a route to India by sea and had then swarmed further east; the Turks had occupied Persia and Egypt and battled with the Portuguese to cut their tenuous routes and destroy their nascent trade; the Portuguese had come into conflict with Muslim princes in the Far East and had seized and fortified Malacca as an earnest of their future intrusive intentions. In short, Mendes Pinto was born and grew up in combative times. As a young man, before he could land in Goa, he became involved in a sea-battle with a Turkish flotilla, was captured and sold as a slave; his first journey took him to Gil Eitor where he met the mother of 'Prester John', Emperor of Ethiopia, an ally in resistance to the Grand Turk. Pinto's many voyages east of Malacca brought him into hostile contact with Muslim kingdoms, his bloody adventures as a buccaneer reached their peak in the pursuit of Koja Hassan, a Muslim pirate. He returned home to witness the last, a Portuguese, crusade, and to suffer the effects of its ruin in the sands of Morocco.

Small wonder then that Mendes Pinto and his Portuguese contemporaries were aware of the long and savage rivalry of Christianity and Islam. The other religions they encountered in the East – 'pagan', Hindu, Buddhist, Shinto, Confucian – did not display the monotheistic exclusivity which Christianity and Islam shared, nor their vehement absolutism. In Mendes Pinto's day, Islam and Christianity were in conflict across the civilized world (the Americas being then of slight importance), and even in Europe the outcome of the struggle was much less certain than it has since seemed.

❦ THE PEREGRINATION ❦

1 : *My boyhood and youth in Portugal.*

FROM TIME TO TIME WHEN I CALL TO MIND THE GREAT MISFORTUNES and countless hardships that have befallen me, beginning in my earliest years and continuing throughout the greater – and best – part of my life, I think I have every good reason to complain about Lady Fortune, who seems to have considered it her particular responsibility to persecute and abuse me, as if that should be a cause of fame and glory to her name.

This fickle lady was not content with allotting me a station in my native land where I had to endure poverty and degradation and not a little danger from the day I was born, but also saw fit to lead me away to the Orient where, instead of the relief from my hardships that I sought there, I found that the hardships and dangers only increased with the passing years.

On the other hand, when I consider that God always chose to rescue me from the midst of all these dangers, I think that rather than complain about evils suffered in the past I have good reason to give Him thanks for my present blessings.

He chose to preserve my life so that I could write this rough and ready narrative which I leave as an inheritance to my children – and it is for them alone that I write it – so they can see for themselves the hardships and dangers I knew when I was thirteen times a prisoner and sixteen times sold as a slave during my twenty-one years travelling around India, Ethiopia, Arabia, China, Tartary, Macassar, Sumatra and dozens of other places along that archipelago on the eastern edges of Asia that the Oriental geographers call 'the eyelash of the world'.

All these adventures I hope to describe in detail and at length in the following pages.

And my readers should find in my story good reason not to become so discouraged by life's hardships that they neglect their Christian duties – because there is no hardship, however great, that human nature cannot cope with when aided by divine grace.

They should also find reason to join with me in giving thanks to Almighty God, Who saw fit to use me of His infinite mercy in spite of all my sins – because I understand now, and readily confess to it, that all the misfortunes I suffered were born of my

1

sinfulness, while out of God's infinite mercy were born the strength and spirit to overcome those misfortunes and escape from them with my life.

Now, I'll take my early life here in Portugal as the starting point of my travels.

Let me tell you that I was born in the town of Montemor-o-Velho and spent my first ten or twelve years living in degradation and poverty in my father's house. It was then that one of my uncles, who was keen for me to improve my lot in life I suppose, brought me to Lisbon and arranged a place for me in the household of a lady of fairly noble lineage. Some of this lady's relatives were famous enough, and my uncle hoped that between the lady herself and her famous relatives I would be able to achieve the advancement that he had in mind for me.

I entered into this lady's service at the time of the ceremony of the Breaking of the Shields, when all of Lisbon was deep in mourning for King Dom Manuel, of glorious memory. That would be St Lucy's Day, December 13th, 1521. I recall that date quite clearly but I can't remember anything earlier than that.

My uncle's scheme didn't work out as he had planned – rather the opposite! After about eighteen months in this lady's service something happened that put my life in such jeopardy that I had to get out of the house at a moment's notice and make myself scarce as quickly as possible. I ran off down the street so beside myself with fear that I didn't know nor care where I was running to, like a man with Death snapping at his heels, ready to swallow him up at every step he takes.

I ended up down at the Pedra quay where an Alfama caravel was anchored, waiting to carry a nobleman's horse and clothes across to Setúbal. King John III, blessed be his name, was holding court in Setúbal at the time, taking refuge there from the plague that was breaking out in many parts of the kingdom. Anyway, I got myself aboard this caravel, and it weighed anchor soon afterwards.

The following morning we were off Sesimbra when we were overhauled by French corsairs. They came alongside and fifteen or twenty pirates boarded and took control of the ship without the least resistance from us.

The pirates helped themselves to all the goods on board (worth more than 6000 cruzados) and then sent the ship to the bottom. Seventeen of us were spared drowning but we were tied hand-and-foot and taken aboard the pirate ship. They told us that we would be sold as slaves in Larache where they were bound with a cargo of arms to sell to the Moors.

We sailed on towards Larache for the next thirteen days; our only rations were the whippings and beatings that the pirates gave us. At sunset on the thirteenth day the pirates' good fortune brought them within sight of a sail which they followed throughout the night by keeping a track of her wake (they were old hands at such tricks of the trade). At daybreak the pirates overhauled the vessel before her watch was alerted and fired three rounds of cannon-shot into her. They pulled alongside with a shuddering jolt, and although the ship's crew offered some resistance it wasn't enough to stop the pirates boarding and capturing the ship, leaving six Portuguese and ten or twelve slaves dead.

This ship was a handsome carrack belonging to one Silvestre Godinho, a merchant from Vila do Conde; it was being used by other merchants from Lisbon to carry a large cargo of sugar and slaves from São Tomé. These unfortunate merchants, bewailing their bad luck, valued the cargo at 40,000 cruzados.

As soon as the pirates realized the value of their prize they changed their plans and turned back for France, bringing some of their prisoners with them to help them handle the captured vessel. The rest of us were left ashore one night at Melides. We didn't have a shoe or a stitch of clothing between us, although some of us were covered with wounds from all the beatings we had received.

The next day we made our way, naked as we stood, to Santiago do Cacém where the local people generously looked after us, especially one lady, Dona Beatriz, daughter of the Count of Vilanova and wife of Alonso Perez Pantoja, the esteemed mayor of Santiago do Cacém.

As the sick and wounded recovered one by one, each man went on his way, seeking a sure cure-all for his life's troubles; and I, poor wretch that I am, made my way to Setúbal along with six or seven others as wretched as myself.

In Setúbal I chanced to be recruited into the service of Francisco de Faria, a nobleman in the Order of Santiago. I stayed with him for four years and he was pleased enough with me to recommend me to the Master of the Order himself, whom I served a further year-and-a-half.

But the allowance that was usually paid in a great lord's household at that time was scarcely enough to keep a man properly fed and clothed – so I decided to take ship for the colonies in India. I set out with little optimism but ready to accept whatever fortune, be it good or otherwise, might befall me.

2 : I take leave of Portugal. The voyage to India.

SO IT WAS THAT ON THE ELEVENTH DAY OF MARCH, IN THE YEAR OF Our Lord 1537, I took my leave of Portugal aboard a carrack bound for India, one in a fleet of five ships.

There was no overall commander for the fleet, the five individual captains just worked together. The captains and their vessels were as follows: Dom Pedro da Silva, nicknamed The Rooster, was in command of the *Rainha*. Dom Pedro was the son of the Lord High Admiral Vasco da Gama and had brought his father's remains back from India in the *Rainha* in 1524. King John III, who was in Lisbon at the time, had ordered da Gama's body to be received with the greatest pomp and ceremony that were ever accorded someone who was not a member of the royal family. The *São Roque* was captained by Dom Fernando de Lima, the son of the mayor of Guimarães, Diogo Lopez de Lima; Dom Fernando died the following year while he was in command of the fort at Ormuz. His cousin Jorge de Lima, who was going out to take over the command at Chaul, was the captain of the *Santa Barbara*. The *Galega*, the ship in which Pêro Lopez de Sousa was to perish later, was captained by Martim de Freitas, a native of Madeira who was killed along with thirty-five companions in Damao the following year. Finally, ordinary sea-captain Lopo Vaz Vogado was in charge of the *Flor de la Mar*.

These five carracks set sail from Lisbon and by the grace of God arrived safely in Mozambique. We met another ship wintering there, the *São Miguel*, owned and commanded by one Duarte Tristão. His ship was laden with riches when it resumed the voyage back to Portugal – but the *São Miguel* disappeared and was never heard of again. For our sins, this has been the fate of many a ship on the 'India Run'.

Our five ships had all been overhauled and were ready to leave

Mozambique when the commander of the fort, Vicente Pegado, presented the captains with a directive from Nuno da Cunha, the Governor in Goa. The orders were that any ship outward-bound from Portugal which stopped over in Mozambique that year was to proceed directly to Diu in India and leave a detachment of men at the fort there. The reason for this was that the Portuguese were expecting to see the Turkish fleet along the Indian coast seeking revenge for Bandur, the Sultan of Cambay, who had been killed by Nuno da Cunha in battle the previous summer.

The five captains immediately called a meeting to discuss the orders from Goa. There was much pleading and protesting from the merchants' agents about breaking and losing their contracts if they went straight to Diu. It was finally decided that the three ships belonging to the Crown would go to Diu as ordered while the two ships owned by merchants would hold their course for Goa.

By the grace of God all five ships reached their respective destinations safely. The Crown's ships appeared off the bar at Diu on September 5th, 1537 and were welcomed with great joy by the commander there, António da Silveira, a brother of Luís, the Count of Sortelha. He treated us all at his own expense with great generosity, providing the food for more than seven hundred men and continually offering us gifts in cash and kind.

When the men from our three ships saw such generosity over and above what they would be receiving for their basic pay and keep, almost all of them stayed in Diu of their own free will so that no compulsion or threats of punishment were necessary to get them to stay – which is nearly always the case at a fort under threat of a siege.

When they had sold their cargoes in Diu for a good price, the ships belonging to the Crown sailed on to Goa with only their crews and the king's officials still on board. In Goa they met up with the other two ships and stopped over there for a few days until the Governor, Nuno da Cunha, sent all five ships to Cochin, where they loaded up and from there returned safely to Portugal accompanied by the *São Pedro*, a ship that had been built in India.

The captain of the *São Pedro* was Manuel de Macedo and he brought back to Portugal the famous basilisk known as 'the gun of Diu'. It was one of three guns captured at Diu in 1537 in the battle when the Sultan Bandur was killed. These were three of fifteen cannon that Rumecan, the Lord High Admiral of the Turkish fleet, had brought from Suez to attack Diu in 1534, the occasion when Dom Pedro Castelbranco had to set sail from Portugal in November with twelve caravels to raise the siege.

3 : *I sail from Diu for the Straits of Mecca. A sea battle.*

SIXTEEN DAYS AFTER I LANDED IN DIU, TWO FOISTS WERE MADE ready to sail for the Straits of Mecca to gather information about the movements of the Turkish fleet, which the colonies in India were so worried about.

The captain of one of the foists was a friend of mine and I enlisted in his command, led on by his great show of friendship and his promises that I would make a lot of money in a very short space of time on the voyage. To make my fortune was my chief ambition and I never stopped to consider the high price we so often have to pay for riches, nor gave any thought to the risks to which I was exposing myself – though with the fate that befell us, a fate caused by the sinfulness of myself and everybody else aboard that foist, I later knew those risks only too well. The immediate hazard was that we were setting out at the wrong time of the year into contrary winds – but I was aboard the foist called the *Silveira* when it sailed out from Diu, confident in my friend's promises but misguided in my hopes.

The two foists set sail together and, since it was the end of the winter, the weather was rough enough with heavy rain storms and the monsoons blowing against us. We passed the islands of Curia, Muria and Abedalcuria, which are utterly desolate and offer nothing for the sustenance of life at all, and had no choice but to sail to the south-west. By the grace of Our Lord we eventually dropped anchor off the island of Socotra, a league from the fort built there by Dom Francisco de Almeida, the first Viceroy of India, on his voyage out from Portugal in 1507. We took on fresh water there and rested and refreshed ourselves, buying food from the local Christians who are descended from the converts made in India and Coromandel by St Thomas the Apostle in ancient times.

We left Socotra and set out for the Straits of Mecca and after

6

nine days of favourable weather we were off Mesena. At sunset on that ninth day we caught sight of a sail and we chased her with such speed that we were abreast of her by the first watch. We wanted to talk to her captain in all good faith to see if he could tell us anything about the Turkish fleet – but he gave us an answer we weren't expecting at all.

We hailed the strangers' ship but without so much as a word they stunned us with a broadside from a dozen assorted cannon and a volley from a mass of arquebuses, like people who didn't have the least bit of respect for us! A succession of loud shouts and hoots and jeers went up from them and they waved their flags and caps in the air, taunting us, while from the poop-deck they made a great display of brandishing short-swords at us, daring us to come and attack them.

At first we were somewhat taken aback by this chest-beating but our two captains and their officers then met to discuss what should be done. Most of them thought the enemy ship would not be able to repulse a boarding-party but that, first, we should do as much damage as possible by using our cannon on them until the morning, when it would be less dangerous to board her and easier to capture her; and that was the plan of attack we followed.

We bombarded the ship for the rest of the night until, by the grace of God, she surrendered near daybreak without further resistance. Sixty-four of the eighty men on board were already dead and most of the others threw themselves into the sea, preferring that watery end to being burnt alive in the fires started by the barrels of gunpowder we were pouring into the ship. Of the original eighty there were no more than five survivors, all of them badly injured, one of whom was the captain.

We tortured this captain and he told us that he was coming from his home in Jiddah and that the Turkish fleet had already set sail from Suez bound for Aden. The Pasha in Cairo (one of whose duties is to act as Lord High Admiral of the Egyptian Fleet) had been ordered by the Sultan in Constantinople to capture Aden and make it his base for an attack on the Portuguese colonies in India. The captain gave us lots of other information about the Turks that we were very interested to hear. We also got him to confess that he was, in fact, a renegade Christian, a native of Cerdenha in Majorca, the son of a merchant there, one Paulo Andrés. It was no more than four years since he had become a

Muslim for the sake of the Greek Muslim he had married.

Our two captains asked this man did he want to return to the true faith and become a Christian again; but his reply was so wild and so crude that you would have thought he had been born and bred in that accursed sect. It angered our captains to see how maddened and blind this wretch was when presented with the truths of the holy Catholic faith, especially when so little time ago he had indeed been a Christian, as he himself had confessed. So with a holy zeal for the honour of God's name our captains ordered the man to be bound hand-and-foot and thrown into the sea with a big stone tied around his neck, from where the devil could drag him down to enjoy the torments reserved in hell for that Mohammed whom he believed in so fervently.

The captured ship was sent to the bottom taking the other four wounded survivors with her. All she had been carrying was a cargo of bales of dyed cloth (in the same sorts of pastel-shades we have in Portugal) which was of no use at all to us, save for a few suits of chamelot that some of the soldiers took for themselves.

4 : *We sail to Massawa, and from there travel overland to Gil Eitor, where we meet the mother of the Prester John.*

AFTER THIS DELAY WE SAILED ON TO ARQUICO, IN THE LAND OF the Prester John, to deliver a letter from António da Silveira, the commander in Diu, to one of his factors, Henrique Barbosa, who had been posted to Arquico from Goa three years earlier by Nuno da Cunha.

This Henrique Barbosa and forty other Portuguese had escaped from the uprising in Xael when Dom Manuel de Meneses and a hundred and sixty of his men were captured along with 400,000 cruzados and six carracks. The Pasha of Cairo used these ships to carry provisions and munitions when his fleet laid seige to Diu in 1538. The King of Xael had sent the carracks and sixty of his Portuguese prisoners as a gift to the Pasha and sacrificed the rest of the captives as an offering to Mohammed. I dare say this whole affair will be discussed at length by the historians who come to deal with the governorship of Nuno da Cunha.

When we reached Gotor, a league below the port of Massawa, we were very well received by the local people and by Vasco Martins de Seixas, a native of Óbidos, who had been sent to Gotor a month earlier by Henrique Barbosa to wait for any Portuguese ship that might call there.

Martins had a letter from Barbosa for our captains containing all the information he had gathered about the movements of the Turkish fleet, and also pleading that at all costs they should send some Portuguese to see him concerning a matter of importance to both God and the King. Barbosa was now in the fortress of Gil Eitor with a troop of forty Portuguese guarding the Princess Tigremahon, the mother of the Prester John, and so could not leave to come to Gotor himself.

Our captains and officers discussed Barbosa's request and it was agreed that four soldiers should go back with Vasco Martins to meet Barbosa and deliver the letter from António da Silveira. I was selected as one of the four.

We set out early the following morning accompanied by Vasco Martins and six Abyssinians. We had good mounts for the journey overland, mules that Vasco Martins had brought with him from Gil Eitor, provided for him by the tiquaxy, the governor of the region, on the directions of the Princess Tigremahon.

That first night we slept in an impressive, wealthy monastery called Saltigan. The next morning we travelled a further five leagues along the banks of a river as far as a place called Bitonto and sheltered for the night in the pleasant monastery of St Michael, where we were warmly welcomed and well treated by the prior and his monks.

While we were there a son of the Negus, the governor of this Ethiopian empire, came to see us. He was a very friendly lad of seventeen and he brought a team of thirty mules with him. He himself rode a horse harnessed in the Portuguese manner, using reins of purple velvet fringed with gold that Nuno da Cunha had sent as a gift to him from India two years earlier with Lope Charnoca, who was later imprisoned in Cairo. The prince had sent a Jewish merchant, a native of Azebibe, to ransom Charnoca, but when the merchant arrived in Cairo Charnoca was already dead. This had deeply distressed the prince, and Vasco Martins told us that in this same monastery of St Michael the prince had arranged a memorial service for Charnoca, the finest that Vasco

Martins had ever seen, with four thousand clergy in attendance besides a great number of 'santileus' (what we call novices). The prince knew that Charnoca had left a widow and three small, helpless daughters back in Goa and he sent them a gift of 300 óqueas of gold (that's about 3600 cruzados).

We left St Michael's the following day on the fresh mules that this prince provided for us, as well as four of his men to accompany us and these fellows were splendid company throughout the journey. That night we slept in great houses called 'betenegus' (which means, 'the houses of the king'). These houses were surrounded by more than three leagues of very tall trees: cypresses, cedars and date- and coconut-palms like those to be found in India. We travelled on from there covering about five leagues a day, passing through enormous, beautiful meadowlands of corn and reaching a mountain range, the Vangaleu, which is inhabited by Jews; they are fair-skinned and well-built but very poor from what we saw of them.

Two and a half days later we reached a pleasant town called Fumbau, two leagues from the fortress of Gil Eitor, and it was here that we found Henrique Barbosa and his men. They greeted us with great happiness but with tears of sorrow as well because although, as they told us, they were there very much of their own accord and were lords and masters of everything in the country, they were still dissatisfied at heart because it remained a land of exile and not the land of their birth.

It was already well after dark when we arrived there so Barbosa thought that the Princess Tigremahon would not yet know of our arrival; the following morning, which was a Sunday, the 4th of October, we went with Barbosa and his men to the royal apartments where the princess lived.

As soon as she heard of our arrival she ordered us to come straight into the chapel where she was hearing mass. We knelt before her and kissed the fan she held in her hand and followed the other ceremonial courtesies of local custom that Barbosa's men had explained to us beforehand. The princess received us joyfully and said:

'The sight of true fellow Christians like yourselves arriving here brings me so much joy precisely because it has always been so keenly desired at every minute of the day by these eyes of mine, just as a dry garden longs for the dews of the night! Come

10

in and be welcome! And may your entry into my household be as joyful an hour as the hour when Queen Helena entered the holy ground of Jerusalem!'

She directed us to sit down on some mats five or six feet away from her and with a big smile on her face questioned us about all sorts of things. Barbosa's men told us this was something she always enjoyed. She asked us about the Pope and what his name was; how many kings there were in Christendom; if any of us had ever been to Jerusalem; why the Christian princes were so negligent in pursuing the war against the Turks; how powerful the King of Portugal was in India; how many forts he had there and where they were. She asked these and many other questions in a similar vein and seemed satisfied with the answers we gave her; then we took our leave of her and returned to our own quarters.

After staying at Gil Eitor for nine days we went to say good-bye to the princess. As we kissed her hand she said:

'Truly it grieves me that you should be leaving so soon; but since it has to be this way, go now, and may your return to India be so welcomed among your own people that they receive you just as in olden times King Solomon in all his glory received our own Queen Sheba into his dazzling palace.'

She ordered that the four of us should each be given 20 óqueas of gold (that's 240 cruzados) and also provided a manservant (or 'naique') and a further twenty Abyssinians to guard us against brigands along the road, and laid on provisions and mounts to take us to our foists at Gotor. As well as all this, Vasco Martins brought with him many gold objects which were an expensive gift from the princess to Nuno da Cunha – but all this was lost on the return voyage, as you will presently hear.

5 : *We set out from Harkiko on the return voyage. An encounter with three Turkish ships.*

AFTER WE REJOINED OUR COMPANIONS AT HARKIKO WE SPENT nine days there overhauling the foists and taking on provisions. We set sail again on Wednesday, November 6th, 1537.

Vasco Martins de Seixas was on board with the gift of gold and a letter from the Princess Tigremahon for Governor Nuno da

Cunha in Goa. We also brought with us an Ethiopian bishop who was to go on from India to Portugal, from there to Santiago de Compostela, then on to Rome, Venice and finally to Jerusalem.

We set sail an hour before dawn and with favourable winds we made our way along the coast until near evening. We had got as far as the Point of Goção, before reaching Arrecife island, when we sighted three ships at anchor. They looked like gelbas or tarrads from the Arabian coast, so we tacked about and headed towards them, using our oars as well as the sails because the wind was dying down. We rowed so steadily that within two hours we were close enough to the ships to make out the shouting from the oar-decks and recognized them to be Turkish galliots – so we turned for land as quickly as we could, like a man wanting to escape from the midst of dangers into which he has already stepped.

The Turks knew or suspected who we were and what we were up to: they gave a great shout and before you could say a Hail Mary all three ships were hoisting their quarter coloured sails. They tacked about into our wake, with their silken banners streaming, and as the wind helped them they soon swung round to windward and with no great effort at all they quickly caught up with us.

Just as soon as we were within range they opened fire on us with all the guns they had and in no time at all had killed nine of our men and wounded twenty-six. Most of our two crews jumped overboard and the two foists were left drifting helplessly so that one of the Turkish ships was able to pull alongside and her soldiers to lean over from the poop-deck and stab at us with their lances.

At that stage we still had forty-two men who were able to fight, and seeing that our only hope of salvation lay in the strength of our sword-arms we boarded the flag-ship of Suleiman Dragut, the commander of the three ships. We attacked with such force and vigour that we ravaged the ship from stem to stern, and killed twenty-seven janissaries, but then the other two ships, that had been standing a little way off, came to the flag-ship's aid: forty more Turkish soldiers boarded her and we were completely routed. We were so badly beaten that of our original fifty-four men only eleven were left alive, two of whom died the following day. The Turks quartered these two bodies and hung the pieces from the yardarms, like trophies, for their entry into Mocha, where the governor was the father-in-law of this Suleiman Dragut who had captured us.

By the time we dropped anchor in Mocha, the governor was already down at the shore-line with all the townspeople to welcome his son-in-law and congratulate him on his victory. The governor was accompanied by his mullah, a quaziz the people considered to be holy because he had returned just a few days earlier from Mohammed's holy city. This mullah arrived down at the shore in a carriage with a silk canopy and, dispensing elaborate blessings and salaams, he urged the crowd to give great praises to Mohammed for this victory over the Christians.

The nine of us who were left came down the gang-plank manacled together in one long chain. The Ethiopian bishop was also with us but he was so badly injured that he died the next day; however he died in a truly Christian manner, which was a great consolation and encouragement to the rest of us.

The nine of us who were left came down the gangplank manacled together in one long chain. The Ethiopian bishop was also with us but he was so badly injured that he died the next day; however he died in a truly Christian manner, which was a great consolation and encouragement to the rest of us.

When the townspeople saw us coming in chains and knew us to be Christians they jeered and insulted us so much that to tell the truth I never thought we would get away from there with our lives: the mullah had told them that they would gain plenary indulgences by insulting and mistreating us. We were paraded like this through the city, in the manner of a triumph, surrounded by a great din of shouting and trumpeting and even the children and the women who were kept indoors came to the windows and emptied chamber-pots over us in order to insult and debase the name of 'Christian'.

When it was almost sunset they threw us into a dungeon where they kept us for sixteen days of misery and deprivation. They never gave us anything more than a handful of barley-flour and, occasionally, some rough grain dipped in water to last us through the day.

6 : *Defeat and capture. I am taken from Mocha to Ormuz.*

ALL NINE OF US WRETCHES WERE SUFFERING FROM BAD INJURIES, and these, coupled with the rough treatment that we received in that miserable dungeon, caused two more of us to die by the following morning. These two were Nuno Delgado and André Borges, gallant men from good families, but they both had deep head-wounds and died so quickly because there was no doctor nor any help at all for them in that prison.

When the 'mocadão' (the gaoler) saw the two corpses he immediately informed the 'wazir' (who is like our chief magistrate) who came down to the prison himself in a great show of fearsome pomp accompanied by a crowd of judicial officials. This wazir ordered the gaolers to take the chains and manacles off the two bodies and to drag them outside with ropes tied around their feet: then the two bodies were dragged like this through the entire city, with crowds of children throwing stones at them, before they were finally dumped into the sea.

One afternoon the remaining seven of us were put up for auction in the market-place where the whole town was gathered and I, poor wretch that I am, was the first one to be brought before the auctioneer as he set about his business. The mullah was there with ten or twelve assistants, all quazizes of that damned sect, and the first bid for me had just been called when he asked Heredim Sofo, the city's governor, to send us as a gift to Mecca, where the mullah was going to make a pilgrimage on behalf of the city. He said it would not be right, nor reflect any honour on the governor himself, for him to visit the tomb of the Prophet empty-handed, with nothing to present to the chief mullah – who would then not want to see him nor grant any pardon at all that he might ask for the people of Mocha, who were so much in need of God's favour on account of their sins.

Heredim Sofo said the prize was not his to dispense as generously as the mullah requested; but he would ask his son-in-law, Suleiman Dragut, who would willingly agree to the mullah's request. The mullah replied that the things of God, and alms asked for in God's name, didn't have to be passed through so many hands but only through those hands to whom the request was made. Heredim Sofo was the governor of the city and of all

14

the people within the city, so it was up to him alone to grant a request that was so just, so holy and so pleasing to the Prophet, since it was the Prophet, and the Prophet alone, who had brought the spoils of that victory to Suleiman Dragut, and not sheer force of arms as the governor had declared.

A captain of janissaries from one of the three galliots was standing there, a fine man called Koja Geinal, who was highly esteemed among his men. He was deeply saddened to hear such a slighting of himself and all the others involved in our capture and he said to the mullah:

'What you say is true. But how much better for your soul if you shared with the poor soldiers the wealth that you have in excess rather than seeking to rob them of their just rewards with your hypocritical words – which is one of your unending activities! And if, as you say, you don't want to go empty-handed to Mecca so that you will be able to bribe the quazizes there to suit your own interests, then take the inheritance your father left you and leave these prisoners, who cost the life-blood of so many who are dead and so much blood from those who are still living. Your red-dyed robes was never so red as the blood-stained robes of myself and these poor soldiers here!'

Such a spirited retort by the captain on behalf of the soldiers so annoyed the mullah that when he spoke again he was so rash and arrogant that he insulted Koja Geinal and the rest of the soldiers who had gathered there, and a great row started between the soldiers and the townspeople, whose support for the mullah had given him the nerve to speak so freely. The arguments lasted for the rest of the day and not even Heredim Sofo himself was able to calm everyone down.

To cut a long story short and to skip over the ins and outs of these arguments, which would take a long time to tell, this uproar eventually broke out into so vicious and wild a riot that more than six hundred people were killed and more than half the city ransacked before it was halted. The mullah's house was attacked and he himself was killed and quartered and thrown into the sea along with seven wives and nine children and any other members of his household that the soldiers could lay hands on, with no mercy shown to anyone at all.

As I've said, when this started we Portuguese were there in the market-place, waiting to be sold to the highest bidder. We decided the safest course was to go back and be locked in the dungeon – and this we did without any officials or guards to escort us: we reckoned that the 'mocadão' did us no small favour when he locked us behind the dungeon-doors! The riot was finally brought under control by Suleiman Dragut, commander of the three galliots, who took charge of affairs in the city because his father-in-law had been wounded in the rioting and was lying injured in his bed.

Thirteen days after peace had been restored we were put up for auction again along with the rest of the spoils from the two foists – clothes and artillery – and this time everything was sold cheaply enough. As for me, poor wretch that I am, perhaps being less fortunate than the others, it fell to my lot to be bought by a Greek who had reneged on his Christian faith, a man whom I will curse as long as I live, because he treated me so badly that during the three months I was his slave. I was tempted to poison myself seven or eight times – and would have done so if Our Lord in His kindness had not kept me safe in His hands – just for the sake of making the Greek lose the money he had paid out for me. He was the most inhuman, cruellest enemy you could ever come across anywhere in the whole wide world.

However, by the grace of God, after three months, this Greek was so worried that I might die and lose him what he had paid for me (which some of his acquaintances had told him might well happen) that he exchanged me for thirty cruzados' worth of dates from a Jew by the name of Abraham Mussa, a native of Toro, which is two and a half leagues from Mount Sinai.

This Jew was part of a merchants' caravan en route from Babylon to Kashan. He brought me as far as Ormuz and took me to Dom Fernando de Lima, who was commander there at the time, and Pêro Fernandes, the Chief Justice in India, who had arrived from Goa on Crown business a few days earlier.

These two men, by giving out of their own pockets and by asking for contributions around the fort, raised 200 pardaus (150 cruzados in our money) which they paid to the Jew for me – and he thought himself very well paid at that!

☐In Ormuz Pinto joined a Portuguese cargo ship bound for Goa. By that time, 1537, the first siege of Diu had already started. In the Arabian Sea, Pinto was involved in naval battles against the Turks. At Honowar, a town to the south of Goa where the local queen had a treaty with the Portuguese vice roy, the Portuguese attacked the Turkish forces in the harbour; they were badly mauled and retreated to Goa. In this city, finding himself wounded and destitute, Pinto decided to quit soldiering.

Pinto now entered the service of Pêro de Faria, newly appointed to be captain of Malacca. In April 1539 Pinto left Goa with Faria's fleet for Malacca, where a wholly new career opened up for him. He was entrusted by Pêro de Faria with the duties of a roving ambassador.

The Portuguese had taken Ormuz from the Turks, Goa from the Indians and Malacca from the Malays, but they had never felt strong enough to attack the Muslim states of the Achin, who occupied the northern half of Sumatra. However, they kept close ties with rulers of the small kingdoms in the southern part of the island who, in their frequent fights with the Achinese, asked for Portuguese military assistance and support. The ruler of one of these kingdoms, the King of Batak, visited some Malay states: in response, Pêro de Faria sent Pinto as his envoy to Batak. His public aim was to obtain the king's good will towards trade; his private mission was to enquire about the military position of the Achin. The king was persuaded that Portuguese support would be forthcoming, although previous experience had showed that the Portuguese made empty promises.

Such missions as these gave Pinto the opportunity of doing his own business while looking after that of others. After taking leave from the King of Batak, Pinto sailed to the Malay state of Kedah and, accompanied by his Muslim agent, decided to visit the Sultan of Kedah, hoping that trade would result.□

19 : We sail to the kingdom of Kedah. What happened to us there.

THE NEXT MORNING WE SET OUT FROM THE SMALL ISLAND OF Fingau and followed the ocean coast-line for twenty-six leagues until we reached the Minhagaru Strait (which we had passed through earlier) and sailed from the open ocean into the channel that lies between Sumatra and the many islands off her western coast. We followed this course until we reached Pullo Bugay and thereafter we followed the coast-line of the Malacca Peninsula.

We called in at the port of Junkseylon and then with two and a half days of favourable winds we came to the Parlés river in the kingdom of Kedah where we were delayed for another five days waiting for a suitable wind.

After talking with some of the local merchants Koja Ali and myself paid a courtesy visit to the King of Kedah, bringing with us an 'odiaa' (that is, a gift) of several appropriate items which he accepted from us with a great show of welcome.

We had arrived in the country at a time when the king was leading the funeral ceremonies for his late father with great pageantry and ostentation – loud music, dancing, shouting and the distribution of food to the many hungry people in the kingdom. Actually, the king himself had stabbed his father to death so that he could marry his mother whom he had already made pregnant. To silence the murmurings of the people about these horrible crimes the king had issued a proclamation that nobody was to so much as mention what had happened, on pain of the cruellest of deaths; on this account already, we were told, as yet another means of tyranny, the king had executed the leading lords of the land as well as a great number of the merchants, whose property was then confiscated by the royal treasury. These crimes had brought in more than two contos in gold to the king. At the time we arrived in Kedah the people were already so terrified that they scarcely dared open their mouths to speak about anything at all.

Now, Koja Ali, the Moor who was travelling with me, had a very talkative nature and he wasn't afraid to say whatever came into his head; and because he was a foreigner and known to be the agent of the Portuguese commander in Malacca he thought he could talk with greater freedom than the local people and that the king wouldn't dare punish him as he punished his own subjects.

One day Koja Ali was invited to the house of another Moor who was some relation of his, a merchant who was a native of Patani. From what I heard afterwards it seems that in the middle of the banquet, when they were already well into their cups, the guests started to discuss the forbidden subject so openly that, through some of the many informers that he employed for this very purpose, the king was very quickly notified about what was going on. He ordered his soldiers to surround the merchant's house and all sixteen guests were arrested and tied and brought

18

before him.

As soon as the king saw them, without caring to hear anything in their defence or offering them any further recourse to justice, he ordered them all to be killed on the spot in the cruellest manner, the 'gregoge': they were sawn into pieces while still alive, feet and hands first, then at the neck, finally clean through the chest to the backbone – as I was later to see for myself.

Once this had been done, the king started to worry that Pêro de Faria, the Portuguese commander in Malacca, would be outraged when he heard that his agent had been killed along with the others and would retaliate by seizing some merchandise the king had waiting in Malacca.

So later the same night he sent a troop of men to get me at the jurupango where by this time I was asleep, completely unaware of all that had happened. They brought me to the palace just after midnight and in the outer courtyard I saw a crowd of men armed with swords, bucklers and lances. This took me by surprise and threw me into great confusion. I suspected treachery from the king and wanted to turn back there and then. My escort wouldn't let me go but told me not to be afraid of the armed men because they were simply a guard sent out to capture a thief. I must confess I wasn't too reassured by that explanation. I started stuttering then, scarcely able to make myself understood, but I asked my guards as well as I was able if they would let me go back to the jurupango to get some keys I had left behind. I said I would give each of them forty cruzadoes in gold, on the spot, if they let me go back. But all seven answered as one man: 'No, not for all the gold in Malacca! If we let you go back the king would have our heads on spikes!'

By now I had been surrounded by another fifteen or twenty armed men and they kept guard over me until daybreak when they informed the king that I was waiting outside. He immediately sent for me to come before him. God alone knows how I was able to take a single step forward, miserable wretch that I am; I walked like a man more dead than alive.

When I entered the inner courtyard the king was there, seated on an elephant and surrounded by more than a hundred courtiers as well as his palace guard who numbered many more than that. When he saw the state I was in the king said to me a couple of times: 'Jangam tacor. Don't be afraid. Come over here and I'll tell you why I sent for you.' At a wave of his hand ten or twelve of the courtiers moved to one side and he gestured to me to look over to where they had been standing. I looked over and saw a pile of mutilated bodies in a big pool of blood and among them I recognized Koja Ali.

I was so shocked and bewildered by the sight that like a man gone beserk I threw myself at the feet of the king's elephant and called up to him, weeping:

'Master! I beg you to make me your prisoner rather than kill me like the ones lying there! I swear to you as a Christian that I do not deserve such a death! Remember as well that I am a nephew of the commander in Malacca and he will pay you whatever ransom you ask for me! And there's a load of goods on my jurupango in the harbour and you can take them all if you want them!'

To all of which he answered:

'May our Gods preserve us! What's this? Do you think I am so evil a man that I'd do anything of the sort to you? You have nothing whatsoever to be afraid of! Come, sit down and rest yourself. I can see you are upset and when you've recovered I'll tell you why I had to execute your Moorish friend. I swear by my gods that if he had been a Portuguese or a Christian I wouldn't have dealt with him in the same way, no, not even if he had killed my own son.'

Then he ordered a jug of water to be brought for me: I drank long and hard from it and then another servant came and cooled me with a fan. After an hour or more, when the king saw I was well enough recovered from my shock to talk sensibly, he said to me:

'My Portuguese friend, I am well aware that you have already been told I killed my father recently. And indeed I did – but only because he himself wanted to kill me on account of the gossip that he heard from evil men convincing him I had made my mother pregnant, something which has never so much as entered my head!

'But he rashly believed all this gossip and had determined to kill me – so I decided to kill him first. The gods alone know how much I did it against my will because I was always such a good son to him – so good a son indeed that his wife will not end her days poor and abandoned like so many widows. Instead, I have

20

taken her for my own wife and to do so I have rejected many a prospective bride in Siak, Patani, Berdiu, Jambi, Tenasserim and Indraguiri, all of them the sisters or daughters of kings who would have brought large dowries with them.

'To stop the impudent gossip of good-for-nothings who maliciously say the first thing that comes into their heads I issued a proclamation that nobody was to speak about this regrettable matter. Yesterday your friend, the Moor there, got drunk along with these other curs as bad as himself and said things about me that I'd be ashamed to repeat to you, telling all and sundry at the tops of their voices that I was a pig and worse than a pig, and my mother a bitch in heat. So, for the sake of my honour I was compelled to seek justice from the Moor and these other whoresons as bad as himself.

'So now I plead with you, as a friend, not to think badly of what I have done because, believe me, I would be deeply hurt if you did. And if you should happen to think I did this in order to seize the merchandise in your boat belonging to the commander in Malacca, believe me, I had nothing like that in mind at all. I swear by my gods that this is the truth of the matter and you can rest assured of it because I was always a great friend of the Portuguese and always will be, for as long as I live.'

When I heard all this I calmed down a little although I was still by no means completely at ease. Then I said to the king:

'Your Royal Highness has done a great favour to his Portuguese brother, the commander in Malacca, in having this Moor executed. He was the commander's agent but he was cheating him of merchandise and had already twice tried to poison me to stop me from telling the commander about the swindling. And the dirty pig was drunk all the time, shouting out the first thing that came into his head like a dog howling at whoever it sees passing by in the street.'

I rambled on wildly, scarcely aware of what I was saying, but the king was so satisfied and pleased with my words that he called me over and said:

'From what you've just said I can see that you really are a good man and a true friend of mine, so what I did to my father doesn't seem evil to you – not like those whoresons lying there.'

Then he took an embellished gold kris from his belt and presented it to me along with a letter for Pêro de Faria in Malacca;

the letter was full of apologies for what he had done to Koja Ali.

I took my leave of the king in as orderly a manner as I was able, telling him that I would be stopping in Kedah for another ten or twelve days – and headed back to the jurupango to set sail immediately. As soon as I was back on board I cast off the moorings and hoisted the sail as quickly as I could. After the terror and mortal danger of the last few hours I still imagined the whole country to be hot on my heels, thirsting for my blood.

□After the hurried departure, Pinto searched off the coast of Sumatra for the Isle of Gold. He did not find it. Returning to Malacca, he gave Pêro de Faria what information he had been able to gather about the island's location.

Then – the year is 1539 – an ambassador from the King of Aru, another small kingdom in Sumatra, arrived in Malacca to ask Pêro de Faria for military aid against the Achins, who were poised to invade his country. The captain refused to give him any assistance; however, the King of Aru was highly regarded by the local Portuguese and Pêro de Faria was persuaded to change his mind. So he entrusted Pinto with a mission to take the king some munitions and guns.□

22 : *I take some arms to the King of Aru, who makes some sharp observations about the Portuguese as allies.*

WE LEFT MALACCA ON A WEDNESDAY MORNING, THE 5TH OF October, 1539, and on the following Sunday we reached the city of Aru on the river Punetican.

As soon as we had dropped anchor I went ashore and met the king at a palisade he was building at the mouth of the river to stop the Achins landing from their ships. He received me with a warm welcome and obvious joy and I gave him a letter from Pêro de Faria.

The whole substance of the letter was Faria's expressed hope of coming personally to the king's assistance at some later date. There were a lot of other easy compliments and encouragements – the letter was full of them – which the king valued greatly because he believed that Faria's promises could be fulfilled. When he saw the personal gifts and the gunpowder and the weapons I had brought from Malacca he embraced me and said happily:

'Let me tell you, my good friend, that all last night I dreamed that from my lord the King of Portugal's fort would arrive this wealth that I now see before me – and with these weapons I hope in God successfully to defend my homeland so that I may be free to do your king as many services in the future as I have done him in the past, services to which all your past commanders in Malacca could stand witness.'

He asked me a few questions about the state of affairs both in India and Portugal then left his aides to continue supervising the building of the palisade, a task that was keeping everyone feverishly busy. The king took my hand and, accompanied by no more than six or seven young noblemen of the court, we walked into the city of Aru, about a quarter of a mile from the palisade. He welcomed me into his palace, banqueted me and even introduced me to his wife, which is a very rare thing in those countries. Then he said to me, through a flood of tears:

'Understand now, Portuguese, why I'm sorry that these enemies of mine are coming here. If I didn't find myself the prisoner of necessity that I am, nor obliged to act for the sake of honour, as I am, I swear to you by the Holy Book of the Muslims that what the King of Achin plans to do to me I should have done to him first, without involving anyone else save my own resources and my own men! I knew a long time ago how treacherous the King of Achin is and just how much he wants to extend his power. What saves him is gold! He uses his gold to buy the services of foreigners who cover up the shortcomings of his own native soldiers. And so that you will fully understand how vile and degrading the misfortune of demoralizing poverty is, and what a serious disadvantage it is to kings like myself, come with me and you will see for yourself just how miserly Fortune has been to me.'

Then he led me to some sheds covered with straw that served as his arsenal. He showed me what he had stored there and it amounted to so little you could honestly say that it was as good as nothing considered against the huge amount he would actually need to defend his kingdom properly against a fleet of 130 ships full of fierce warriors like the Achins, Turks and Malabaris.

Then, with his sadness plain to see and like a man aware of the enormous humiliation he faces, unburdening himself of his great

23

worries, he told me in detail the resources he had at his command: five thousand of his own men, without any outside help whatsoever, and forty pieces of small artillery like falconets and mortars. The artillery also included a metal demi-cannon that had been sold to him by António de Garçia, who had been the Crown Agent at the fort in Pasay. This Garçia had later been drawn and quartered in Malacca by Jorge de Albuquerque for some treacherous correspondence he had entered into with the King of Bintang.

The king told me that he also had forty muskets, twenty-six elephants and fifty horses, ten or twelve thousand pointed stakes tipped with poison ('saligues'), something like fifty lances, and a mass of earthen bulwarks to protect the men fighting at the palisades. He had a thousand pots of powered quick-lime to use instead of firebombs when the ships were fighting at close quarters and three or four longboats loaded with rocks to use as missiles. There was a miserable pile of other bits and pieces which was so inadequate to meet his needs in this extremity that I knew there and then how little trouble the Achins would have in seizing his kingdom.

He asked me what I thought of the abundance of arms in his arsenal and if it would suffice to give a warm welcome to the guests he was expecting. I told him that he had more than enough to keep them well entertained, but then he said to me, shaking his head after a few moments thought:

'I'm sure that if the king of you Portuguese really knew just how much he would benefit by my being saved, and just how much he will suffer by the Achins capturing my kingdom, then he would punish the habitual negligence of his commanders, blinded and mired in their greed and self-interest, who have allowed his enemies to develop such might and power that when he wants to restrain the Achins I fear he will not be able to or, if he is able to, it will only be at great cost to himself and his men.'

I started to defend the Portuguese after what he had said so sorrowfully to me but he demolished all my arguments with such obvious truths that I didn't have the nerve to prolong the discussion – I knew myself that there was no contradicting his complaints.

He pointed out to me some of the evil criminal deeds that certain Portuguese have been guilty of – but I'll say no more about that here because such details are not relevant to my purposes and I'm not writing this just to uncover other people's faults. However, at the end of this lecture he taunted me with the mild punishment given to the guilty parties and the great rewards that had come to people who didn't deserve them. He concluded by adding:

'For a king who wishes to fulfil his obligations and responsibilities properly, and who has conquered and has to defend peoples far removed from his own kingdom, it is as necessary to punish the bad as it is to reward the good; but if he is seen to be the sort of man who gives the name of clemency to neglect and tardiness in the matter of discipline then his subjects will very soon be doing just what they want without fear of the consequences and this, as time goes by, could bring all his colonies into situations like that to be found in Malacca at the moment.'

When he had finished he went into a house and sent me to stay with a pagan merchant, a native of Indraguiri. I stayed with him for five days and he looked after me in a splendid fashion – although at the time I would have been happier eating any old scraps somewhere else where I felt a bit safer, because in Aru there were alarm bells ringing and rumours of the enemy's approach at every hour of the day and night.

In fact the day after I arrived in Aru the king was informed that the enemy fleet had set out from Achin and would reach Aru within eight days. This news made the king press ahead with greater urgency to complete his defences and to evacuate the city of all the women and other non-combatants. He ordered all these to take refuge four or five leagues into the jungle, and they made their way out of the city in utter confusion, their misery and helplessness so pitiful to see that I was numbed by it all: God knows I was heartily sorry that I had ever gone there in the first place. The queen left the city on an elephant, accompanied by just forty or fifty old people, and they were all so stricken with fear that I knew the Achins couldn't fail to capture the kingdom and at very little cost to themselves.

After five days the king sent for me and asked me when I wanted to leave. I replied:

'I will go when your Highness directs me to leave – but it would suit me to leave shortly because Pêro de Faria has ordered me to sail on to China to trade his merchandise.' The king just said: 'How right you are.'

He took two finely worked bracelets (or 'loias') of solid gold off his arm. They were each worth eighty cruzados but he gave them to me saying:

'I beg you not to think it meanness that I give you such a trifle because I tell you truly that my hope now, as always, has been to possess abundantly in order to give abundantly. And give this letter with this diamond to Pêro de Faria and tell him that the rest of what I know I owe him for the love he has shown me in sending these arms here I will leave until I bring it to him myself, when I am rid of these enemies and have more time to spare than I have now.'

23 : We leave Aru. Shipwreck.

WE SET SAIL FROM ARU SHORTLY AFTER BIDDING FAREWELL TO the king, leaving around sunset and rowing downstream as far as a village in the estuary. This village was composed of fifteen or twenty thatched houses and the people were all very poor without any means of subsistence, other than killing lizards and making a potion from the livers that is used to poison arrowheads: this poison from Aru – and above all from this region of Pocausilim – is considered the deadliest to be found anywhere because there is no medicine that can counteract the effects of it.

The next morning we left the village and sailed along the coast with favourable land-winds until late in the evening when we rounded the islands of Ankepisan and, still making use of the south-east wind (although it was now a slight head-wind), we kept our course out at sea for what remained of the daylight and some part of the night.

When it was little more than half-way through the first watch a thunderstorm broke from the north-east, which is the commonest kind of storm around Sumatra for most of the year. The squall overwhelmed us and wrecked the boat with the mast and the sails smashed to pieces by the wind and three holes battered in the hull. She went straight to the bottom before we could save any of the cargo. As for the people: of the twenty-eight men on board, twenty-three were drowned before you could say 'Hail Mary' and the five of us who survived – through nothing else but the mercy of Our Lord – spent the rest of the night where we were, washed up on the rocks, all of us injured in some way or another, weeping and bewailing our wretched condition.

We were in no fit state to discuss things among ourselves or to decide what we should do, and we didn't know in which direction we should go because the shore there was swampy and covered with such dense undergrowth that not even the smallest sparrow could get through the thickets of brambles. We were stranded there on the rocks with nothing to eat but the weeds we snatched out of the foam.

After three days of this suffering and bewilderment we set off along the shore-line, up to our waists in the mud, not knowing what was going to become of us. It was near sunset when we came to the mouth of a small river, little more than a crossbow's shot in width, but because it was very deep and we were all very tired we dared not risk crossing it that night. So we spent the night there in water up to our necks, tormented by the mosquitoes and flies so that every one of us was covered in blood from their bites.

When it was daylight I asked my four companions if any of them knew where we were and if there were any towns or villages up-river. One of them, a man of a good age with a wife and family back in Malacca, answered me weeping:

'Oh sir, the city that is closest to us right now – unless God should work a miracle to save us – the city that is staring us in the face is the city of painful death, the place where before very long we will have to render an account of our sins! And for that accounting it is necessary that we make ourselves ready with all haste, like men who have to go through another, much greater trial than that in which we find ourselves at this moment. Accept everything with patience as coming from the hand of God and don't be discouraged by what you see nor by the images that fear puts into your mind because, when all is said and done, there is little difference whether your going be today or tomorrow!'

Then, embracing me tightly and with many tears in his eyes, he asked me to baptise him a Christian because he had realized that such was the only way he could be saved, and not by following the wretched Mohammedan sect of which he had been a member until then – for which he asked God's mercy. He died right after asking this. He was very weak and his head was split open, the brains were mashed and almost rotten because the wound had not been treated and was full of salt-water and exposed to the bites of the flies and mosquitoes. I, for my sins, was never able to baptise him because he died so quickly and I myself was falling with every step I took, weakened and faint from the blood I had lost through my injuries and wounds. However we buried him there in the mud as well as we were able.

The other three men and myself decided to cross the river, intending to sleep in some tall trees that we could see on the far side because we were afraid of the numerous tigers and wolves roaming the country, besides all sorts of poisonous animals and all the cobras and some other snakes with green and black spots, so poisonous that their breath alone can kill a man.

I asked two of the others to lead the way and the third to stay with me and help me across because I was so weak. The first two plunged into the river one after the other, telling me not to be afraid and to follow. They were little more than halfway across when two enormous lizards attacked and pulled them under, tearing them to pieces in no time at all and leaving the water stained with blood.

Such a sight so stunned me that I wasn't even able to scream, and I don't know who got me out of the water nor how I escaped because I was already up to my neck in the river along with the negro who was holding me by the arm – and he was so frightened he didn't even know his name.

24 : *I am rescued by fishermen and sold to a Moor.*

AS I SAID BEFORE, I WAS SO STUNNED AND SHOCKED BY WHAT I HAD just seen that I wasn't able to weep, let alone speak, for upwards of three hours; the other sailor and myself turned back from the river and waited in the sea until the following morning when we saw a fishing-boat approaching the mouth of the river.

As soon as the boat was close enough we pulled ourselves up onto some rocks and on our knees, naked, with our hands raised in the air, we pleaded with the men on the boat to take us on board. When the men saw us they stopped rowing and rested for a little while; and then, when they saw our wretched condition and realized that we were victims of shipwreck, they pulled in close to the rocks and asked us what we wanted.

We told them that we were Christians from Malacca who had been wrecked nine days earlier on our way back from Aru and we begged them, for the love of God, to take us with them wherever they were going.

The man who seemed to be in charge of the boat answered us:

'From what I can see of you both from here you'll not be worth the food that you'll eat, so for your own good you'd better hand over any money you've got hidden away – and then we'll treat you just as brotherly-like as you're begging us to! Otherwise just forget it!'

Then they made as if to sail off, but we started weeping and pleading with them again just to take us as prisoners and sell us as slaves wherever they wanted. As for myself, I added that I was a Portuguese and a close relative of the commander in Malacca, so wherever they sold me they would certainly receive whatever price they asked for me.

Their leader answered:

'Fair enough. We'll take you, but if you're not who you say you are we'll whip you to shreds and throw you bound hand-and-foot into the sea!'

We said yes, that was all right by us, and four of them jumped ashore and carried us aboard. By this time we were both so weak that we could scarcely lift our hands.

As soon as they had us on board they tied both of us to the foot of the mast. They had planned all along to take any money that we might have and thought that if they whipped and beat us we would break down and tell them where any valuables were hidden. They beat us mercilessly until the blood was pouring out of us. I was as good as dead already, in a worse condition than my companion, so I was spared drinking the potion that they gave to him, poor wretch. It was a mixture of quicklime and piss that made him bring his guts up and he died inside the hour.

They didn't find any trace of gold in what my companion had vomited up (as they had been convinced they would) so by the grace of Our Lord they didn't bother to give me the same treatment; instead they used the same mixture to rub my body all over so that I wouldn't die of my wounds – though the pain was so great that I was as good as dead to the world.

We finally left this river, the Arissumhee, and at evening on

29

the following day we came into sight of a large town of thatched houses called Siaca, in the kingdom of Jambi.

The seven fishermen who had rescued me and who now all had a share in me kept me in their house for twenty-seven days and, praised be Our Lord, I recovered from my wounds; but when they realized that I wouldn't be of any use to them in their fishing they put me up for auction.

On three separate occasions they brought me to the market but didn't so much as get a bid for me. They decided they wouldn't be able to sell me at all: I was of absolutely no use to them, and they threw me out of the house to save the expense of having to feed me.

I spent the next thirty-six days living out in the open like an old donkey without a master, begging from door to door for crumbs and morsels that I was rarely given because the people of Siaca were very poor themselves.

Then one day when I was down on the sea-shore bewailing my misfortune Our Lord saw fit that a Moor should pass by, a merchant from the island of Palembang who had been to Malacca several times and traded there with the Portuguese. When the Moor saw me lying there, naked on the shore, he asked me if I was Portuguese – and said not to be afraid to tell the truth if I was.

I told him that I was, indeed, Portuguese – and one with very rich relations in Malacca who would pay as much ransom as he asked for me if he brought me there. I said I was a nephew of the commander there, the son of one of his sisters.

The Moor replied:

'If you are who you say you are, what wrong have you done that you have come to the miserable state I see you in here?'

I gave him a detailed account of my shipwreck and how the fishermen had brought me to Siaca and then turned me out of their house because they couldn't find anyone to buy me.

He was amazed by my story and after thinking things over for a while he said:

'As you might have guessed, I am a poor trader, so poor that, with my income not being more than a hundred pardaus I went into the shad's egg business, thinking that it could be the path to an easier life – although with my bad luck it didn't work out that way. Now I know that I could make a good profit at the present time trading in Malacca and I would be glad to go there – if the commander and customs men don't treat me as badly as I've heard they treat some of the traders who go there. So if you think that on your account I could do business in Malacca, secure against any obstacles and abuse, then I will go and see about buying you from these fishermen.'

I answered him through flooding tears:

'You know very well yourself that there's no good reason why you should believe what I have told you. Indeed, you might well think that in order to escape from this poverty and miserable captivity I would make myself out to be more important in Malacca than I actually am. But if you will trust my word – and I have no other bond to give you – I will swear a written oath that if you take me to Malacca the commander there will reward you and will not confiscate the least part of your merchandise and, furthermore, will pay you twenty times over whatever sum you pay to the fishermen for me.'

The Moor replied:

'All right. I'll be glad to buy you out and take you to Malacca but don't say anything to the fishermen about what we have just arranged. We don't want them to raise your price so high that I won't be able to do you the favour I want to do!'

I swore to him that I would do just as he said and added a lot more besides that I thought would help to win him over, and he accepted all my promises readily enough.

25 : *The Moorish merchant buys me. My return to Malacca.*

FOUR DAYS AFTER I MADE THESE ARRANGEMENTS WITH THE MOOR he began to bargain for me with the seven fishermen through a third party, a native of Siaca.

The fishermen were already fed up with the sight of me because I was very sick and of absolutely no use to them. It was more than a month since they put me out of the house and by this time the seven who had a share in me were no longer all working together nor even as friendly with each other as they had been. Through these and other means God brought it about that they were not bothered to keep me at all. They asked the Moor's man for seven mazes of gold (that's three and a half cruzados). It was paid straight away and the Moor brought me to his house.

Five days after I was freed from the clutches of the fishermen, and when I was somewhat recovered due to the good treatment I received from my new master, this Moor went to a place called Surabaya, five leagues away, to finish loading up a boat with a cargo of shads' eggs – which is what he traded in, as I mentioned earlier. Shad are so abundant in the local rivers that the people don't make use of anything but the females' eggs, of which they export more than two thousand boat-loads every year, each boat carrying a hundred and fifty or two hundred jars, and each jar holding a thousand eggs, which is as much as the traders are able to handle.

When the merchant had finished loading the lanchara (the type of Malayan boat he used for carrying his merchandise) we set sail for Malacca and arrived there three days later. He straight away brought me to the fort to see Pêro de Faria and told him everything that had happened to me.

Pêro de Faria was astonished when he saw the condition I was in, and with tears in his eyes he told me to speak up and let him know that it was really me – because I was so emaciated and changed in face and body that he couldn't believe his eyes. It was more than three months since they had heard from me and they had given me up for dead, but now so many people wanted to see me that there wasn't room in the fort for them, all of them weeping and asking me what on earth had brought me into the sorry state in which they now saw me. When I gave them the full story of my voyage and the ill-fortune that had befallen me they were so amazed that they were left speechless and went on their way again, blessing themselves.

As was the custom at that time there was a collection taken up for me afterwards, so that I ended up a lot better off than I had been.

Pêro de Faria ordered sixty cruzados and two rolls of damask be given to the Moor who had rescued me and he decreed, in the king's name, that the Moor's merchandise be exempted from whatever custom duties might be due on it (which was worth another sixty cruzados to him). The Moor wasn't impeded or harassed at all while he was in Malacca, so he was content and more than satisfied, considering himself very well paid for the bargain he had struck with me.

Pêro de Faria sent me to stay in the house of a married man, a clerk in the trading-post. He thought I would be better looked after there than anywhere else in Malacca – indeed I was: I spent upwards of a month in bed, and I was fully restored to health, thanks be to God.

☐Pinto was now sent on trade missions to the large kingdoms of Further Asia. In these remote regions, his chances of making money greatly increased but so did the perils he had to risk.

As an agent of Pêro de Faria (who, like all Portuguese employed by the government, engaged in private trade on the side) Pinto sailed for Pahang, the Malay state on the east side of the peninsula, to meet Tomé Lobo, another of Pêro de Faria's agents. Pinto borrowed some money from friends and took a cargo boat under his charge. Near the Tuman Island they rescued twenty-three people from a Portuguese ship which had been sunk. Pinto arrived in Pahang and made over Pêro de Faria's merchandise to Lobo.

Pinto wanted to move on to Patani, as his instructions required, but Lobo did not want to leave Pahang because he had a local enemy who threatened his property. Pinto was forced to wait a few days. Suddenly the Sultan of Pahang was murdered by men hired by an ambassador of Borneo, who had discovered that his wife had had an affair with the Sultan. There were riots in the city and the enemy of Tomé Lobo attacked him and his house. Pinto and Lobo fled the place and sailed to Patani, the seat of a Malay Sultan who was friendly to the Portuguese. The Sultan gave the Portuguese permission to seize Pahang merchandise to the value of what they had lost. Thus Tomé Lobo and Pinto were reimbursed for their losses.

One day a Portuguese ship arrived. On board was another emissary from Pêro de Faria, come to discuss a trade agreement with the Sultan. The emissary was António de Faria (a relative of the captain of Malacca) with whom Pinto was destined to have many adventures.☐

36 : *Misfortune befalls us off the bar of Ligor.*

I HAD BEEN IN PATANI FOR TWENTY-SIX DAYS, AND HAD JUST dispatched a small amount of merchandise that had come from China for me to return promptly, when a foist arrived from Malacca, captained by one António de Faria de Sousa. He had been sent by Pêro de Faria to renew the peace treaty with the King of Patani and to thank him for the good treatment the Portuguese had received there, with other shows and tokens of friendship important for the development of trade – which, to be truthful, was the most important consideration of all. However, this commercial interest came wrapped up in official letters and accompanied by impressive gifts as if it was a diplomatic mission in the name of our master, the King of Portugal. It was certainly paid for out of his treasury – which is the usual practice among all the Portuguese commanders in Asia.

This António de Faria had brought with him ten or twelve thousand cruzados' worth of Indian clothes which had been loaned to him in Malacca, but the clothes were so unmarketable in Patani that he couldn't find anyone who would give him a sou for the whole lot of them. When Faria saw he had no hope of selling the clothes he decided to winter in Patani until he found some way or another out of his predicament.

Some of the men who had been in Asia longer than himself told Faria to send the clothes to Ligor, a large port a hundred leagues to the north in the kingdom of Siam, where there would be merchant junks from Java, Lave, Tanjampur, Japara, Demak, Panaruca, Sidayo, Passaruan, Solor and Borneo, some of whom would surely buy Faria's clothes in exchange for jewels and gold.

Faria thought this was good advice and decided to do as they suggested. The foist in which he had come from Malacca was not suitable for the voyage to Ligor so he arranged another vessel in Patani to carry the cargo and appointed as his agent Cristovão Borralho, a trader experienced in Asia. Sixteen other traders and their merchandise sailed with Borralho as well, besides the usual complement of soldiers, all of whom had their own goods to trade, thinking at the least they would make six or seven times over what they had laid out. As for myself, poor wretch that I am, I happened to be among the company for this voyage.

We left Patani on a Saturday morning, sailing along the coast with favourable winds and reaching the bar of Ligor on the Thursday morning. We entered the mouth of the river and anchored there for the rest of the day: before going ashore we wanted to make detailed enquiries about the prospects both for trading and for our own personal safety. From what we were told, the prospects for trading looked so good that we hoped to

34

get our money back six times over, and our safety was also assured with free movement and exemption from taxes for the whole of September, in accordance with a decree of the King of Siam, September being the month of 'the kings' homage'.

To understand this situation properly, you should know that the whole of this peninsula is dominated by a powerful king whose title, famous above all others, is Prechau Saleu, Emperor of the Sornau (which is a region of thirteen kingdoms, commonly known among us as Siam.) Fourteen minor kings are subject to him and pay him a tribute every year. By ancient custom these fourteen kings were obliged to go in person every year to Ayathia, the capital city of the Sornau empire, bringing their tributes and doing him homage (or 'sumbaias') which involved kissing the short-sword that he carried in his belt.

However, this city of Ayathia is fifty miles inland and the river currents are so contrary that often these fourteen kings had to spend the whole winter season there at great cost to their treasuries. The kings petitioned the Prechau about this burden and he thought it best to change such a heavy imposition into a lighter one. He announced that he would appoint a viceroy (what they call a 'poyho') to the city of Ligor and henceforth the fourteen kings could come in person every three years and pledge their loyalty to this viceroy just as they had done to the Prechau himself, and also pay in one sum the tribute due for the three years. The Prechau furthermore declared that during the month when the kings came to pay homage he would exempt from paying taxes any merchants, be they foreign or native, who used the port of Ligor.

As I said earlier, we arrived in Ligor during the month of the 'sumbaias' and there were so many merchants there that someone told us more than fifteen hundred vessels from all over the Orient had entered the port, carrying an infinitude of expensive merchandise. We learned all this after we anchored in the mouth of the river and we were so excited and delighted that we decided to enter the port itself just as soon as a landward breeze arose. However, to pay for our sins, Fortune ordained that we should never enjoy what we all looked forward to so much.

It was almost ten o'clock and we were just ready for dinner; we were tightly anchored and ready to hoist sail as soon as we had finished eating. It was then we saw a big junk coming downstream, just foresail and mizzen hoisted; they tacked to windward and dropped anchor abreast of us. As soon as the junk knew we were Portuguese and saw our small numbers and our small boat they slackened their anchor and let themselves drift towards us. When they were alongside our starboard bow they hurled across two grappling-hooks on long chains that fixed onto our gunnels. Since the junk was so much bigger than our boat we were held tight under their bows.

Then seventy or eighty Moors, and some Turks among them, came out from under the awnings on the junk's deck where they had been hiding. They gave a great shout and then fired a hail of arrows, spears and spiked clubs down at us. It seemed like a shower falling from the skies and before you could say a Hail Mary it had killed twelve of the sixteen Portuguese on board, besides thirty-six slaves and sailors. The four of us who were left alive jumped overboard into the sea. One of us quickly drowned but the other three of us got to the riverbank, absolutely exhausted, wading ashore up to our waists in mud and then making our way into the jungle.

The Moors had quickly boarded our boat and without offering any quarter killed the six or seven slaves that they found lying wounded on the deck. They loaded the junk as quickly as possible with all the merchandise they found on our boat, then holed her and sent her to the bottom. They hauled in the grapple-hooks that had trapped us, then weighed anchor and put to sea straightaway for fear that they might be seen and recognised.

37 : *In deep distress, we head off into the jungle.*

THREE OF US HAD ESCAPED THIS CALAMITY BUT WHEN WE SAW OUR injuries and no sign of any relief we started weeping and cursing ourselves, stunned and maddened by what we had seen less than half an hour earlier; and that's how we spent the rest of that miserable day.

The land around us was swampy and crawling with lizards and snakes, so we decided that it would be best to stay where we were for the night, which we spent up to our chests in mud. At daybreak we made our way along the river-bank until we came to a small creek which we did not dare to cross because it was very deep and we could see it was full of crocodiles. We spent that night and the next five days stuck there, overcome with exhaustion and hunger and unable to move forward or go back because the ground was so swampy and the undergrowth impenetrable.

While we were there one of my companions died, a wealthy and highly respected man by the name of Bastião Henrique, who had lost eight thousand cruzados in the lanchara. This left just myself and Cristovão Borralho and we stood there on the banks of the river weeping over the half-buried corpse. We were so weak by now that we couldn't even talk but had decided to see out the few hours of life left to us there on the river-bank.

Near sunset on the following day, the seventh of our misfortune, we saw a barge carrying salt being rowed upriver. The barge slowed down when it was opposite us and we pleaded on our knees with the oarsmen to take us on board. When they saw us they stopped rowing, staring in astonishment to see the state we were in, on our knees with our hands raised to heaven like men praying. They didn't answer us but made as if they wanted to continue on their way – seeing which both of us shouted at the tops of our voices, weeping and pleading with them again not to leave us there to die.

At the sound of our shouting a woman came out from beneath the canopy on the barge. She was of a fair age and her appearance and bearing truly showed her to be the woman we later learned she was. When this woman saw our plight, like someone who took pity on us and suffered our misfortune and our wounds with us, she picked up a stick and made them row the barge to the shore, striking out two or three times at the sailors when they wouldn't obey. Then six of them jumped ashore, lifted us onto their shoulders and brought us onto the barge.

When this worthy woman saw our wounds and our clothes covered with mud and blood she immediately ordered her men to wash us and gave us some sheets to cover ourselves for the time being. She made us sit down beside her, ordered food to be brought and then served it to us herself, saying:

'Eat up, forlorn strangers, and don't be discouraged at seeing yourselves in this state – because here am I, a woman of no more than fifty, and it's not six years since I saw myself imprisoned and robbed of more than a hundred thousand cruzados, and saw my husband and three sons killed – the husband whom I treasured more than these eyes that gazed upon him! – saw every last one of them – husband, children, two brothers and a son-in-law – mashed to pulp by the King of Siam's elephants! Now with a sad, weary life I endure all these evils and ills and others besides which are almost as great – the sight of my three maiden daughters, my mother and father and thirty-two nephews, neices and cousins thrown into blazing furnaces by the same king with screams that split the heavens, calling on God to save them in their unbearable torment – but my sins were so great they blocked the ears of the Lord above all Lords so that he never heard their cries for His Infinite Mercy, cries that to me seemed so just. Yet the truth is that whatever God ordains, that is for the best.'

We told her that it was on account of our sins that God had let us fall into our present condition; she replied to this in a flood of tears, which we weren't short of either:

'It is good that you should always see the hand of the Lord in your adversities because it is in that truth itself, spoken by the mouth and believed by the heart with a clear, firm forbearance, that very often the reward for our trials lies.'

She changed the subject then and asked us the cause of our misfortune and how we had come to be in that wretched state. We told her everything that had happened to us although we didn't know who had attacked us nor why they had done it – but her crew were able to tell us that the big junk we mentioned belonged to a Gujerati Moor by the name of Koja Hassan, who had sailed from Ligor the morning we were attacked, with a cargo of brazil-wood for the island of Hainan.

The worthy lady beat her breast in great amazement and said:

'May I be struck dead if that's not who it is! That Moor you're talking about was bragging in public to whoever would listen that at different times he had killed great numbers of Portuguese from Malacca, and that he wished them so much ill he had promised Mohammed to kill a great many more of them!'

We were astonished to hear such a thing and asked her to tell us about the man and why he wished so much evil on the Portuguese. She told us she knew nothing about his motives other than that he had said one of our great captains, Heitor de Silveira, had killed his father and two brothers in the Straits of Mecca when they were sailing from Jiddah to Dabul; and for the rest of the journey to Ligor she told us in detail about the great hatred this Moor had for the Portuguese and the things he said to abuse and insult us.

38 : *António de Faria swears to hunt down the pirate Koja Hassan.*

WHEN WE LEFT THE PLACE WHERE THIS FINE WOMAN HAD FOUND us we made our way by sail and oar some two leagues upstream to a small village where we stayed the night. The following morning we set out for Ligor, another five leagues further on, and arrived there around noon. When we went ashore the woman brought us to her house and we stayed there for twenty-three days, very well cared for and provided in abundance with whatever we needed.

This woman was a widow and of noble lineage. We learned afterwards that she had been the wife of the Xabandar of Prevedim, who was killed in the city of Bancha in 1538 by the Pate of Lasapara, King of Quaijuan on the island of Java. At the time she rescued us she was unloading a junk which was too large to get past the sandbanks, moving its cargo of salt a bit at a time upstream to Ligor in the barge.

After twenty-three days during which we completely recovered, thanks be to God, we thought we were fit to travel again and the lady sent us to a relative of hers, a trader who was going to Patani, eighty-five leagues away. He brought us with him on a calaluz (which is a type of galley) and sailing along a great freshwater river called the Sumihitan we arrived in Patani seven days later.

António de Faria's eyes were nearly popping out of his head looking for some sign of us on the horizon and waiting for news about his merchandise. When he saw us and we told him what had happened he was completely stunned, unable even to talk to us for more than half an hour. By then there were so many Portuguese gathered around that there wasn't enough room for them in the building: most of them had had goods aboard that ill-starred lanchara, so she must have been carrying more than sixty thousand cruzados' wortth, most of it in minted silver to be used for buying gold.

António de Faria had been robbed of the twelve thousand cruzados he had borrowed in Malacca and saw he could do absolutely nothing about it. Some of the others tried to console him but he confessed that he didn't dare return to Malacca to face his creditors. He was afraid they would hold him to the credit notes he had written them – and right now there was absolutely no possibility of his being able to repay them. He thought it made more sense to go and find the man who had robbed him rather than return to Malacca unable to pay back his creditors.

Then he swore an oath on the Holy Gospels in front of everybody and said that besides the oath, he also vowed to God to leave immediately in search of the man who had stolen his property and to make that man repay him down to the last sou, whatever good or ill came of it – although he knew very well before he started that it couldn't possibly be for the good because when a man killed sixteen Portuguese and thirty-six slaves and sailors, all of them Christians, it wouldn't be right for him to get off lightly without any punishment – otherwise a hundred others similar to this fellow would be doing the same thing to us every day.

Everybody standing there praised Faria for this determination and many young men and fine soldiers offered their services for this mission, while others offered to lend him money to buy weapons and supplies. He accepted these offers from his friends and set about making preparations as quickly as he could, and within eighteen days he had fifty-five soldiers ready to sail with him.

It was necessary for me, poor wretch that I am, to take part in this expedition because I had been left without a sou to my name, nor even a friend who would give or lend me one, and I owed more than five hundred cruzados to friends in Malacca. Their five hundred and as much again of my own money had, for my sins, been taken by that Moorish dog along with everyone else's. I had nothing except my own poor hide – and that had three arrow wounds and a deep gash from a stone that hit me on the head, from which I had almost died three or four times, and back in Patani they had to take a piece of bone out of me before I was fully recovered.

My companion Cristovão Borralho was much worse off than I was: he had received more wounds than me in return for the two and a half thousand cruzados that Koja Hassan had stolen from him.

As soon as António de Faria was able he set out from Patani. It was Saturday, 9th May, 1540, and he made his way nor'-nor'-west to the coast of Tsien-pá, planning to explore the ports and inlets of that coast and also, with some profitable pillaging, to gather up some of the supplies he still needed. His departure from Patani had been a little hurried and he had not left well supplied, so that he still needed to stock up on many things – mainly food, weapons and gunpowder.

□Beyond Malacca the Portuguese Viceroy had no official control: pirates, Portuguese adventurers and other unscrupulous operators could act there with total impunity. On this voyage with António de Faria, in pursuit of Koja Hassan, Pinto saw for the first time the coast of Champa (Indochina) and entered lawless seas.

One morning they were at the bar of a river, when a big ship arrived. The Portuguese saluted, but the crew of the other vessel did not respond. Feeling insulted by this behaviour, Faria assaulted the ship and found out that the captain, Similau, had been the killer of Gaspar de Mello, a Portuguese officer. Similau was put to death.

Faria continued to explore the coast of Champa, moved up to the Gulf of Ton-king and reached the island of Hainan, where he attacked a second pirate ship. An old man (who rebuked Faria for his un-Christian ways) told him the story of the pirate he was pursuing, Koja Hassan, and of the harm he had done to the Portuguese.

António de Faria entered the bay of Quemoy. With the merchandise they had seized, the Portuguese were potentially rich, but they needed to sell their goods. António de Faria decided to exchange the merchandise for pearls, if he could, with the pearl fishers of Quemoy.□

44 : *We arrive in the Bay of Quemoy, where pearls are gathered for the Emperor of China.*

THE FOLLOWING AFTERNOON WE WEIGHED ANCHOR AND STARTED scouring the coast of Hainan again. We sailed along the coast for the next day and night, in a depth of twenty-five to thirty fathoms, until we dropped anchor at daybreak in a large bay where there were some barges fishing for pearls.

António de Faria wasn't sure about his next move and spent the whole morning discussing with his officers what we should do. There were a lot of different views and opinions expressed: some thought it would be all right to go ahead and sieze the pearl-boats, others thought we should trade with them, because in exchange for their pearls we could get rid of most of the merchandise that we were carrying. In the end Faria chose the best and safest of these options and hoisted a trading flag – this is the Chinese custom. Shortly afterwards two lanteas (which are like foists) came out from the shore with plenty of food and drink for us and, after saluting us, the men in the lanteas went aboard the big junk to meet António de Faria.

These men were astounded because they had never seen people like us before. They asked us who we were and what we wanted. We told them we were traders from Siam who had come to trade with them, if they would give us permission to do so.

An old man who seemed to have most authority among them told us we could trade all right but that we couldn't do it there with them: we would have to go to a port further along the coast called Guamboy where there was a trading post for foreign merchants. There were similar trading-posts for foreign ships in Canton, Chinchow, Lamau, Comhay, Sumor, Ning-po and other ports along the coast.

Then the old man said to Faria:

'And now, sir, I advise you, as a good commander of your men, to sail on to Guamboy immediately because this bay where you have stopped is exclusively reserved for the fishing of pearls for the royal treasury of the Son of the Sun. By order of the Tu-Tung of Comhay, the supreme governor of Cochinchina, no boats apart from those that have been granted a royal licence can fish for pearls; any other boats discovered in the bay are to be burnt immediately, along with everybody in them. Since you are foreigners and don't know the customs and laws of this country, I advise you to set sail quickly before the mandarin's fleet arrives here in three or four days' time. At present the fleet is taking on stores in a place called Buhaquirim, seven leagues away.'

'How many ships and men are there in this fleet?' Faria inquired.

'There's forty big junks and twenty-five galleys; two

thousand sailors and five thousand soldiers.'

Faria then asked the old man a few questions about pearl-fishing and the pearl trade. He told us that the season lasted about six months, from early March to the end of August. The fishermen paid duties at the following rates: two-thirds on pearls of five carats and over, a half on pearls of less than five carats, and a third on seed-pearls. As for their income over a season, it varied a bit from year to year but it probably worked out at around four hundred thousand taels (that's six hundred thousand cruzados).

António de Faria was very keen to know in detail about all these things and he made the old man very welcome. He ordered us to bring two balls of wax, a bag of pepper and an ivory tusk for the old man, which pleased both him and the others who were with him. Then Faria began questioning them again about this island of Hainan, about which he had heard so many marvellous things already; but they said to him:

'First of all tell us who you are and what you have come here for and then we will answer your questions! We assure you, by the true religion, we never saw as many young men in trading ships as you have with you here, nor any so refined and well-mannered; and it seems to us that in your country Chinese silks are either so cheap as to be worthless or else you paid a lot less for them than their full value – because while they're amusing themselves at dice your men carelessly hurl down a roll of damask for a bet like men who don't value it at all.'

António de Faria smiled somewhat drily at this because he saw they had already guessed the silks were stolen, but he replied that we behaved like this because we were only young men and the sons of wealthy merchants, too young to appreciate the proper worth of such things; and the Chinese pretended not to know what they knew perfectly well: 'Yes,' they said, 'probably it is just as you say.'

Then Faria nodded to the soldiers to stop the dicing and gambling and to put away the silks they had been laying as bets so that the Chinese wouldn't get a good look at the pieces and know us all to be thieves for sure. The soldiers promptly stopped the dicing. Faria wanted to quieten the Chinese mistrust of us by not completely confirming what they already suspected – that we were people who were up to no good! He ordered us to open the hatches and show the holds loaded with pepper. When the

Chinese saw the packed holds they were indeed somewhat re-assured and less suspicious, saying among themselves:

'All right, now that we know they are genuine traders we can answer all their questions freely. We don't want them to go away thinking we're too stupid to answer them at all, like men who know nothing except how to catch oysters and fish.'

45 : *A pearl-fisherman tells us about the island of Hainan.*

THIS OLD MAN WANTED TO SATISFY AT LEAST SOME OF ANTÓNIO DE Faria's curiosity so he began talking to him again:

'Now that I know who you are, sir, and that you want to know all these things in good faith, I will tell you what I have heard and learned at different times from men who used to serve in this province as royal supervisors and inspectors; in our language they are called "tu-tungs" and "chiangs".

'These men told me that Hainan used to be a sovereign king-dom in its own right, ruled by a very wealthy king called Prechau Gamu, the most famous and most revered monarch of his time. When he died without leaving an heir there was widespread disagreement among the people about who should succeed to the throne. This disagreement eventually developed into civil war and there was so much bloodshed that the chroniclers who deal with the period state that in just four and a half years about one million, six hundred thousand people were killed.

'This slaughter left the country so short of fighting men and so vulnerable that the King of the Cochins conquered and made himself master of the island with an army of just seven thousand Moguls, who had been sent to him by the great Tartar from Tumikhan, which at that time was the capital of the Tartar empire.

'When he had conquered Hainan the king returned to Cochin but left one of his captains as governor of the island, a man called Hoyha Paguarol. Eventually this man was more than justified in leading the island in revolt against the king. He sought out the King of China as his protector, paying a tribute of four hundred thousand taels a year' (that's six hundred thousand cruzados) 'in return for which the Chinese king was pledged to defend Hoyha

Paguarol from his enemies as the need arose. This agreement lasted for thirteen years during which the King of the Cochins was defeated in battle five times.

'Hoyha Paguarol died without a natural heir but in his will he appointed the King of China as his legitimate successor and heir, on account of the benefits he had received during his life from the king. From that time on – a period of two hundred and thirty five years – the island of Hainan has been subject to the sceptre of the great Chinese king.

'You also asked me about the treasures, trade and people of the island: I know nothing except what I've heard from these old men. They told me that the total income from trade, silver-mines and customs duties in the ports amounted to two and a half million taels.' (That's three and three-quarter million cruzados).

António de Faria and the rest of us were visibly astonished by what the old man had just told us but then he added:

'If you are all so impressed by such small matters what would you do if you saw the city of Peking, where the Son of the Sun is in permanent residence with his Court. All the revenue from each of the thirty-two kingdoms of the empire goes to Peking and the gold and silver alone taken from the eighty-six royal mines is stated to be worth more than fifteen thousand piculs.'

António de Faria thanked the man for answering all his questions so fully and then he asked where he would recommend us to try to sell our merchandise – we wanted the safest port with the friendliest people, since we did not have the monsoons to take us to Ning-po. The man replied:

'Speaking to you as a friend, I wouldn't advise you to go to any of the ports on Hainan, nor to trust any of the Chinese on the island, because I tell you there's not one among them will deal honestly with you. You can trust me because I am very rich and don't need to try swindling you like a poor man. I'd advise you to follow the shore-line of this bay – and keep your hand on the tiller because it is full of dangerous shallows – until you come to a big river called the Tanauquir which has good anchorages. You'll be safe and at your ease there and in two days you'd be able to sell all the cargo you have and much more besides if you had it. But I'd advise you not to go ashore at all because very often the sight of traders arouses envy in the people, and if envy tempts honest people how much more will it tempt disgruntled, dishonest people who are more inclined to grab from another person than, for the love of God, to give of their own to those who need it.'

When he had said this the old man and his companions took their leave of us with abundant expressions of good will (the Chinese generally are not miserly with their courtesies). In return for António de Faria's gifts the old man gave him a tortoise-shell box, small as a salt-cellar, filled with seed-pearl grains, and twelve decent sized pearls as well. He asked us to forgive them for not trading with us but he was afraid they would be discovered and executed if they did so, in accordance with the emperor's severe laws, and he begged us to move on quickly before the mandarin's fleet arrived, because if it discovered us there he knew for certain that we and our ships would be burned.

António de Faria didn't want to ignore this advice in case what the old man had said was true. We quickly hoisted sail and followed the coast southwards; with west winds we reached the Tanauquir river in two days and dropped anchor near the small village of Neytor.

□António de Faria's ships were working their way up the Tanauquir river when they were attacked by two pirate junks. In hand-to-hand fighting the Portuguese prevailed, many of the pirates jumping overboard to escape. In one of the holds, sixteen Christian captives were found, two of them Portuguese, naked and in chains. The pirate chief, they said, was a Chinese who had converted to Christianity, taking the name Fransisco de Sá. He had reneged on his vows, seized the ship he was commanding for his own purposes, slaughtered most of the crew, and established himself on the Tanauquir river to prey on passing ships. The rescued prisoners identified the renegade among the corpses, and António de Faria had the body beheaded and quartered.□

47 : *We intrude upon a wedding party.*

AFTER WE HAD DEFEATED FRANSISCO DE SÁ WE TENDED THE wounded and arranged a guard for the prisoners and then made an inventory of the cargoes in the pirates' two junks. We discovered that the value of what we had captured amounted to just over forty thousand taels (sixty thousand cruzados) and it was all loaded onto the boat of António Borges, who was in charge of all our booty. This sum didn't include the value of the two junks themselves but although they were only newly built we had to burn one of them because we didn't have enough sailors to man both. We also came across seventeen bronze artillery pieces (including four falconets, one camel and twelve bases), nearly all of them stamped with the royal emblem, because that piratical dog had taken them all from three ships in which he had killed forty-six Portuguese.

The next morning António de Faria wanted to try sailing up-river again but he was warned by some fishermen whom we had captured during the night not to go anywhere near the city of Tanauquir because the people there already knew what Faria had done to Francisco de Sá, and the provincial governor, the chileu, had been accustomed to do business with the pirate, receiving a third of all the prizes he captured. The city was now in such an uproar that even if Faria offered to give them his goods for nothing they wouldn't take them – never mind thinking that he could sell the stuff! Already there were two huge jangadas lying in wait for us at the entrance to the harbour, laden with firewood and barrels of pitch and tar to attack us when we came to the harbour, besides a further two hundred war-canoes full of archers and warriors.

After hearing this report António de Faria followed the advice of some of his officers who had more experience in Asia than himself, and decided to move on to another port, forty leagues to the east, called Mutipinam. It was a very busy trading centre with merchants from Laos, Gueos and Pafuas arriving in caravans bearing large shipments of silver. So we set out in our three junks and the lorcha in which we had come from Patani and sailed along the coast against headwinds until we came to a headland called Tilaumera, where we dropped anchor because the currents were so strongly against us.

We had been anchored there for thirteen days, well wearied by the storms across our bow and already running low on provisions, when by our good fortune four lanteas (which are like our foists) sailed towards us in the evening, carrying a bride to a village called Panduri, nine leagues away. They were celebrating as they sailed along and the noise of their drums and whistles and bells and singing was so great that you couldn't hear yourself speak.

We didn't know what to make of it all – we thought they might be spies from the governor of Tanauquir's fleet that had come looking for us. António de Faria promptly ordered the anchor to be tightened and told the men to stand to, ready for anything; then he bedecked the ship with flags and put on a show of merry-making, and waited for the lanteas to pull alongside.

As soon as the bride's party saw our four ships all together, festooned and festive as themselves, they took us to be the bridegroom's party come to meet them along the way and happily headed straight towards us. After saluting each other from the mast-tops (which is the custom among these people), they turned away and sailed to the shore, where they dropped anchor.

We didn't know at the time what the true situation was, so we all agreed with our commander that the lanteas were spies scouting ahead of the Tanauquir fleet and that it wouldn't be very long before the fleet itself arrived. We spent what little remained of the daylight and almost two hours of darkness waiting there, nursing our suspicions. Meanwhile the bride was impatient to see the bridegroom, but when he did not send for her, as anyone would have expected him to, and wanting to show him how much she loved him, she sent one of her uncles over with a letter in one of the lanteas. This letter read as follows:

'If my frail, womanly nature would permit me, without staining my honour and virtue, to go from here now to stand before you, believe me that my body would fly to kiss those feet that tarry there, flying like the starved goshawk in its first surge of freedom.

'However, my lord, since I have already left my father's house to come here to meet you, it is you who should now come to this ship of mine – where I no longer truly am because it is only in meeting you that I will be restored to myself. But if you cannot come to me in the darkness of this night I don't know if in the brightness of the morning you will still be able to find me among the living.

'My uncle Licorpinau will tell you what my heart keeps silent about, since even now I am unable to speak because my soul will not suffer me to be the orphan of your eyes that your sterile indifference makes me.

48

'So I beg you to come to me now or give me leave to come to you and don't deny this love which I keep for you and have always kept – for fear that God in His justice, to punish your ingratitude, should take from you the treasure you inherit now in the first flowering of my maidenhood and which, through matrimony, you will reign over until death.

'May our Lord and God for pity's sake keep death from you for as many years as the sun and moon have circled the earth since the time of creation.'

When Faria saw the lantea approaching he ordered all the Portuguese to hide, leaving just our Chinese sailors on deck so that the visitors would not be wary of coming alongside.

When the lantea was safely alongside our junk three men quickly climbed aboard and asked where the bridegroom was – our reply was to grab all three and throw them under hatches. Most of the others in the lantea were too drunk to notice any noise our men made, nor were they fit to pull away quickly enough to stop a rope being thrown from our poop around the top of their mast, holding them tight to our junk without the least chance of them being able to break free.

We hurled a few grenades down onto the lantea which made everybody on board jump into the sea. Six or seven of our soldiers and as many sailors immediately jumped aboard the lantea and took control of her; the first thing they did was to pick up the unfortunates in the water who were screaming that they were drowning.

When these were picked up and settled safely on board António de Faria went after the other lanteas that were anchored a little more than a quarter of a league away. He pulled alongside the one carrying the bride; there was no resistance whatsoever because there were no soldiers on board, only the crew and six or seven relatives of the poor bride, noblemen by the look of their clothes, and also two fair-skinned, good-natured little boys, the bride's younger brothers. The rest of the passengers were old women who hire themselves out to provide music for such occasions, which is a Chinese custom.

The other two lanteas heard the uproar, and hauled in their anchors by hand and fled, as fast as if the devil himself was in them, making use of both oars and sails – but even so they weren't fast enough to prevent us capturing one of them, so that of the four vessels we had seized three. After this we returned to our other ships.

By this time it was almost midnight, so we did no more than load our booty onto António Borges' junk and put all the prisoners below decks. In the morning when António de Faria saw these people were just unfortunate innocents, most of them being old women who were no use for anything, he ordered them to be left ashore. He kept only the bride and her two little brothers as well as twenty of the sailors who would be very useful to us in manning the junks, where we were a bit short-handed.

We learned afterwards that this bride was the daughter of the Anchacy of Colem (who is like our district judge) and she was betrothed to a young son of the Chifu of Panduri. The son had written to tell her that he would meet her there, off Tilaumera, with three or four junks belonging to his father (who was very rich) and that was why they had mistaken us for the bridegroom's party.

The following afternoon, after we had left there, the bridegroom himself passed us in five gaily decorated ships on his way to meet his wife. He hailed us with loud music and transparent joy, not knowing the least part of his ill-fortune nor that we were carrying his bride away with us. So with all his banners flying and bedecked with coloured silks he doubled the point of Tilaumera, there to await his future wife, just where we had met her the day before at the place that came to be known as 'Lost Bride's Point'.

We sailed ahead on our course and, thanks be to God, in three days we safely reached Mutipinam, where António de Faria had been told he would be able to sell our merchandise.

48 : We reach Mutipinam and gather information about the country thereabout.

WHEN WE REACHED MUTIPINAM WE ANCHORED IN AN INLET NEAR a small island that lies to the south of the entrance to the bar. We stopped there without letting anyone know we had arrived or giving any sign of our whereabouts. We intended, as soon as it was dark, to check the river depths and gather information about what we wanted to know.

As soon as the moon came out, which would have been around eleven o'clock, António de Faria despatched one of the captured lanteas with a good crew and a dozen soldiers under the command of Valentin Martins Alpoim, an alert and capable man who had given a good account of himself in other similar operations. Alpoim set out and took soundings along the river as far as the city's harbour, where he seized two men he found sleeping on a porcelain-barge, and then returned to our ships without being noticed.

He gave Faria a report of all he had seen: the great size of the city, the small number of ships in the harbour, and he said he thought we could go into the harbour without any fears for our safety because if, for some unforseen reason, we weren't able to trade as successfully as we had hoped to, no-one would be able to stop us from leaving whenever we wanted to, because the river was very wide and clear of traffic with no shallows or sandbanks to cause us any trouble.

Faria and his officers discussed what to do with the two Moors that Alpoim had seized and most agreed that it was best not to interrogate them under torture, as had earlier been planned: they thought it best not to start outraging anyone and, besides, torture didn't seem necessary.

By now it was clear daylight and with great devotion we all recited a litany to Our Lady of the Mount in Malacca and promised her expensive gifts to adorn her shrine. Afterwards António de Faria went along by himself to see the two Moors. First of all he calmed them down and encouraged them, reassuring them that they had nothing to fear, then he questioned them in great detail about everything he wanted to know.

They told him that he had nothing to fear entering the river because it was the biggest along the entire coast-line: very often much bigger vessels than ours went in and out without any bother, because the shallowest parts in the river were between fifteen and twenty fathoms deep. They also told him he needn't be afraid to go ashore, because the local people were very mild-tempered by nature and they didn't carry any weapons, and most of the foreigners there at present were merchants from the kingdom of Benam who had arrived nine days earlier in two caravans, with five hundred oxen in each caravan, carrying a great load of silver, perfumed wood, silk, linen, ivory, wax, lacquer, benzoin gum, camphor and gold-dust like that found in Sumatra; and these merchants had brought all this to trade for pepper and medicines and Hainan pearls.

Faria asked if there were any fleets patrolling along that coast. They told him:

'There are no fleets because most of the wars fought by the Prechau, King of the Cochins, are fought on land, and when they do fight on the rivers they use small galleys, not big seagoing ships like yours, because the rivers are not deep enough for them. The prechau is just twelve days away by road, in the city of Quanjiparu, where he is in residence for the greater part of the time with his household and court, ruling his kingdom with justice and peace.'

'The prechau – what sort of treasure and revenues does he have?' Faria inquired.

'The royal mines yield a good fifteen thousand piculs of silver a year, a half of which, by the divine decree of the Lord who made all things, belongs to the poor people who work the land, to help them support their families. However, for the good and contentment of all the peoples of the kingdom, they had freely relinquished this right to the prechau, in return for which, from that time on, the prechau never constrained them to pay any tribute or imposed anything which might oppress them, and the prechaus long ago swore an oath in court to fulfil this agreement for as long as the sun should give light to the earth.'

António de Faria saw that the two Moors were willing to talk about anything he wanted to know, so he asked them:

'What do you know about that which you see with your eyes, by night in the heavens and by day in the light of the sun, that which you have just spoken about at length?'

They replied:

'The one truth above all other truths is to hold and believe that there is but one all-powerful God, Who just as He created all things, so He sustains all things; and if at times our understanding of this truth is weakened by the chaos and tumult of our desires, that is not the work of the Creator – in Whom there can be no imperfections – but the work of the sinner, whose impatience makes him follow the humours of his own evil heart.'

Faria asked if their religion taught that God had ever come to earth and taken on himself the flesh of the human form. They said:

'No, because nothing could oblige God to go to such an extreme. The excellence of the divine nature is free of our wretchedness and completely oblivious to the desire for worldly treasures. All things are as nothing in the presence of the divine splendour!'

Through such questions as these we learned that these people had heard nothing about the truths of our faith: they simply professed with their tongues what they saw with their eyes in the colours of the heavens and the beauty of the day, to which they continually raised their hands in adoration saying:

'For your works, O Lord, we proclaim Your glory!'

When he had finished questioning the two Moors, António de Faria ordered them to be put ashore safely, and he gave them some gifts before they left with which they were very pleased.

A landward breeze had now arisen so we hoisted our sails with great rejoicing and high spirits; we bedecked the topsails with silken banners and flew the trading-flag from the top of the mast so that everyone who saw it would understand we were merchants and only interested in trade. An hour later we dropped anchor in the harbour in front of the city quays and made our salute with a little round of cannon-fire.

It wasn't long before ten or twelve canoes came out from the shore loaded with food and drink. The men in the boats found us a great novelty: they could see from our clothes and complexions that we weren't Siamese, Malayan, Javanese nor like any other race that they had ever seen before. They exclaimed:

'May the dawn of the fresh morning be as advantageous to us as this afternoon that seems to be smiling on us in the presence we behold before us!'

One canoe came alongside and the men asked for permission to come aboard. We told them to do so without any fear at all, because we were all their brothers. Then three of the nine men who were in the canoe climbed aboard our junk. António de Faria welcomed them warmly and sat them down on a large carpet. He told them he was a merchant from the kingdom of Siam and that, when he was travelling to the island of Hainan, people had told him he could trade more safely and profitably in Mutipinam than anywhere else because the merchants and local people there were more honest than the Chinese of Hainan and the neighbouring coast. They replied:

'You are not mistaken in what you say. If you are a merchant, as you seem to be, rest assured that all our dealings with you will be conducted in the most honourable fashion. So you can safely enjoy your untroubled sleep; you don't have to worry about anything at all.'

□António de Faria was anxious not to unload his cargo ashore, as was the normal practice, to pay customs and trade piecemeal: that would make a quick escape impossible should news of the battle in the Tanauquir river arrive. Instead he managed to sell his cargo as a whole, and to unload it into five barges which had arrived laden with silver as payment. Faria's caution proved wise: news of the battle arrived and the Portuguese could no longer pose as peaceful merchants. By sailing at once, they manage to avoid arrest.

They sailed up the Cochinchina coast, taking prizes as opportunity offered, always seeking news of Koja Hassan. This was the season notorious for typhoons and when the weather began to look especially threatening, the Portuguese took shelter in Mandel harbour. Other junks also sailed in. As one of these passed by, five boys rushed to the rail and called out to the Portuguese for rescue: they were captured Christian slaves. António de Faria tried to negotiate the boys' freedom by purchase but, failing in this, he attacked the junk at night, killed many of the crew and captured the rest, including the captain.

This Chinese captain had once been converted to Christianity, but he found the Portuguese so haughty that, when on a visit to a port in a Muslim country, he took to Islam. After this, he became a pirate with a particular cruelty to Christians and Portuguese. The pirate captain, after strenuous interrogation, finally revealed the whereabouts of the five Christian boys: they were to be found in the forward hold. And so they were – beheaded, disemboweled; and other young children were found in the same state, too, with their mothers. The pirate captain suffered a similar fate.

This and other victories, led to António de Faria achieving the status of a sort of *de facto* ruler of the coastal waters in that region; he even began to issue guarantees of safe passage to ships' captains – on their payment of suitable protection money.□

53 : *Shipwrecked on Thieves' Island.*

WE HAD BEEN SAILING AROUND THE GULF OF TONKIN FOR SEVEN and a half months, continually changing course, up to the north and down to the south, going from one river to another, and around the coast of Hainan – but in all this time António de Faria hadn't come across a single report or rumour of the whereabouts of Koja Hassan.

By now the ordinary soldiers were fed up with having had to endure their hardships for so long without respite. They went in a group to Faria and pressed him to give them their shares of all the booty we had captured, divided according to an agreement he had made with them at the start of the expedition. They wanted to take their shares and go back to India or wherever seemed best for them. There was more than a little irritation and ill-temper about this but in the end it was agreed that we would all go to winter in Siam, where we could trade our prizes for gold and then share out the gold as the soldiers had requested. This agreement was sworn to and signed by everyone.

We were anchored off a place called Thieves' Island, the furthest of all the islands from the coast of the gulf, waiting there for the early monsoons to start our voyage to Siam. We had been there for twelve days, with everyone on board really eager to get on with the plans we had made, when Fortune chose to send a storm of such winds and rain, coupled with the tides of the October new moon (which are always to be feared), that you would have thought there was nothing natural about it at all. We were short of ropes and cables and those that we had were nearly all worn thin and half-rotten; as soon as the sea began to brew up, a violent south-east cross-wind caught us out in the open and drove us towards the shore. We did everything we possibly could to save ourselves from the gigantic waves crashing over us: we cut down the masts, smashed the cabins and castles in the poop and the prow, jettisoned everything on the top-deck, manned the pumps, threw all the cargo overboard and fixed cables and capstan-ropes to the heavy cannon that had broken loose of their mountings, to use them as anchors – but to no avail. It was so dark and cold, the sea was so rough, the winds so strong, the waves so enormous and crashing right across our ships – simply, the storm was so terrible that nothing less than the mercy of Our

Lord would have been able to save us, and we all called on Him unceasingly with great weeping and wailing.

But our sins did not merit us such mercy and His divine justice ordained that at about two o'clock in the morning we should be caught by such a strong blast of wind that all four ships were driven straight onto the shore and broken into pieces with the loss of five hundred and eighty-six men, including twenty-eight Portuguese.

Those of us who had been spared by the mercy of God spent the rest of the night lying in rock-pools, naked and injured. There were fifty-three of us in all: twenty-two Portuguese and thirty-one slaves and Chinese sailors. When it was daylight we returned to the beach and found it strewn with dead bodies – such a sorrowful, shocking sight that there wasn't a man among us who didn't fall stunned to the ground, crying out pitifully and beating our heads in grief.

We remained there like that until it was almost evening. Then António de Faria – who, thanks be to God, was among the survivors, which was some small consolation to us – suppressing in himself the grief that no-one else was able to hide, and dressed in a scarlet woollen robe that he had taken from one of the dead, walked around among us and, assuming a joyful face and with dry eyes, made a short speech to us:

'Comrades, how fickle and deceptive are the ways of the world! How fickle! Yet I plead with you, as a brother speaking to his brothers, to try your utmost to forget these calamities because to dwell on them serves no other purpose than to cause further grief to ourselves. If you consider carefully the miserable state that, for our sins, Fortune has reduced us to, then you will recognise and understand just how necessary is this response that I urge you to make. Yes, how fickle are the ways of the world! But, for myself, I trust that the Lord Our God, in this dense, desolate jungle, will bring us the means to save ourselves because I firmly believe that God never permits an evil that doesn't lead to an even greater good. So I firmly believe that if we have lost five hundred thousand cruzados on this shore, then before very long we will find ourselves with more than six hundred thousand!'

This short speech rang out amid all our inconsolable weeping; then we set about burying the corpses strewn around the beach, which occupied us for two-and-a-half days. We also salvaged some provisions from the wreck: there was more than enough to feed us for the fifteen days we were stranded there but the food had been soaked by the seawater and after no more than five days started to rot so rapidly that there was no benefit to us in eating it.

We spent fifteen days there on the shore in great hardship; then the Lord, who never fails those who truly believe in Him, miraculously delivered us the means to save ourselves, helpless and naked though we were, as I will presently describe.

54 : *After dire hardships, we are miraculously saved.*

THOSE OF US WHO HAD SURVIVED THE WRETCHED SHIPWRECK I have just described wandered naked and barefooted around the shore and through the undergrowth, suffering so badly from hunger and exposure that many of us collapsed and died of sheer exhaustion as we were standing around talking to each other. It wasn't the lack of food that caused this but rather that the food we had salvaged and eaten was mouldy and rotten after a few days, with an unbearable stench and so foul a taste that nobody was able to keep the stuff down if they had managed to swallow it.

However, the Lord Our God of His very nature is infinite goodness and there's not a place on earth, no matter how remote or desolate, that can hide the sufferings of sinners from Him, nor a place where He will not be able to succour those same sinners through the workings of His infinite mercy that are so far beyond our comprehension; and if we could but discern the means through which His mercy works we would clearly see that they are the miraculous work of His divine hands rather than the workings of mere nature – although our frail judgement very often confuses the two.

I say all this because one day – it was the Feast of St Michael the Archangel – we were all weeping wildly and, in the weakness of our wretchedness and lack of faith, as despairing of any human help as we could be, when a kite-hawk happened to fly past over our heads, coming from the direction of a headland on the south of the island. Hovering in the air with its wings outstretched, the kite dropped from its claws a fresh mullet of almost a palm's length which landed on the ground close to António de Faria, who was a little startled and confused until he realized what it was.

Faria stared at the fish for a little while then fell to his knees and, through the tears that were pouring down his cheeks and heaving a sigh from the depths of his breast, he said:

'Lord Jesus Christ, eternal Son of God, I humbly beg You by the sufferings of Your sacred passion, not to punish the lack of faith into which the misery of our exhaustion has thrown us, because I firmly believe that in Your mercy what You were to Daniel in the lions' den when You sent the prophet Habbakuk to test him in days of old, You will be to us here today, and will be so wherever and whenever a poor sinner calls on You in steadfast faith and hope. And so, my Lord and my God, I beg You, through the intercession of your holy angel whose feast Your holy church celebrates today, not to consider what we deserve but rather what You have earned for us: because then You will be granting us the help that we can hope for from You alone, sending us the means for You to deliver us from here to Christian lands where, ever persevering in Your holy service, we shall finish our days as true Christians.'

Then he picked up the mullet, cooked it over a wood fire and shared it out among the sick, who were most in need of it. When we looked over in the direction the kite-hawk had flown from we saw great numbers of them hovering, swooping and climbing, so we surmised that on the other side of the hill there was prey or carrion that the kite-hawks were feeding on. We all wanted to bring some relief to the many injured men among us and we set off in a disorganized procession towards the hill, singing a litany as we walked that was drowned in our tears.

When we reached the top of the headland we were looking down on a flat valley, crowded with all kinds of fruit-trees and with a stream of fresh water flowing through the middle; and before we had reached the stream Our Lord revealed to us a freshly killed deer that a tiger was beginning to eat. We all gave a great shout and the tiger fled into the thickest part of the under-growth, leaving the deer's carcass behind. We took this as a good omen and walked down to the stream and rested that night on its banks, making a great feast out of the deer and the numerous

58

mullet we got for ourselves by shouting at the kite-hawks who very often dropped their catch to the ground in fright.

We discovered this stream on a Monday and we lived off the fish from it until the following Saturday when, early in the morning, we saw a sail approaching the island. Since we didn't know whether or not it would come into shore we headed back down to the beach where we had been wrecked and after about a quarter of an hour we could make out that it was only a small vessel, so we turned back and hid in the undergrowth in case they saw us.

This boat was a fine-looking lantea and when it reached the island the crew tied her from her poop and bow to the steep bank on the side of the headland so that they could put out a gangplank. Then all of the crew came ashore – about thirty men in all – and set about gathering water and firewood, washing their clothes and cooking up a dinner, while others amused themselves with wrestling and other games – nothing was further from their minds than there being anyone else on the island to disturb them.

When António de Faria saw how careless and carefree these sailors were and that there was nobody left on the boat to offer us any resistance, he called us together and said:

'My brothers and comrades, you are very well aware of the unhappy situation that our sins have brought us to – though I believe, and confess to you, that my sins alone were cause enough. But since Our Lord is infinitely merciful I trust in Him not to suffer us to end our days here in such a wretched fashion.

'Now, I know very well that there is absolutely no need for me to remind you how important it is for us to try and take this ship that Our Lord has just miraculously brought to this island – but I will remind you just the same so that all of us here, with God's Holy name on our lips and in our hearts, will rush at the ship as one man and be aboard her before they know what is happening.

'And once we are aboard don't worry about anything except getting hold of all the weapons we can find – because with those weapons we can defend and remain masters of this ship in which, after God Himself, lies our only hope of salvation. So as soon as I say three times, "Jesus, Most holy name of Jesus", just follow me!'

We all agreed to do exactly as Faria said. When we were all

prepared and ready to go he gave the signal and burst out of the jungle running towards the boat with all of us behind him. We reached the boat and took control of her without any resistance whatsoever, casting off the mooring ropes and pulling the distance of a crossbow's shot from the shore.

The Chinese noticed nothing at first but as soon as they heard the commotion on the boat they rushed back down to the shore and were so stunned to see their boat taken that none of them made any move to stop us. We fired a round at them from a demi-base we had found on board and they scattered into the undergrowth – and we left them there to weep over their ill fortune, just as we had wept over ours until then.

55 : *A brave Chinese boy. We set sail for Ning-po, stopping at the Xingrau river.*

ONCE WE WERE ALL SAFELY ABOARD AND OUT OF REACH OF THE Chinese we sat down to eat at our leisure the dinner an old man on board had prepared for them. There were two pots of rice with wild duck and minced ham – which all tasted very good to us because we were so hungry.

When we had finished eating and given thanks to God for the favour He had shown us, we looked at the cargo and found silks and silken thread, satins, damask and three big jars of musk, which we valued all together at about four thousand cruzados; there was also a good store of ships' provisions – rice, sugar, ham and two coops of chickens – which we valued more than anything else at the time for the sake of our sick and injured, of whom we still had a good number. Each man sorted out some clothes for himself without more ado and we all took whatever we needed.

There was a Chinese lad of thirteen or fourteen who had been trapped on board. He was fair-skinned and good-natured and Faria questioned him about the lantea: whose it was, where it was coming from, where it was going to and why it had called in at the island. The boy replied:

'This boat belonged to my luckless father, whose sad fate and misfortune it was to have you steal from him in less than an hour what had taken him more than thirty years to earn. The boat was coming from Quoaman where he had traded silver for all the merchandise you have here, and he intended to sell it again to the Siamese merchants who are now in the port of Comhai – but his misfortune was to call in here for fresh water just so that you could seize his property without a trace of fear of divine justice.'

António de Faria told the boy he shouldn't cry and comforted him as best he could, promising to treat him as his own son because from now on he was responsible for the boy's welfare.

When he heard this, the boy looked at Faria and answered with a scornful smile:

'Don't imagine that because I am only a boy I am so foolish as to care for someone who has deprived me of my father and yet would now treat me like a son! And if you are worried about my welfare I beg you with all my heart, for the love of your God, to let me swim back to that sad shore where the one who gave me life remains, because he is my true father and I would rather die with him in the jungle – where I see him weeping for me now – than live among people as evil as you are.'

Some of the men standing there told the boy to shut up and not to be saying such things. He replied:

'Do you know why I say these things to you? Because I have seen you praising God after stuffing yourselves, with your hands joined in prayer and your lips covered in grease, like men who think it suffices to mouth words to heaven without doing justice to the man they have just robbed. What I understand is that God Almighty doesn't want us to make a lot of noise with our mouths but to restrain ourselves from taking what isn't ours, never mind actually robbing and killing, which are two sins whose gravity you will discover when you die and receive the severe punishment of His Divine Justice.'

António de Faria was amazed at the boy's answers and asked him if he wanted to become a Christian. The boy looked at him and said:

'I don't understand what you're talking about and I don't know what you are suggesting to me. Explain it to me first and then I will give you an answer.'

António de Faria explained to the boy about Christianity and baptism with his customary well-chosen words. The boy didn't reply to Faria but he looked up to the heavens, raised his hands and said, weeping:

'O Lord God, blessed be your patience that suffers there to be people on this earth who speak so well of You and yet have so little regard for your law – like these blind wretches who think that flattery and evasion can satisfy You like some tyrant prince who lords it on this earth.'

The boy didn't want to talk any more at all and went away into a corner to weep; and in three days he never took a bite of any of the food that we brought to him.

We discussed among ourselves where we should go to next and whether it was best to set our course to the north or the south; there were several very different opinions about this but in the end it was agreed that we should go to Ning-po, two hundred and sixty leagues to the north, because along the Chinese coast we might be able to arrange another, larger vessel more suited to our needs. The boat we had just captured was too small for such a long voyage and we were fearful of the many storms that the new moon brings to the coasts of China, with ships being lost regularly.

With this plan agreed upon we hoisted sail when it was almost sunset, leaving the stunned Chinese behind us on the beach and sailing east-nor'-east through the night. Around daybreak we were off the island of Guintu where we commandeered a fishing-boat with a big haul of fresh fish. We took as much fish as we needed and press-ganged eight of the twelve fishermen to help us sail the lantea – we were still too weak and exhausted from our earlier hardships to handle her properly.

We questioned these eight fishermen about the ports along that coast as far as Chinchow. We thought we might come across a Portuguese carrack from Malacca in one of these ports. The fishermen told us that eighteen leagues away there was a big river called the Xingrau. It was a good anchorage and was frequented by lots of junks carrying salt, pumice stones, olive oil, mustard and gergerlim, and we could stock up there with everything we needed. There was a poor fishing village called Xamoy at the mouth of the river but three miles upstream there was a city with plenty of silk, musk, porcelain and other goods that the people used for trading in different places.

In the light of this information we set our course for the Xingrau river and arrived there the following afternoon. We anchored about a league out to sea because we feared that our sins might bring another calamity down on our heads, like the ones we had suffered in the past.

That night we seized another fishing-boat and questioned the fishermen about the junks anchored in the river: who owned them, how many there were, how many men were aboard each one and other such matters that had some bearing on our plans.

The fishermen told us that at the moment there were only about two hundred junks anchored upstream outside the city because the rest had already set out for Hainan, Sumbor, Lailu and other ports in Cochin-China; but in the village of Xamoy we would be safe enough and the villagers would sell us whatever supplies we needed. So we entered the river and dropped anchor near the village, resting there for about half an hour until around midnight.

António de Faria was well aware that the lantea we had captured was not suitable to take us all the way to Ning-po, where we had decided to lay up for the winter, so we all agreed that we should find ourselves another larger vessel; and although at this time we were still not fit enough to start any trouble, our necessity obliged us to attempt more than was advisable, given our recent exhaustion and debilitation.

There was a small junk anchored by itself outside the village and at this time of the night the few people aboard her were all asleep. Faria saw this was a good opportunity to arrange for a larger boat so he hoisted anchor and drew alongside the junk. He picked fifteen of our twenty-seven soldiers as well as eight slaves and we climbed up onto the deck of the junk without anyone on board hearing us.

We found six or seven Chinese sailors sleeping on deck. We tied them up hand and foot, threatening to kill the lot of them if they made any noise – so they were all too frightened even to whisper. Then Faria cut the moorings and as quickly as we could we sailed out into the open sea and kept moving for the rest of the night, heading out to sea all the time so that by daybreak we were off the island of Pullo Quirim, nine leagues from the Xingrau river.

God aided us with fresh winds to fill our sails and three days later we dropped anchor off the island of Luxitai where we had to stop over for fifteen days to give our sick and injured the chance to recover completely. The air there was very healthy, and we had plenty of fresh water and fresh food that local fishermen brought to us in exchange for rice.

While we were at Luxitai we searched the junk thoroughly but found she was carrying nothing more than a cargo of rice that the Chinese had been selling in Xamoy. We dumped most of this rice into the sea to make the junk more buoyant and safer for the voyage to Ning-po, then transferred everything from the lantea to the junk. We beached the lantea to careen and caulk it; we could use it for going ashore in the ports where we would be stopping.

As I've said, we spent fifteen days at Luxitai doing all this until our sick were completely restored to health; then we set out on the voyage to Ning-po where, according to the reports we received, there were plenty of Portuguese from Malacca, Sunda, Siam and Patani, all of whom at that time usually wintered in Ning-po.

56 : *We meet a Chinese pirate friendly to the Portuguese and strike an alliance with him.*

WE HAD SAILED ALONG THE COAST OF NING-PO FOR TWO DAYS with favourable winds and tides when by chance – and praised be Our Lord – we met with a junk coming from the Ryukyu islands, captained by a Chinese pirate called Kai Panjan, a native of Patani. This Panjan was a great friend of the Portuguese, very fond of our customs and our clothes, and had thirty Portuguese in his command, hand-picked by himself, who all received regular allowances, besides many other favours that Panjan did them all the time, so they all had plenty of money.

As soon as Panjan's junk caught sight of us they made ready to attack, because they didn't know we were Portuguese. Kai Panjan was an old hand, well-versed in the art and science of piracy: he manoeuvred into position for boarding us, making use of the cross-wind with all sails hoisted and tacking around to windward. Then he bore down to ram us astern between masts, closing on us until he was little more than a base-shot away, when he fired a salvo of fifteen guns, mostly falconets and bombards, causing great confusion among us.

António de Faria encouraged us all with his bravery and fine Christian spirit and positioned us at key points on the top-deck, the bow and the stern, with other men held in reserve to fight wherever they were most needed. We were ready to see through to the end whatever Fortune might bring us – but then Our Lord mercifully granted that we should notice the junk carried a large flag with a cross on it and a lot of men in the fo'c'sle wearing red berets, which at that time was what our men very often wore when they were going into battle. We guessed then that they were Portuguese sailing from Ning-po to Malacca, which is a regular voyage with that monsoon. We signalled to them to see what response they made. As soon as they saw we were Portuguese a great shout went up from them and they furled their foreward mainsail in acknowledgement. They quickly despatched a pinnace with two Portuguese aboard to find out who we were and where we had come from. As soon as they were sure we were Portuguese they came directly towards us and saluted us. When we had returned their salute they came aboard.

António de Faria gave the two Portuguese the warmest of welcomes and because they knew some of our soldiers they stayed a long time, swapping stories and information with us. Cristovão Borralho went back with the two Portuguese to meet Kai Panjan, bringing him a letter from Faria full of compliments and great offers of friendship. This letter made Panjan so pleased and proud that he couldn't contain himself for vanity.

The pirate junk came abreast of us and furled its sails, then Kai Panjan came across in a sampan (that served as a longboat) to meet António de Faria, accompanied by twenty Portuguese. He brought Faria gifts of amber, pearls and pieces of gold and silver, worth more than two thousand cruzados; and Faria welcomed Panjan and his Portuguese with great warmth and joy, and made a great fuss of them.

After they had exchanged pleasantries for a while they all settled down and António de Faria gave them the full story of his losses at the hands of Koja Hassan, and his shipwreck and all our other misfortunes since we had left Malacca. He said he was determined to go to Ning-po and gather up men and galleys there so that he could start searching the coast of Hainan again and go upriver from the coast of Cochinchina to the mines of Quanjip-aru where, he had been told, there were six big warehouses full of minted silver, besides the great amounts being worked at in the foundries on the banks of the river. There, without any risk at all,

65

we could all make ourselves very, very rich.

To all this Panjan answered:

'Sir, I do not have as much wealth as some people think I have. At other times I have indeed been very rich but the malicious blows of Fortune – like those you have just told us about in your own case – took away the greatest part of my wealth. And now I am afraid to return to Patani, where my wife and children are, because I know for sure that the king there will seize everything I bring back with me. You see, I left without his permission and he will cause trouble about that, just to provide an excuse to rob me, as he has already robbed other people on several occasions, with much less reason than he has in my case.

'So if you would be happy with the arrangement, I propose to accompany you on your planned expedition. I have a hundred men and fifteen cannon and thirty muskets aboard my junk, and my Portuguese have another forty muskets of their own. I will gladly join forces with you in return for a third of all the spoils. If this is agreeable to you, Sir, give me your written guarantee and swear on oath by your religion that you will keep your part of the bargain.'

Faria willingly accepted the offer. He complimented Panjan with many fine phrases and embraced him repeatedly before swearing an oath on the Holy Gospels that he would honour the agreement down to the last detail; and he quickly gave Panjan a written guarantee with ten or twelve of the most reputable men there as witnesses.

With the pact signed and sealed the two junks sailed to the Anay river, five leagues away, where we were able to buy all the supplies we needed after bribing the commander of the city with a hundred cruzados.

☐And still there was no sign of the elusive Koja Hassan. One day a small fishing boat was seen adrift at sea. On board were eight Portuguese, barefoot, wounded, in dire straits. They were the sole survivors of three large Portuguese trading 'naus' (carracks) that had been seized off the nearby island of Sumbor by a pirate fleet of seven ships led by – Koja Hassan. The pirate ships had repeatedly rammed the naus; the tactic had been successful, but the pirates had suffered some damage and had put into port for repair.

Here, at last, was news of Koja Hassan! Antónia de Faria dropped anchor in Lailo, and spent two weeks in preparation for battle. He part-exchanged his battered vessels for two larger, newer junks and two oar-propelled lanteas; they bought gunpowder, shot, fire-pots, grappling hooks and the rest. On board, counting soldiers and sailors, there were five hundred men, ninety-five of them Portuguese.

After three days sailing, the flotilla reached the river Tinlau and heard that Koja Hassan was still in port. One of the Portuguese, disguised as a Chinese, was rowed gently up river to spend the day fishing, and in making leisurely observations of the Moorish ships. The attack on them was launched under cover of darkness, just before dawn, and achieved complete surprise.□

59 : *We catch up with Koja Hassan. His fate.*

WE SAILED UPSTREAM HELPED BY A WIND AND A TIDE THAT GOD sent us, and in less than an hour we were bearing down on Koja Hassan's junks where they lay at anchor. As yet we had still not been seen, but the pirates were always on their guard, fearing the local people might retaliate for the crimes and suffering inflicted on them daily, and when their look-out finally spotted us a bell started ringing wildly and there was so much commotion and uproar, both on the junks and on the shore, that you couldn't hear yourself speak.

When António de Faria saw all this he shouted to us:

'Now, my comrades and brothers! Let's strike at these pirates, for the name of Christ, before their lorchas get out from the shore to help them! Saint James be with us!'

And straightaway we fired a full round of artillery which was so accurate, praised be Our Lord, that most of their bravest men – who had rushed to their positions in the fighting-castles – were blown to pieces. We took this as a good omen for the rest of the battle. Then our musketeers, one hundred and sixty men in all, received the signal to fire and they almost swept clean the top-decks of the two pirate junks, so that our enemies didn't dare show their faces on deck. After this our two junks pulled alongside the pirate junks and hand-to-hand fighting was joined on all sides.

To be honest, I wouldn't presume to give a detailed account of all that happened, even though I was there myself: it was not yet clear daylight when the battle started and the confusion of fighting at close quarters was so great, besides all the noise of trumpets, gongs, and bells, and the shouts and cries from one side and the other, and the cannon booming and the muskets cracking, and all of this tumult then echoing across the hollows of hill and valley all around – it made my flesh quiver with fear.

The hand-to-hand fighting on the junks continued for a quarter of an hour so that four lorchas had time to set out from the shore to help Koja Hassan with plenty of reinforcements. Diogo Meireles, who was on board Kai Panjan's junk, spotted these lorchas but saw that his gunner was so beside himself with excitement that he was wasting shot and incapable of hitting any target at all. The distracted gunner was just about to fire again when Meireles pushed him so hard to one side that he knocked him through a hatchway and shouted down to him: 'Get out of the way, you good-for-nothing oaf! At a time like this a gun like this is meant for a man like me and not for the likes of you!' Meireles was well used to handling a culverin and he quickly took aim and fired. The shot hit the leading lorcha on the starboard side, ripping through the hull from bow to stern along the waterline so that she quickly filled with water and went straight to the bottom, drowning everybody on board including the officer in command of the four lorchas. With his next shot Meireles hit the deck of the second lorcha and killed her captain and six or seven of the men standing beside him. The other two lorchas were terrified by this and were in such a panic to turn and get to the shore that they got badly entangled in each other's rigging and were stuck there together, unable to move either backwards or forwards.

Gaspar de Oliveira and Vicente Morosa, the captains of our own two lorchas, saw the time was right for them to play their part and, spurred on by an honourable desire for glory, they launched themselves into the attack and hurled firebombs into the two snared lorchas, setting them both on fire so that they burned right down to the water-line. Most of the men aboard them jumped into the sea where they were picked off by our bow-men, and not a single man of them was left alive.

In these three lorchas alone more than two hundred men died; and the other lorcha, whose captain had already been killed by Meireles, had no chance of escape because Kai Panjan went after it in his sampan, the small boat attached to his junk. He caught up with the lorcha when it was almost ashore but there was nobody aboard – they had all jumped into the sea to escape but most of them were smashed to death on some rocks near the shore.

There were still about a hundred and fifty pirates fighting on their two junks, all Muslims from Luzon, Borneo and Java, but when they saw the fate of the lorchas their resistance began to weaken and some were already jumping overboard to escape.

Until now we hadn't known which of the heathen dogs was Koja Hassan himself but he reacted very quickly to the disarray that he saw among his men. He was wearing a breastplate covered in crimson satin fringed with gold – taken off some unfortunate Portuguese – and he shouted three times at the top of his voice so that all his men could hear him:

'*La ilaha illa-Mahu Muhammad rasūl Allahi!*' 'Muslims! Honest followers of Mohammed's holy law! How can you let yourselves be beaten by such weaklings as these dogs, who have no more heart in them than white hens and bearded women? Arise and attack them! Arise and attack them! We have the certain promise of the Book of Flowers where the prophet surfeited with delights the holy men of Mecca: and he will do just the same for every one of us here today if we bathe ourselves in the blood of these godless savages!'

The devil's words so encouraged his men that they formed themselves into a body and charged back into the fight so ferociously that it was astonishing to see how they threw themselves at our swords.

Now António de Faria shouted encouragement to his own men:

'Fellow-Christians and comrades! If these dogs take strength from the damnable religion of the devil, let us take strength from Christ Our Lord Who died on the cross for us, because He will not abandon us, however great our sins may be, for in the end we belong to Him and these curs do not!'

And in his fervour and zeal for the faith, Faria hurled himself at Koja Hassan and struck the pirate a fierce blow on the head with his two-handed sword, cutting right through his chain-mail helmet and sending him crashing to the deck. Then he rolled Hassan over with his sword and chopped off the pirate's two legs so that he would never get up from the deck again. When Hassan's men saw this they gave a great shout and rushed towards Faria. Six or seven of them got near him, so spirited and reckless that they took no heed of the thirty Portuguese who were around him; Faria received two blows which almost had him down but our men rushed to save him and Our Lord so strengthened their sword-arms that in little more than the time it takes to say two Hail Marys forty-eight of the enemy were killed there alongside their leader, for the loss of just five Portuguese and nine slaves, all good men and faithful Christians.

By now the remaining pirates were weakening and they withdrew in disorder to the fo'c'sle, intending to barricade themselves in there; but twenty of the thirty soldiers in Kai Panjan's junk moved swiftly and engaged the pirates face to face before they could secure the fo'c'sle. Our men fought so fiercely that the pirates started jumping overboard into the water in so much panic that they were crashing on top of one another.

Our spirits were now so quickened by the name of Christ Our Lord, on whom we called continually, and by the victory and the honour we knew were ours that we ended up by killing all the pirates except for five who were taken prisoner. We tied these up hand and foot and threw them into the hold, intending to torture them later for information – but they bit each other's wrists and bled themselves to death rather than face torture and death at our hands. So these five bodies were quartered by our slaves and the pieces thrown into the sea along with that cur Koja Hassan, pirate-captain, chief mullah of the King of Bintang and 'spiller and drinker of Portuguese blood', as he titled himself at the beginning of his letters and publicly declared to all Muslims, which made him greatly revered among the members of that accursed, superstitious sect.

□António de Faria and Kai Panjan spent twenty-four days in the Tinlau river after the bloody battle against Koja Hassan. The Christian dead were buried, other corpses were shoved overboard to 'the huge lizards' that infested the river and its banks, and Koja Hassan's body was drawn and quartered. The booty from the battle was enormous, for it included the dead pirate's accumulated acquisitions, by trade and seizure, including many chests of Japanese silver coins. Three of the captured vessels were needed to carry the spoils.

The victorious flotilla now resumed the journey to Ning-po, where the leaders planned to winter, before voyaging to the rich mines of Quanjiparu, the agreed next target now that the feud with Koja Hassan had been ended. Soon after leaving the shelter of the river, however, they were struck by a furious tempest. António de Faria's ship (with Pinto on board) struck a reef. At night, in the violent tumult, they had to chop away the masts and superstructure and then, to lighten the ship still further, to cast everything overboard, even finally the chests of silver. Next day, they were taken aboard by the other ships, most of which had suffered damage and loss. One of the lanteas had broken away from the junk to which it had been lashed, and it had sunk, with the loss of all hands. Many other men had been swept overboard by the huge waves breaking across the decks.

The reduced and damaged flotilla put into Nouday. There, so António de Faria had been told, thirteen Portuguese members of his crew, captured in previous engagements, had been imprisoned. He sent two Chinese messengers to the mandarin in charge offering to purchase the release of the prisoners. The offer refused, he sent the messengers again, this time with money and gifts and an elaborate letter. In the letter, he happened to refer to his being a servant of the King of Portugal, the friend and 'brother' of the Emperor of China. Such presumption so infuriated the mandarin that he had the messengers whipped, their ears cut off, and sent back with orders to the Portuguese and their allies to leave at once.

António de Faria and Kai Panjan decided to attack. They could still muster some three hundred people, seventy of them Portuguese; these they put ashore within a short march of the city. □

65 : *We attack and sack the city of Nouday.*

THE FOLLOWING MORNING, WHEN IT WAS ALMOST CLEAR DAY-light, António de Faria sailed up-river with his three junks and lorcha, and the four barges we had seized. We anchored in six and a half fathoms of water close to the walls of Nouday.

We furled the sails without firing a salvo or giving any other kind of salute but hoisted the trading flag, after the Chinese custom, so that by making this peaceful gesture we wouldn't have to offer any further courtesies. However, Faria was well aware that nothing he did was likely to make any difference because he was already damned as far as the Mandarin of Nouday was concerned. He sent yet another gift to the mandarin with promises of a larger ransom for the prisoners and pledges of lasting friendship: but this so outraged the heathen dog that he ordered our poor Chinese messengers to be crucified and put on show to all our ships from the top of the walls.

When Faria saw this he gave up the last hopes of a peaceful outcome that some of his men had still encouraged him to have, and the soldiers started to get angry and impatient and told him that since he had agreed to make a raid ashore, he should make it now without waiting any longer and giving the enemy time to gather up more men. Faria thought this was sound advice and went ashore shortly afterwards with all the men picked for the raid, who had been standing around, ready to go. He ordered the junks to maintain a steady bombardment of the city, directing their fire to wherever they saw the largest numbers of the enemy gathered, until they saw the raiding party join battle with the enemy.

Faria landed about the length of a base-shot below the harbour, meeting no resistance whatsoever, and marched along the beach towards the city where there was already a great number of people gathered on the walls, with a mass of swirling silken banners and blaring trumpets and shouting. They were like men relying more on noise and show than on anything they were actually going to do.

When we were little more than a musket-shot's distance from the ditches outside the walls, about a thousand men (though some of us reckoned it was nearer twelve hundred) sallied out against us from two gates. Between a hundred and a hundred and twenty of them were mounted on horses – or, to be more accurate, on undernourished nags – and these horsemen began to skirmish with us on our flanks. They executed this manoeuvre so deftly and expertly that most of the time they rode straight into one another and many of them went crashing to the ground three and four at a time. From this performance it was obvious to us that these men were the scrapings of the barrel and had come out to fight because they had been forced to rather than through any desire of their own. So Faria happily encouraged his men about the prospects for battle and gave the signal to the junks to stop their bombardment. He halted and waited out in the open because, judging by all the fanfares and showing off, it was there that the mandarin wanted to pit his forces against us.

The enemy started skirmishing again, circling round us like men threshing corn with their feet, as if they thought that was menacing enough to make us turn back. When they saw that we were not retreating as they had expected or, which is more likely, as they had hoped, they all gathered into one body and, crowded together in a disorganized mass, they halted for a while without advancing any further.

When António de Faria saw how badly organized they were he ordered our musketeers, who hadn't been used at all until then, to fire a volley and, thanks be to God, they took aim so well that more than half of the horsemen in the vanguard were brought to the ground. We took heart from this and charged into the attack, calling on the name of Jesus as we ran, and in His mercy He ordained that the enemy should abandon the field, fleeing in such panic that they were falling over one another, and when they reached a bridge over the ditches they were in such confusion that they weren't able to get to the gates or turn to flee elsewhere!

The main force of our men caught up with them at this bridge and charged so fiercely into them that very soon there were more than three hundred of the enemy piled dead one on top of the other – a pitiful sight to see because not one of them had even drawn his sword.

Emboldened by this success we then rushed at the city gates where we were met by about six hundred men led by the mandarin himself, mounted on a fine horse and wearing a breastplate covered in red velvet and old-fashioned gold-work. We learned afterwards that this armour had belonged to one Tomé Pires, whom King Dom Manuel of glorious memory had sent as an ambassador to China in 1516 aboard the carrack of Fernão Peres d'Andrade, during the time that Lopo Soares d'Albergaria was governor in India.

The mandarin and his men chose to face us at the gates and such a fierce struggle ensued that for the time it takes to say four or five Hail Marys they fought us much more bravely than their comrades on the bridge – until one of our slaves knocked the mandarin from his horse with a musket-shot in the middle of the chest. This so frightened the Chinese that they all turned tail together and began rushing pell-mell back inside the gates, with us at their heels, stabbing them with our lances, and not one of them had the presence of mind to try and close the gates. So we drove them before us like a herd of cattle down a very long street and then out through a gate on the other side of the city into the open country, where they all scattered and hid, with not a single man left behind in the town.

António de Faria sounded the recall and lined his men up into an orderly troop so that he could keep them under control and then marched straight to the 'chifanga', the gaol where our men were being held prisoner. When the prisoners saw us coming they cried out so desperately, 'Lord God have mercy on us!' that it made our flesh tremble. Faria ordered the doors and bars to be smashed with axes and we were so willing and enthusiastic for the task that in a few moments the place was smashed to pieces and the irons were knocked off the prisoners' hands and legs and our comrades were unchained and free.

Faria told us all that every man should grab what he could for himself: there wasn't going to be any organized share-out of the spoils, just every man keeping for himself anything and every-thing he could carry. He just warned us to be quick about it because he wasn't allowing us more than half an hour. We were all more than happy with this arrangement and immediately began ransacking the houses. António de Faria himself went for his share to the mandarin's house where he found eight thousand taels in silver-plate alone and five big jars of musk that he ordered to be taken away. All the rest he left to his servants, and this included a lot of silk, silken thread, satin, damask and boxes of delicate porcelain which everyone helped themselves to until they could carry no more.

The four barges and three sampans in which we had come ashore had to make four trips back and forth to the junks and there wasn't a man among us who didn't talk about the boxes and boxes of loot he had taken aboard (besides all the rest that every man kept quiet about).

After an hour and a half Faria ordered everyone to get back to the junks as quickly as possible but the men couldn't bring themselves to leave behind the smallest piece of loot that they were carrying – and this was most obvious among the people of highest rank. António de Faria saw what was happening and, because it was getting dark already and he was fearful of some

74

calamity overtaking us, he ordered fires to be started in ten or twelve different places. The city for the most part was built of pine and other kinds of wood and in less than a quarter of an hour it was burning like the fires of hell.

So everyone then ran down to the beach and got back to the junks without any opposition whatsoever. We were all very rich and very happy. We had also captured a lot of beautiful girls for our use later on and it was pitiful to see them coming along in groups of four and five, hands tied up with musket-fuses, the girls all weeping and our men all singing and laughing.

☐Sailing from Nouday, the Portuguese were attacked by a pirate, Premata Gundel but, with the help of their ally, Kai Panjan, won the battle. They arrived at two islands, which were known as the Gates of Ning-po (near Canton). Faria asked formal permission to come ashore, for he feared that the news of his sack of Nouday might prejudice the Chinese authorities against the Portuguese and prevent peaceful trade. Faria was welcomed by the Portuguese community at Ning-po, who gave him a splendid reception, as if he were a king or a viceroy.

Faria and his men stayed there five months. Alas, Kai Panjan died, which greatly saddened Faria. He gave up a plan they had formed together to seek the gold mines of Quanjip-aru: instead he decided to look for the island of Calempluy, celebrated for containing seventeen tombs of the Emperors of China. On 14 May 1542 Faria set sail from Ning-po.☐

75 : *We reach the island of Calempluy. The tombs of the kings.*

WHEN WE ROUNDED THE POINT OF GUINITARAN WE SAW AN island about two leagues ahead of us. It was as flat as meadow-land, sitting in the middle of the river, and from that distance there seemed to be little more than a league around its entire shoreline.

António de Faria sailed closer, his great enthusiasm mixed with more than a little fear because until then he hadn't under-stood the enormous danger into which he had led us all. It was after three o'clock in the morning when we finally dropped anchor a base's shot from the island.

At daybreak there was a meeting of the officers and they all thought it impossible that something as spectacular and majestic as the tombs of the kings would be left without some sort of a guard. They decided that the best thing to do was first of all to scout right round the island without drawing attention to ourselves, looking out for suitable landing-places and trying to discover anything that might hinder us from going ashore; then, in the light of this information, they would decide what to do next.

With this intention António de Faria, making as little noise as possible, sailed in close to the shoreline and right around the island, taking his time and noting in detail everything that was visible to the eye.

The land was levelled off inside a wall of carved jasper built right around the island. This wall rose up to a height of twenty-six palms above the river and was made of slabs of very high quality stone which were so tightly set in place that whole wall looked as if it was made of just one single enormous piece of jasper. Such skilled workmanship utterly amazed us because we had never seen the like of it before, not in Portugal nor in India nor anywhere else. In fact the wall had been built up from the actual riverbed, a depth of another twenty-six palms, so its full height was fifty-two palms in all from base to top. Along the rampart on the top of the wall there was a rounded parapet, also carved of jasper, the girth of a twenty-four-gallon barrel and twisted like a friar's cord. This parapet ran the length of the wall with railings of lathe-turned brass set into it. There were little brass niches set into the railings at intervals, each one sheltering an idol of a woman holding a round ball in her hands (we only learnt the meaning of these idols later). Inside these railings there was an enormous number of cast-iron monsters, all standing in a line and holding each others' hands as if in a dance, completely encircling the island which, as I've said, was about a league in circumference.

Inside this huge circle of monstrous idols there was a circle of finely wrought arches with an abundance of decoration for the eyes to study and take delight in. Inside these arches the rest of the island was covered by a grove of dwarf orange trees – there was no other variety of tree at all – and in the middle of this orange-grove stood three hundred and sixty hermitages dedicated to the gods of the year, about whom these pagans in their chronicles tell great stories in justification of their ignorance.

About a quarter of a league further inland on a steep hill to the east we could see some buildings with seven façades, in the manner of churches, and every inch of them that could be seen was covered in gold-leaf. They had very high bell-towers (or so we presumed them to be) and were encircled by two rows of arches of the same design as the façades of the buildings and these too were decorated with gold from the tops of their spires down to the bases of their pillars. From all of this we reckoned that the buildings must be a lavish temple of immense wealth.

After we had scouted and studied the island António de Faria decided to go ashore, although it was already very late, to see if he could get any information in one of the hermitages, because that information would decide whether we went any further or withdrew. He left the necessary guard on the two boats and went ashore with forty soldiers and twenty slaves, half of them with arquebuses, half with lances. He also brought four Chinese who had been to the island several times, to act as guides and interpreters. He left Fr Diogo Lobato, a lively and intelligent man, in command of the two boats.

When they had landed – still without having seen a single person or having heard the slightest noise or movement – António de Faria quickly went through one of the eight gateways in the wall and made his way through the orange-grove towards a hermitage he could see in the distance, perhaps the length of two musket-shots from the place where we had landed. What he found in the hermitage you will hear presently.

76 : *We meet a hermit guarding a tomb.*

ANTÓNIO DE FARIA LED THE WAY TOWARDS THE HERMITAGE, moving as quietly as possible. We were all a bit wary because we had no idea what we were getting ourselves into, and we all advanced with the sweet name of Jesus on our lips and in our hearts. We still hadn't seen a trace of a living soul when we came to a small clearing in front of the hermitage.

Broadsword at the ready, Faria went up and tried the front door. It was locked on the inside. He told one of the Chinese in our company to knock. The man knocked twice and a voice called out from inside:

'Praised be the Creator Who shaped the beauty of the heavens! Please, walk around to the back of the hut and tell me what it is you want.'

The Chinese walked round and went in through the back door, then came and opened the front door where Faria was waiting.

We all went in and found an old man sitting there; at a guess he was over a hundred years old. He wore very long robes of purple damask and had the bearing of a man of noble character – as afterwards we indeed found him to be.

When the old man saw this crowd of armed men in his little hut he was so beside himself that he fell face-down on the ground, hands and feet quivering, unable to utter a single word. It took a long time for the old man to calm down again and for his shock to pass, but eventually he fixed his gaze on us and, with a serene face and brisk speech, he asked us who we were and what we wanted.

Faria replied through a Chinese interpreter:

'Kind sir, I am the man in command of all these foreigners, natives of the kingdom of Siam. I have come here on pilgrimage now to keep a promise I made to give thanks to God for bringing me safely through the great dangers of a shipwreck in which I lost a full cargo of merchandise. I also came here begging for alms to redress my present poverty – but on that score I swear that within three years I will repay twice over to you all that I take now.'

The 'hiticu' (as the old hermit was called) considered for a little while what he had just heard, then looked straight at Faria and said:

'I have heard clearly what you have to say for yourself. I have also clearly understood the devilish intention by which your blind folly, like a pilot from Hell, is leading every last one of you down to the Deep Cave of the Lake of Night – because rather than praising God for the great favour you admit he has shown you, and have come here to rob Him.

'So I'll ask you now: if you do rob Him, what do you expect the divine justice to do with you after you breathe your last? Step aside from this evil path and don't let even the thought of such a

78

foul sin enter your heads! If you hold back from sin, God will hold back His punishment from you. Believe me, I am telling you the truth of the matter, may it protect me as long as I live!'

António de Faria pretended to think that the old man had given him sound advice. He replied:

'Kind sir, I ask you not to be so upset. Let me assure you that I am only doing this because at the moment I simply don't have any other means of livelihood than what I can take while I am here.'

When he heard this the old man raised his hands, looked up to the heavens and started to weep, saying:

'Blessed are You, O Lord, that You suffer there to be men on earth who take to sinning against you as a way of life and not even the promise of eternal glory will make them serve You for so much as a single, solitary day!'

The old man was pensive for a little while until distracted again by the noisy, disorderly scene around him as we rifled and raked through the coffins. He turned and asked Faria (who was standing nearby, leaning on his broadsword) to sit down beside him. Faria obliged him with a display of courtesy and reverence, although he kept nodding to us all the while to get on with the business in hand of sorting out the silver from the bones in the coffins.

The sight of us rummaging through the coffins was so unbearable to the hermit that he fainted and fell off his bench, like a man outraged to be a witness to so grave a sin. He got up wearily and sat down again beside Faria and continued talking:

'You're a man who seems intelligent enough to understand what I'm going to say. I want to explain clearly to you just what is involved in the forgiveness of sins. I want to tell you so that you won't perish for all eternity when your mortal body has breathed its last.

'You tell me that necessity alone compels you to commit grave sin and that, granted the time to do so, you will restore everything that you take. If you are indeed sincere you will do these three things that I tell you.

'First: you will return everything that you take from here before you die so that your robbery will not impede the mercy of the Lord on High on your behalf.

'Second: you will sincerely beg His forgiveness because what you have done is repugnant to Him and deserves unceasing punishment for your body in Hell.

'Third: you will treat God's poor as liberally as you treat yourself, giving alms with discretion and prudence from your own store so that the slaves of darkness will have no accusations to lay against you on the Day of Judgement.

'And now I beg you to tell your men to gather up the bones of these saints so that their remains are not left scattered and disgraced.'

António de Faria promised that he would do everything that the hermit had urged him to do, which reassured the old man somewhat although he was not altogether satisfied. Then Faria drew close and embraced the old man, soothing him with mild sentiments and talk of love and courtesy, saying that after hearing such wise counsel he greatly regretted having undertaken this journey at all but his men had threatened to kill him on the spot if he tried to pull out of it. The hermit said:

'God wishes it to be so! At least you will not have so much to suffer as these other slaves of darkness, who are like famished curs; by the look of them all the silver in the world would not be enough to sate their greed.'

77 : *The hermit condemns our desecration of the tomb.*

WE GATHERED UP ALL THE LOOT WE COULD FIND IN THE HERMITAGE and sent it back to the boats. We decided not to go looking for any more because it was nearly dark and we were unfamiliar with the terrain; but we hoped to continue looting at our ease the next day.

António de Faria was ready to go back to the boats but first he wanted to bid farewell to the old hermit. He consoled the old man with well-chosen words, begging him, for the love of God not to be too scandalized because it was only the dire poverty into which Faria had fallen after the shipwreck that made him act as he did, and such behaviour was not a true reflection of his character.

Faria said that after listening to the hermit earlier he had repented of what he had done and had wanted to go back to the boats straightaway but his men had sworn to kill him if he did turn back; so he had kept his mouth shut out of fear and agreed to go along with them in what he himself clearly saw to be as great a sin as the hermit said it was. He had resolved, however, that just as soon as he was rid of all these others he would travel through the world doing as much penance as was necessary for the expurgation of so grave a sin.

The hermit said:

'May it please the Lord, Who lives and reigns over the beauty of the stars, that He should not hold it against you that you understand His ways as much as your words show you to do: for I tell you solemnly, the man who knows God's laws and yet commits evil, that man is in much greater danger than the godless heathen whose ignorance excuses him before God and the world.'

At this point one of our men, Nuno Coelho, joined in the conversation and told the old man not to worry his head so much about so little.

The hermit replied:

'If you call this sacrilege a small matter then your fear of eternal death is a great deal smaller yet, because you spend your life committing such foul deeds – deeds as foul as I believe your soul to be, rotten all the way in from that dunghill you call your body!

'And if your overpowering greed wants yet more silver to finish stuffing your infernal appetite to the full, then in those other buildings you will find enough silver to fill yourselves till you burst – which would be the most appropriate thing to do because if you are damned for what you have taken already, you should go and take the rest as well so that the more you are carrying, that much quicker will you sink to the bottom of hell!'

Nuno Coelho told the old man he should show forebearance in the face of evil, just as God had commanded us to do in His holy law. The hermit put his hand to his forehead in amazement and shook his head five or six times, smiling at what he had just heard. He said:

'Believe me, I have just heard and seen what I thought I would never hear nor see: evil posing as virtue, robbing God and preaching His holy law at the same time! Your folly must be great indeed because you put your trust in such fine words while you spend your lives committing evil! I doubt if God will bother trading words with you on the Day of Judgement!'

The hermit didn't want to hear any more from Nuno Coelho and turned to Faria with outstretched arms and begged him to stop his men from spitting on the little altar in the hut, a sight that hurt him far more than if they were to kill him a thousand times over. Faria said he would tell his men to spare the altar and this consoled the hiticu a bit.

It was very late by now but before we left Faria questioned the old man about the other hermitages; he wanted more information about the place to allay some of his fears and uncertainty. The hermit said there were three hundred and fifty 'talagrepos', one in every hermitage, and forty 'manigrepos' who looked after the hermits, bringing them provisions and looking after any of them who were sick. Faria had asked if there were any weapons in the huts but the hermit said that people who endeavoured to make their way to heaven had no need of weapons, only forebearance.

Another question Faria asked was whether the King of China ever came to Calempluy. The hermit explained that the king had no need to come to the island because, being the king, he was the Son of the Sun and could absolve everyone of their sins, while no-one could accuse the king himself before the Sun.

The hermit also told us why so much silver was left mixed in with the old bones in the coffins: the silver was the alms the dead brought with them to the Heaven of the Moon, to distribute there as the occasion arose.

Faria asked many other questions but his final one was, did the hermits marry?

The hermit replied:

'For those who seek eternal life it is essential that they have no fondness for the pleasures of the flesh. In the sweet, sweet honey-comb the bee is born whose sting will hurt and scandalize those who eat the honeycomb!'

Then Faria embraced the hermit and took his leave with a great deal of formality, as is the Chinese fashion. It was completely dark by the time we were back on our boats. We were determined to go ashore again the following day and ransack the other hermitages where, as the old man had told us, there was an enormous amount of silver and some idols made of gold.

On account of our sins, however, we were prevented from

bringing our expedition to Calempluy to a successful conclusion – something we had worked towards for two and a half months, enduring so much hardship and danger.

78 : *The alarm is raised on Calempluy. Our plans are foiled.*

WE WERE ALL BACK ON OUR BOATS JUST BEFORE THE EVENING Angelus and rowed to another part of the island, dropping anchor about a falconet's shot offshore. We waited there until around midnight. As I have already mentioned, we were determined to go ashore again as soon as it was daylight and loot the rest of the tombs (which were about a quarter of a league away from us) and load up our two boats with the booty.

And perhaps our plans could have ended well enough if we had acted more wisely or if António de Faria had followed the advice he was given and brought the old hermit back with us to stop him from getting word to the bonzes about our arrival and what we had done; but Faria didn't want to do this. He said he felt quite safe on that score because we had all seen how old and gout-stricken the hermit was, his legs so swollen that he could scarcely stand.

But the truth wasn't at all what Faria imagined it to be. We learned later that as soon as the hermit saw us aboard our boats, and being too doddery to walk, he had crawled on his hands and knees to the next hermitage, which was a little more than a crossbow-shot away from his own, and told the hermit there what he had done and asked him to go and alert the bonzes because he was too old and feeble to go that far himself; and the other hermit had set out for the bonzes' house without a moment's delay.

We ourselves soon understood that the alarm had been raised, because at one o'clock in the morning we could see a long line of bonfires – obviously some kind of signal – along the wall of the great pagoda of the tombs of the kings. We asked our Chinese sailors what they thought the fires meant and they said that without a doubt we had been discovered and they urged us to hoist the sails immediately and get away.

António de Faria had been sleeping but when we raised the

alarm he jumped up straightaway, beside himself with surprise, then slackened the anchor-cable by hand and took the tiller, steering us into the shore to see if there were any signs of activity. When we reached the landing-jetties we heard the great clamour of the bells ringing in all the hermitages and every once in a while the sound of people running and shouting. Our Chinese sailors said to him:

'Sir, there's nothing more you need to see or to know! Let's get away now, for the love of God, sir! Don't cause every last man of us to be killed here!'

Faria paid no heed to what they said but leapt ashore with six other men carrying swords and bucklers. He raced up the steps from the jetty, dismayed at the turn of events and beside himself with anger. He clambered wildly over the railings on top of the wall that encircled the island and ran all over the place like a madman without discovering anything at all. Then he came back to the boats, still raging, and argued with everyone about what should be done next.

Some of our soldiers gave him reasons why we should leave at once – none of which he wanted to accept; and most of them simply demanded that we set sail. He agreed to this because he was afraid of a mutiny but first, he said, for the sake of his honour, he had to find out just who or what he was running away from, so he begged them the favour of waiting for him there while he went ashore and tried to confirm beyond all doubt that we had indeed been discovered. He asked for just another half-hour's grace to do this, which would still leave us plenty of time to get clear away before daylight.

A few men spoke out against this further delay but he wouldn't listen to them. He swore his oath to us on the Holy Gospels and took our word of honour in return, then he left us all and plunged off into the orange grove with the six men who had accompanied him earlier.

Faria had gone a bit further than the distance of four musket-shots into the middle of the grove when he heard a bell ringing ahead of him. He followed the sound until he came across a hermitage far more ornate than the one we had looted the previous day. There were two men inside the hermitage, both of more or less the same age and wearing religious robes with their beads around their necks, so Faria presumed they were hermits.

Faria caught these two by surprise and seized both of them; one of them was so shocked that for a long time he wasn't able to talk sense at all. Four of Faria's companions went into the hermitage and grabbed a fair-sized silver idol from the altar. The idol had a mitre of gold on its head and a wheel in its hand, though they didn't know what these symbolized. They also took three silver oil-lamps with long silver chains attached to them.

Then Faria headed back with all speed to the boats, almost dragging the two gagged hermits along the ground behind him. Once he was back on board we hoisted sail as quickly as we could and made our way back down towards the open sea. Faria questioned the hermit who was most in control of himself, threatening him with violence if he caught him lying.

The hermit told us that a holy man called Pilau Angiru had indeed arrived in the middle of the night at the bonzes' house and started banging in a frenzy on the door and shouting:

'O unhappy men, soaked in the drunken stupor of the flesh! You who have professed a solem oath to honour the goddess Amida, richest prize of all our labours! Hear me, hear me! Hear the most miserable wretch that ever yet was born! Hear from me that strangers from the ends of the earth, with long beards and bodies of iron, have broken into the House of the Twenty-Seven Pillars, where the holy man who told me this sweeps the floors! And while these barbarians steal the saints' treasure they contemptuously throw the sacred bones to the ground and defile them by spitting out their rotten stinking phlegm upon them, laughing madly all the while like demons hardened and obstinate in their original sin. So I beg you to protect yourselves because they have sworn to kill us all when the morning comes. You must either escape right now or else call on those who will defend you because you are religious and it is not your place to take anything in your hands that might draw blood!'

The prisoner went on:

'Everyone in the bonzes' house was woken up by this shouting. They rushed straight to the door and found this old hermit stretched out on the ground, almost dead from sheer misery and exhaustion. It was then that the 'grepos' and 'manigrepos' lit all the bonfires that you can see now, and as quickly as it could be arranged they have sent out messages to the cities of Corpilem and Fumbana, asking them to send us as soon as possible all the men they can muster, and to call on all the surrounding countryside to do the same.

'And I can assure you without fear of contradiction that those two cities will not delay a moment longer than is necessary in sending help and, indeed, if it were possible, they would fly here with the speed and power of famished goshawks just freed from the leash.

'And believe me that this is the truth I am telling you about what has happened: so I beg you not to kill us but to let us go, because killing us will be an even greater sin than the sacrilege you committed yesterday; and remember that God has so much taken us into His care, on account of the penances we have done, that He keeps us in His sight all the hours of the day.

'So strive to save yourselves as best you can because I tell you solemnly that the earth, the air, the winds, the waters, the peoples and the animals of the earth, the fish of the sea, the birds of the air, the grasses and the plants and everything that grows in the ground, indeed every single living thing in God's creation – today these will all hinder you and hound you so mercilessly that only the Lord in heaven Himself will be able to help you.'

This hermit finally convinced António de Faria that we had been discovered and we immediately set off downstream as quickly as we were able, while Faria tore at his beard and raged at himself for having ruined, through his carelessness and folly, a plan that would have been a tremendous triumph if he had been able to carry it through to its finish.

79 : *Typhoon in the Gulf of Nanking. Faria's fate – and ours.*

FOR THE NEXT SEVEN DAYS WE MADE OUR WAY ALONG THE Gulf of Nanking, keeping to the middle of it in order to take most advantage of the swift currents, as if our only hope of salvation lay in those currents; but we were like men distracted: we were all so unhappy and disgruntled that none of us could talk reasonably about anything.

When we reached a village called Susoquerim we were able to anchor in the harbour because the villagers didn't know who we were and had no idea we were coming from Calempluy; so we kept our true identity a secret and were able to load up with provisions and make enquiries about what route we should follow. After two hours we set out again and as quickly as we could sailed into an estuary which was less used by ships than the main channel. This estuary was called the Xalingrau and we travelled along it for nine days, covering a hundred and forty leagues.

When we re-entered the main channel – and here it was more than ten or twelve leagues wide – we kept on our course with westerly cross-winds for another thirteen days. We were all well and truly weary of the troubles and fear we had lived with since we escaped from Calempluy and, furthermore, there was little enough food for us to eat. Finally, when we were within sight of the mines at Conshinacow, lying at $41\frac{2}{3}°$ we were caught by a southerly gale – what the Chinese call a 'typhoon'.

The driving rain and the winds of this typhoon were so violent that it didn't seem a natural storm at all; and because our galleys were small and undermanned we were so hard-pressed that we just lost faith in being able to save ourselves and let ourselves roll towards the shore, thinking it preferable to die on the rocks than drown in the sea.

We left things to run their course to this fatal end but evening came and we still hadn't reached the miserable goal we had chosen as the lesser of the two evils and least troublesome. At last a wind burst from nor'nor'east that made the seas so turbulent and wild that it frightened us just to see the height of the waves. We were so terror-stricken that we began to ditch all our cargo overboard, and our panic was so great that even the provisions and boxes of silver were thrown into the sea. Then we cut down the two masts – by this time the sails had been torn down anyway – and we drifted like this for the rest of that day.

It was almost midnight when we heard great cries of 'Lord God, have mercy on us!' coming from António de Faria's boat. We supposed that they were going under and shouted just as loudly across to them – but we didn't hear another sound, so they must have been swamped even then. This left us so stunned and beside ourselves with fear that for a long time nobody could speak a single word.

We passed that saddest of nights in agony and affliction until an hour before daybreak when our boat sprung a leak above the keel and we were soon drawing eight palms of water. We now knew we were going to sink without the least chance of a reprieve, and we accepted that Our Lord judged it meet for that our lives and our hardships should end there, at the bottom of that sea.

When it was clear daylight and we could see all around us, there wasn't a trace of António de Faria's galley; we were all so shocked that none of us was fit to do anything more. Our agony and trials lasted until almost ten o'clock and our fear and woe were such that I wouldn't dare try to use words to express them. Then our half-swamped boat was almost up to the shore and, at long last, the heaving waves threw us onto a rocky point and smashed our boat to pieces. We were all thrown into the sea clinging to each other and crying, 'Lord God have mercy on us!' But only fourteen of us were saved. Eleven Portuguese, eighteen baptised slaves and seven Chinese sailors were all drowned there together.

This calamity occured on a Monday, August 5th, 1542, for which Our Lord be eternally praised.

80 : *After the shipwreck.*

THE FOURTEEN OF US WHO HAD ESCAPED THIS WRECK, THROUGH the mercy of Our Lord Jesus Christ, spent that whole day and the following night weeping over our sad fate and the wretched state in which we found ourselves, not knowing what to do next because the surrounding terrain was very rugged and mountainous and we hadn't yet seen a single person whom we could ask for help.

When we discussed among ourselves what we should do, it was agreed that we should make our way inland because it was obvious that sooner or later we were bound to come across people who would at least take us prisoner and feed us until Our Lord saw fit to put an end to either our lives or our hardships.

We set off through some mountains and after six or seven leagues we were able to see a great swamp on the far side, stretching as far as the eye could see with no sign of solid ground on the far side of it. We had no choice but to turn and go back to the place where we had been wrecked. We arrived there near sunset on the following day and found the bodies of all our comrades washed up onto the shore: and once again we all fell to the ground and wept without restraint at such a sight.

The next morning we buried the bodies to prevent the tigers that abounded there from eating them. This task, with all its attendant grief and labour, took us the greater part of the day to complete because there were thirty-six corpses – and they were already bloated and decomposing, so the stink was unbearable – and we had no tools for digging other than our own bare hands. We scratched out holes in the sand to put the bodies in and it took all of us nearly half an hour to dig each grave.

When we had buried the corpses we took refuge in a pool of water for fear of tigers and stayed there until daylight. Then we set out again, heading northwards through woodland and brush that was so thick in parts that we could only get through with a great deal of trouble.

We kept going for three days without seeing a single person in all that time and eventually we came to a river. We decided to swim across, but the first four men who dived in – three Portuguese and a slave – were drowned almost immediately because they were weakened and frail, while the river was wide with a strong current: they didn't have enough strength to get more than a third of the way across. These three Portuguese were all well respected men, natives of Ponte de Lima: two were brothers, Belchior and Gaspar Barbosa, and the third was their cousin, Francisco Borges Caeiro; all three were fine men of physical strength and good character.

When we saw the miserable fate of our companions and how our number was being cut down hour by hour, the fourteen of us who were left – eleven Portuguese and three slaves – broke down, lamenting and weeping over what we had just seen happen to our comrades and what we expected to happen to ourselves very soon. We spent that dark night racked by the rain and the wind and the cold and our own tears and groans until, all praise to Our Lord, just before daybreak we saw a big bonfire over to the west. When it was daylight we headed off in the direction of the fire, guided by some of our number who were still capable of thinking clearly, and entrusting ourselves to that all-powerful Lord from whom alone we hoped for the relief of our trials and sufferings.

We continued our miserable trek along the banks of the river for most of the day and it was almost sunset when we arrived at a clearing in the woods where five men were working, burning charcoal. We went up to them and threw ourselves at their feet, begging them for the love of God to tell us where we could get help for ourselves. One of the men said:

'God grant that there's not more than the one evil of hunger killing you, but I see so many of you that all the sacks we have here will not be enough to cover all your battered, naked bodies. But may God receive our souls willingly, because for His sake we will give you the bit of rice we brought with us for our supper and hot water instead of wine: that will get you through the night, if you want to take it, but really the best thing for you to do – even though it is a bit more trouble – would be to go on ahead to that building you can just about see from here. It's a hostel for the travellers who pass through this country all the time.'

We thanked them gratefully for the eager and generous charity they had shown us and accepted the alms of rice from them, though it amounted to no more than two mouthfuls for each one of us. Then, without more ado, we bade farewell to them and headed off along the path to the hostel they had pointed out to us, walking as quickly as our exhausted bodies would allow.

□Pinto and his companions went begging on their way to Nanking, where they expected to find a ship. Generally they were given shelter in the poor-houses, but in one village they were taken for thieves and thrown to the leeches in a cesspit. Finally, they were set free; exhausted, they continued their journey.□

83 : *We arrive at a farm belonging to a very sick nobleman.*

WE LEFT THE VILLAGE OF XIANGULI AND CAME TO SOME POOR hovels where three men were pounding flax. As soon as they saw us these men ran away into some pine trees on a hill and from there they shouted down to passers-by:

'Robbers! Robbers! Watch out for yourselves – there's a band of robbers down there!'

When we saw this we were afraid that we were going to be mistaken for thieves again and stoned and thrown in a cesspit, as had happened in Xianguli, so we moved on straightaway, even though by now it was almost dark and we didn't even know where we were going. We continued on our way in great weariness, not knowing which was the right path to follow, walking in the hail and rain through the middle of the night until we came to some cowsheds where we stopped and rested on a dung-heap until daylight, when we continued along the same path.

After the sun had fully risen we found ourselves at the top of a hill with a great plain below us. The plain was covered with trees and in the middle, beside a stream, stood several imposing buildings with lots of towers and spires and golden weather-vanes. We made our way towards them, with the name of Jesus always on our lips, and sat down beside a fountain at the entrance to a courtyard outside the buildings. We hadn't seen a soul yet, and we spent a good part of the day sitting there in confusion and uncertainty.

At long last we saw a youth of seventeen or eighteen riding towards us on a fine horse and accompanied by four men on foot, one of whom was carrying two hares and the other three or four 'nivatores', which are a kind of pheasant. He had a falcon perched on his forearm and a pack of six or seven dogs followed at his heels. When this young man reached us he reined his horse and asked us who were and what we wanted. We answered by telling him all the details of our misfortunes. We could see by his reaction that he was deeply moved by what we told him and he rode on into the courtyard, saying to us:

'Wait there and for the love of the One who, with the glory of his great wealth, lives and reigns in the highest heavens, I'll arrange everything you need in a moment.'

A short while later an old woman came out and called to us. She was wearing long robes and beads around her neck, like one of those women that the people at home call 'a holy Mary'. This woman said to us:

'The son of our lord and master, who feeds us of his store, sent me out to you. Come in with me modestly so that you won't look like idlers who would rather beg than work for a living.'

So we followed the old woman into an inner courtyard that was much more impressive than the one where we had been waiting: it was enclosed all the way round by upper and lower verandas, like cloisters in a monastery. These verandas were decorated with paintings of hunting scenes depicting women on horseback with falcons on their arms. At the far end of this courtyard there was a very broad staircase rising under a great arch of finely wrought stonework to the upper floor. Hanging from the apex of the arch on a long silver chain was a shield bearing a coat-of-arms that portrayed a man with the features of a tortoise inside a circle: the man's feet were above and his head below, and there was a motto: *Ingualic Fingau Potim Aquarau*, which means, 'Everything of mine is thus'.

We were told that this monster, which the Chinese paint upside down, is an image of the world in which worldly things are deceitful. To disillusion those who pay too much heed to the world this beast proclaims, 'Everything of mine is thus', that is to say, upside down, with its feet where its head should be.

We climbed the stone staircase and went into a large room where there was a woman of about fifty sitting on a dais with two beautiful girls beside her, all finely dressed and with strings of pearls around their necks. An old man was lying on a cot between these women and one of the young girls was cooling him with a fan. The young man we had spoken to was standing beside the cot as well, and nine young girls in white and crimson damask were sitting around the dais, working at embroidery frames.

As soon as we reached the dais we fell to our knees and begged the old man for alms. We began our plea with a few tears and used the choicest words that the circumstances and our necessity taught us. The old woman said to us, waving her hand:

'Enough! Enough! It pains me to see you weeping like this and I can see for myself that you genuinely need to beg for alms.'

Then the old man called out to us, asking if anyone among us knew how to cure fevers. The girl who was fanning him – she was his daughter – smiled across at her mother and said to the old man:

'Honestly, father, these men are more in need of food for their hunger than of being asked to do something which they probably know nothing about in the first place. The right thing to do would be first to provide them with what they most need and then, afterwards, attend to what is less important.'

Her mother told her off, saying:

'Hold your tongue! You're always speaking out of turn! One of these days I'll put an end to that cheek of yours!'

But the daughter laughed and said:

'First put an end to their hunger because you can put an end to the other any time you want!'

However the old man, obviously weakened by his sickness, turned to us again and asked us who we were, where we were from, where we were going to, and other questions in the same vein. We framed our answers to suit our needs, just telling him about our shipwreck and all our comrades who had been drowned, and how we were now stranded there without the slightest idea of what to do next. The old man was pensive for a little while then turned to his son and said:

'What do you think of what you've just heard from these foreigners? I'd ask you to bear it in mind so that you will be able to recognize and please God and thank Him continually for the father He gave you, the father who with his life and wisdom won the best three estates in this province in order to save you from trials such as these men endured and the countless other trials that there are in the world. The least of these estates is worth more than a hundred thousand taels – but you would rather go hunting hares than have all this!'

The son made no response other than to smile across to his sisters.

The old man ordered food to be brought in for us and gestured to us to start eating – which we did most willingly; he obviously enjoyed seeing us eat heartily while he himself was so sick and frail. However, the ones who most enjoyed the sight of us eating were the old man's daughters, because while we were eating they exchanged many amused remarks with their brother when they saw that we ate with our fingers: in the Chinese empire they don't eat with their fingers but use two short bits of wood, like spindles, to bring the food to their mouths.

The old man noted that when we had finished eating we gave thanks to God and he raised his hands to the heavens and said in a flood of tears:

'With a humble heart I praise you, O Lord, who lives and reigns in the serenity of your highest wisdom, because You allow alien peoples from the far ends of the earth without any knowledge of your laws to give you thanks and praise according to their own frail lights, which you will accept as readily as if it was an elaborate offering of sweet music to your ears!'

Then he ordered three pieces of linen and four taels of silver to be given to us and asked us to sleep there in his house that night because it was already too late for us to be setting out again. We accepted his offer and thanked him profusely in the manner they are accustomed to – and this obviously satisfied him and greatly pleased his wife and daughters.

84 : *We reach Taipur, and get arrested.*

WHEN WE LEFT THIS NOBLEMAN'S HOUSE WE TRAVELLED ON TO a place called Guinapalir and then wandered on from place to place for almost another two months, keeping clear of the cities and towns lest our true identity be discovered, until we came to the town of Taipur, where we were destined to pay for some of our past sins.

When we arrived in Taipur it so happened that a chumbi was staying in the town. The chumbi is the president of the district courts and every three years he visits the districts within his jurisdiction to review the conduct of the judges and other officials of justice. The chumbi in question noticed us begging in the street from a window and ordered us to be brought before him. He questioned us in the presence of three clerks of the court and a lot of other people who had quickly gathered to see what was going on. He asked us who we were, and where we came from and why we were begging in the streets of Taipur. We told him:

'We are natives of the kingdom of Siam. We were shipwrecked in a storm at sea and are travelling through the country begging from door to door, trying to keep ourselves alive with the charity of good people and to make our way to Nanking, where we should be able to get a merchant-ship for Canton and there meet up with other Siamese merchants and return home with them.'

The chumbi was satisfied with this and was ready to let us go on our way – but one of the clerks spoke up:

'Your Honour, you must not release these loafers! These men are vagabonds who spend their days tramping from house to house, taking advantage of honest people's charity which isn't due to them at all! Under the laws relating to vagrancy in the Seventh Book of Laws you cannot release these vagabonds under any circumstances on pain of being severely censured by your

94

superiors. So I advise you, as your trusted servant, to order us to give these fellows a little something to stop them running off to start their begging somewhere else!'

The chumbi followed the clerk's advice with all the cruelty that you would expect from a godless heathen. He promptly started legal proceedings against us, with false witnesses making ugly, incriminating statements about us – which is a common trick amongst them – and ordered us to be thrown into prison.

We spent twenty-six miserable days in this prison, with chains on our feet, manacles on our hands, collars round our necks and tormented by hunger and beatings. Finally, the chumbi directed us to be sent for trial to the High Court in Nanking because in his own judicial capacity he was not empowered to pass a death-sentence on us.

85 : *We are taken to Nanking and receive a severe sentence.*

THE TWENTY-SIX DAYS WE SPENT IN THAT MISERABLE, MERCILESS prison seemed like twenty-six thousand years to us! It was plain to see that if we weren't rescued we would all meet our end there – indeed, that was the fate of one of our number called João Rodrigues Bravo, who was eaten alive by lice without our being able to do a thing to save him. It was a miracle that the rest of us escaped from that plague with our lives.

One morning they led us out of the prison, still weighed down with our chains and so sick and feeble that we could only speak with great difficulty, and put us on a boat along with thirty or forty other prisoners who were also going to the High Court in Nanking to stand trial for serious crimes.

Nanking is the second city of the empire and a chiang is based there permanently. After the emperor himself, a chiang holds the highest position in the empire, like a viceroy, and in Nanking he has charge of a hundred and twenty 'jerozemos' and 'ferucuas' who are like High Court judges, Crown Magistrates and review judges, and who deal with all civil and criminal legal affairs, allowing no review, appeal or complaint other than to the Supreme Court of Appeal which has jurisdiction over the emperor himself. An appeal to this Supreme Court is just like crying out to heaven and indeed it is called *Xinfau Nicor Pitau*, which means, 'The Breath of the Creator of All Things.'

So that you can better understand the Chinese system, you should know that the High Court in Nanking (and others like it in all the major cities of the empire) has complete authority from the emperor in civil and criminal law, bound by no appeal or complaint. However, the high courts set up a court superior to their own – and the emperor's – jurisdiction to which appeals can be made in important cases of the utmost gravity.

The Supreme Court judges are twenty-four 'menigrepos' or monks, known as 'the twenty-four of the Austere Life', which is a religious order like the Capuchins. If these men were Christians much would be expected of them on account of the hard, frugal life they lead and all the penance they do. Usually these menigrepos are at least seventy years old before they can sit on this bench and even then they need the permission of their religious superiors, who appoint the menigrepos to the position. In all the cases brought before them the judgement of these menigrepos is so to the point and impartial that there simply isn't anything left to be said: if they gave a judgement against the emperor himself, or against any power on earth that you care to name, absolutely nothing could entice them to deviate in the slightest from what they understand to be the justness of the case.

We left Taipur to sail to Nanking, as I mentioned earlier, and that first night we stopped at a large town called Potimlu. We had to spend the next nine days in the gaol there because the new moon brought torrential rainstorms that made it impossible to navigate the river safely.

While we were held in the Potimlu gaol Our Lord desired us to meet a German who was also being held prisoner there and he welcomed us with great charity. We were able to understand each other by speaking Chinese and we asked him where he was from and how he had come to be there. He told us:

'I am a native of Muscovy, from a city called Hikajin. I've been in prison here for the past five years, serving a life sentence for killing a man; but on account of my being a foreigner I have lodged an appeal in Peking with the court of the Ay-tau of the Batampina, who is the most senior of the thirty-two ay-taus who govern the thirty-two provinces of the empire. This ay-tau has particular responsibility for the law-cases involving foreign travellers and sailors. That is my last hope of being set free to return and die as a Christian among Christians.'

After spending nine days in the gaol at Potimlu we set out again, sailing along a very large river for another seven days until we reached Nanking, which is the second city of the empire and the main city for the provinces of Ning-po, Fanjus, and Sumbor.

We spent another month and a half in prison in Nanking, enduring more than enough hardship and want because we had come to such an extremity of wretchedness that we were dying of neglect and abandonment before our own eyes, and there was nothing for us to do but weep and call out to heaven.

The first night we arrived in the prison we were very quickly beaten up and robbed and left without even a stitch of clothing to cover ourselves. This prison was very large and yet so crowded (we were told it had more than four thousand inmates) that there wasn't a single corner where a man could sit down in peace without being quickly robbed or else covered in lice and vermin.

After a month and a half an ordinary magistrate gave his judgement on our case. His verdict was read out to us in the prison and went as follows:

'As required by the Guardians of Justice, I have studied the evidence of your crimes, submitted by the Chumbi of Taipur, which proved your malicious intent. You have not been able to contradict the least part of this evidence and what you did have to say for yourselves could not be given enough credence to satisfy the demands of the law.

'You are hereby sentenced to be whipped on the buttocks in public, in the hope that this punishment will make you mend your ways. You are further sentenced to have your thumbs cut off because there are well-founded suspicions that you would use your hands to commit robberies and crimes so evil that the Sovereign Judge who reigns in Heaven would punish them with the might of His just law on the day to end all days.

'The rest of the punishment you merit I will leave to be decided by the High Court, as justice requires, because it has greater powers than mine to sentence you.'

We would rather have died than suffer the terrible, cruel whipping they gave us after the sentence was read out. We bled until our blood covered the floor; we bled so much we counted it a miracle that nine of us survived the whipping – although two

Portuguese and a slave did die of their wounds three days afterwards.

86 : *The care we received in prison.*

AFTER WE HAD BEEN WHIPPED THE GUARDS CARRIED US INTO A
building that served as the prison-infirmary, where there were
many sick and injured people lying in cots and on the floor. Our
wounds were soon treated there, cleaned and rubbed with oils
and bandaged, which eased the pain of the lashes a little.

We were nursed by good men who belong to something like
our Fraternities of Mercy. They visit the prisons for the love of
God and with great charity provide the sick with an abundance
of clean clothing and food.

We had been in the infirmary for eleven days and were beginning to feel a good deal better – although naturally lamenting the
loss of our thumbs as demanded by the sentence we had received
– when God saw fit that one morning two men in very long, red
satin robes should come into the ward. They carried white rods
in their hands like sceptres and when they entered all the sick
prisoners shouted as with one voice:

Pitau hinacur makuto chindu! which means, 'May the ministers of God's works bring God with them!'

The two men raised their white rods and called in reply:

'And may He grant patience to all of you in your trials and
adversities!'

They started handing out money and clothing to the prisoners
nearest to them and eventually reached us. They greeted us
pleasantly and were obviously moved by the sight of our tears;
they asked us who we were, where we were from and why we
were imprisoned. Amid a flood of tears we told them everything
about our shipwreck, our begging from place to place through
the countryside, our arrest by the chumbi in Taipur and our trial
and punishment in Nanking.

They listened carefully and then thought about what we had
told them for a few minutes; then they looked up to Heaven and
called out, as their eyes filled with tears and they fell on their
knees to the ground:

'O powerful and patient Lord of the highest heavens, you
allow the cries of the weak and powerless to shatter your ears so

that the grave insults the ministers of our justice continually offer you should not go unpunished, insults that by our faith in your Holy Law we believe will be punished sooner or later!'

They questioned some of the people in the prison about what had happened to us and then immediately sent for the clerk of the court who had handled the case. He was threatened with severe punishment if he didn't bring the complete record of our arrest, prosecution and sentence with him. He came over to the prison straightaway and told the two men everything that had happened and just how far this perversion of justice had gone.

It was too late, of course, to do anything about the whipping but these two Attorneys of God's Charity for the Poor (to give them their official title) lodged a petition of complaint with the chiang. He replied with a statement on behalf of the High Court: 'Mercy is inappropriate where justice is badly served – as it will be if we accept your petition.' The statement was signed by the chiang and eight conchalis, who are criminal magistrates.

These two advocates wanted to free us from this injustice and when they saw the unfavourable response from the chiang they quickly wrote another petition to the Supreme Court of Appeal, 'the Breath of the Creator of All Things.'

In this petition we confessed like sinners to the charges against us but pleaded for mercy. They sent it without delay to the Supreme Court. The menigrepos who sit on the bench are religious like our Capuchin friars and they have great authority and prestige with both the emperor and the ordinary people. In this court they review all the cases involving poor people and people who have much less influence than those taking them to court.

As soon as the petition was delivered a bell was rung to call the twenty-four menigrepos together. When they read all the details about the conduct of our case they saw at once that justice had gone by the board completely. They quickly sent two clerks of the court with a sealed letter to the chiang to halt the proceedings in the High Court and transfer the case to the jurisdiction of the Supreme Court of Appeal. The chiang accepted the directive in a public statement that ran as follows:

'This court of the Might of the Lion Crowned on the Throne of the World accepts the petition of the twenty-four of the Austere Life that these nine foreigners should be sent to appear before the court of the Ay-tau of the Batampina in Peking, so that his mercy will alleviate the sentence they have received. Given on the seventh day of the fourth moon in the twenty third year of the reign of the Son of the Sun.'

This statement was signed by the chiang and eight conchalis from the criminal court. It was brought to us soon afterwards by the two Attorneys of God's Charity for the Poor who had taken charge of our case. We took the document from them and exclaimed:

'God reward you for all you have done for us for His sake!'

The advocates replied:

'And may he guide you to a knowledge of His works because it is in that knowledge alone that you will gather the fruit of your hardships like those who fear His name.'

88 : *We set out from Nanking for Peking. The glories of Nanking.*

THE BROTHERS OF CHARITY GAVE US THE LETTER OF INTRODUCTION to their house in Peking and we set out before dawn the following day, chained up together in threes to our oars. We travelled in irregular daily stages on account of the treachery and great strength of the currents in the Batampina at that time of the year.

One day we anchored near sunset at a little village called Minhacutim, the home of the chifu who had charge of us. He spent three days there attending to some business; then his wife and family and household came aboard and we continued on our way in the company of a large number of other vessels travelling along that river to different provinces and domains of the empire.

The fact that we were chained to the oars of our lantea didn't prevent us from seeing some truly remarkable things in the cities, towns and lands that lie along the banks of this great river, so I'll say a few words about the fraction of the marvels that we saw and I'll begin with the city of Nanking itself, where our journey started.

Nanking is situated at 39⅓° north on the banks of the river Batampina, which means, 'the flower of the fish'. We were told – and I later saw it for myself – that this river has its source in Tartary in Lake Fanstir which is nine leagues from the city of Lansam, where Tamburlane, the king of the Tartars, holds court for most of the year.

Lake Fanstir is twenty-eight leagues long, twelve leagues wide, of enormous depth and gives rise to the five greatest rivers in the known world.

The first of these rivers is the Batampina that flows for three hundred and sixty leagues through the middle of the Chinese empire and enters the sea in the Bay of Nanking at 36° north.

The second river, the Laichung, cuts its way with great force through the Pancrum mountains that separate the lands of Cauchin from the domain of Catibenan, whose interior has borders with the kingdom of Tsien-Pá at 16° north.

The third river, the Taukiday, which means 'mother of the waters', flows to the north-east through the kingdom of Nakatas (as I will explain later, that is where the original inhabitants of China came from in ancient times.) The Taukiday flows into the sea in the empire of Sornau (which is commonly called Siam) at the bar of Quy, a hundred and thirty leagues to the south of Patani.

The fourth river is the Batobasoy, which flows through Sansim province and enters the sea at Cosmin in the kingdom of Pegu. I will describe later how the Batobasoy flooded Sansim province in 1556.

In the opinion of Chinese geographers the fifth river, the Leysacotay, flows westwards as far as the province of Shinshipu, that borders on the kingdom of Muscovy, and they say it flows into a sea made unnavigable on account of the water temperature being more than 70°.

To return now to the matter in hand: the city of Nanking stands on the banks of the Batampina, built on a steep, fair-sized hill from where it commands the surrounding countryside. The climate of the region is a bit cold but nonetheless very healthy. The full length of the city walls is eight leagues, enclosing an area three leagues long by one league wide.

The ordinary houses have only one, or at most two, floors but the mandarins' houses are built completely at ground-level, enclosed by walls and moats with fine stone bridges giving access to the gates, which all have expensive, elaborate arches, and on the roofs there is an enormous variety of decoration. All these buildings, when seen together, present a vista of great majesty.

Chiangs, anchowsis, ay-taus, tu-tungs and chumbis are the

officials who govern the provinces and kingdoms of the empire and their houses have very tall towers of six and seven floors with spires covered in gold leaf. Here they have their private chambers, stores of arms, treasures, furniture, stores of silk and other expensive cloth and an infinity of exquisite porcelain, which the Chinese regard as highly as we do precious stones. This kind of porcelain never goes outside the kingdom, on account of it being worth a lot more among the Chinese themselves than it is among foreigners, and also because anyone caught selling it to foreigners receives the death penalty. The only exception to this rule is the Persians of Shatamas (which the Chinese call Sofio) who have been granted a licence to export some of the porcelain and who buy it at a very high price.

The Chinese told us that Nanking has eight hundred thousand inhabitants, twenty-four thousand mandarins' houses, sixty-two large squares, a hundred and thirty meat-markets with eighty butchers in each one and eight thousand streets, of which the most important six hundred are lined on either side of their full length with thick lathe-turned brass railings.

They also told us that the city has two thousand, three hundred pagodas, a thousand of which are monasteries for people in holy orders. These monasteries are most impressive buildings with towers housing sixty to seventy enormous metal and cast-iron bells – and to hear all those bells ringing at the same time is a frightening sound indeed.

The city also has thirty large, secure gaols, each one holding between two and three thousand prisoners; to each of these prisons there is attached a kind of Fraternity of Charity which attends to the needs of the poor, providing attorneys for them in all the civil and criminal courts, and handing out generous alms.

Each of the six hundred main streets have arches at either end and gates that are closed at night-time; most of them have fountains of the cleanest water and the streets themselves are prosperous and very busy indeed. At every new and full-moon these streets have their own markets where an infinite multitude of people from countless regions meet and mingle together, and there is an abundance of as many fruit, vegetables and meats as you can name available for sale.

The fish in the Batampina, above all the sole and the mullet are so plentiful and of such high quality that it seems impossible to describe them. The fish are sold live, hanging from hooks through their noses. Besides these fish fresh from the river there is also an infinity of salted and dried sea-fish for sale.

Something else the Chinese told us was that there are ten thousand silk-looms in Nanking, and the silk is sent out from here to the rest of the empire.

The whole city is enclosed by a very stout wall of fine stonework, with a hundred and thirty gates and bridges leading out over the moat. At each gate there are a gatekeeper and two halberdiers to keep a watch on everyone and everything that enters or leaves the city. There are twelve blockhouses along the walls built in a style very similar to our own with bulwarks and very high towers but not housing any artillery at all.

The Chinese told us that Nanking pays two thousand taels of silver to the king every single day. I will say nothing about the royal buildings in the city because I only saw them from the outside and I know nothing about them except what I was told by the Chinese – although that was enough to make me tremble to tell it all over again.

Further on I will describe everything that we saw in Peking – and I have to confess that I am already dreading describing even the little of what we saw of that city: not because it might seem strange to someone who has seen other marvels in China, but because I fear people who have not seen the grandeurs of China might measure them by the mediocrity to be found in their own native lands; and these people might want to cast doubt upon or perhaps deny any credibility at all to those things that don't fit in with their limited knowledge and narrow experience.

90 : *Our river journey continues. We come to Junquileu. A tomb we saw there.*

WE LEFT POCASSAR THE FOLLOWING MORNING AND SAILED ON to the city of Xinligau, which was just as large and impressive and full of very fine houses. The city was enclosed by brick walls and a moat; there were forts of stone at either end, very strong and well-built in a style similar to our own, with towers and bulwarks and drawbridges at the entries held by thick iron chains.

In the middle of each of these forts was a tower with five

floors, highly decorated with paintings in many colours, and the Chinese assured us that in each of these towers there were fifteen thousand piculs of silver – the income from this province that the present king's grandfather had ordered to be left there in commemoration of a son who had been born there. This son's name was Luquinau, which means, 'the joy of all', and the Chinese consider him to have been a saint because he died in religious orders. He was buried in Xinligau in a temple dedicated to Kai Varatel, the god of all the fish in the sea, about whom these people in their blindness have so much to relate concerning the laws he handed down and the precepts he gave. All these stories are a source of wonder and I will discuss them in their own place.

In Xinligau and another city five leagues up-river they weave the greater part of the silk produced in the empire, on account of the local water which they say makes the colours of the dyes more vivid than the waters to be found anywhere else. They told us that there were thirteen thousand silk-looms in the two cities yielding three hundred thousand taels (that's four hundred and fifty thousand cruzados) to the Emperor of China each year.

We continued on our way upriver and it was almost evening on the following day when we came to some enormous pastures where there were great herds of cattle and nags and mares, tended by a great number of horsemen who rear and eventually sell them to merchants who cut them up along with other sorts of meat in the meat-markets .

When we had sailed by these pastures – which stretched along the banks for ten or twelve leagues – we came to Junquileu, a town surrounded by a brick wall with spires on it but without any battlements, bulwarks or towers like those to be found in the other towns I have described.

On the river bank at the very edge of the town we saw some fortified houses, now old and dilapidated, that had been built on thick wooden stakes in the water. On a small terrace in front of the city gate there was a stone monument inside a fence of red and green iron railings. There was a roof of exquisite black and red porcelain tiles raised over the monument, supported by four columns of finely polished stone. On top of the monument were five cannonballs from a falconet and two other cast-iron balls from a demi-culverin. There was a plaque on the front of the monument with large lettering in gold that said:

'Here lies Tuan Hassan Mudelliar, uncle of the King of Malacca. Death carried him away before God could give him vengeance against the boldest pirate on the seas, Afonso de Albuquerque.'

We were all astonished by the sight of this plaque and we asked what story lay behind it. One of the Chinese, who seemed to be held in high esteem by the others there, told us:

'The man that lies buried there came here forty years ago as an ambassador from the king of a place called Malacca. He came seeking help from the Son of the Sun against men from an unknown land who had come across the sea from the ends of the earth and seized Malacca from his nephew, the king. He described this and gave details of other incredible horrors in a book that he wrote about the whole affair.

'He was at the court for almost three years pressing his request for aid; then, just when his request had been granted by the chiangs of the government, his misfortune was such that he took sick from a chill he caught while dining out one night and lived no more than another nine days.

'He was aggrieved at not having achieved what he had come to China to do, but he declared his lineage on the plaque on his tomb so that until the end of time the people of this country should know who he was and why he had come to China.'

We left Junquileu shortly afterwards and continued on our way. The river here is narrower than it is at Nanking but the surrounding countryside has many more villages and farms than any other stretch of the river and there's not a stone's throw between buildings, whether they belong to the pagoda or to a farm labourer or a workman.

Two leagues further on we came to a large terrace surrounded by a fence of very thick iron railings. In the middle of the terrace were two gigantic smelted bronze statues of a man and a woman. The statues were leaning against cast-iron columns seven fathoms in height and the thickness of a barrel. The base of these statues was seventy-four palms in diameter. The name of the male statue was Kai Xingatalor and the female was called Apancapatur. They both had their hands on their mouths, their cheeks were puffed out and their eyes looked so bloodthirsty they would frighten anyone who saw them. We asked about these statues and the Chinese told us that the man with his cheeks full of wind was the man who blew on the fires of Hell to torment the souls of those who had not given alms in this life; the woman was the gatekeeper in Hell and she allowed those people who had given alms in this life to escape from Hell to a very cold river called the Ochileuday, where she hid them without the devils of Hell doing them any harm at all.

One of us wasn't able to restrain himself from laughing at such nonsense and devilish folly. This so scandalized three bonzes (as they call their priests) who were standing nearby that they went to the chifu who was in charge of us and told him that if he didn't punish our irreverence to satisfy the two gods then without the shadow of a doubt the chifu's soul would be vilely tortured by the two of them, nor would they ever allow his soul to escape from Hell.

This threat so frightened the cur of a chifu that there and then he ordered all nine of us to be bound hand and foot and gave each one of us more than a hundred lashes. We were left lying covered in blood and from that time on we never laughed at anything we saw or heard.

At the time we arrived there twelve bonzes were burning incense to these two fiendish monsters, their silver censers full of myrrh and bejoin, and singing in high, discordant voices:

'Thus as we serve you, so you help us!'

A large number of bonzes responded with great shouts:

'Thus I promise you as a good master!'

In this manner they walked in procession for more than an hour around this large terrace, making these discordant noises and all the while ringing a great number of cast-iron and metal bells that were usually to be found in bell-towers. Other bonzes beat on drums and played citterns. All this made such a noise I must honestly admit it frightened me.

92 : *The strange origins of the Chinese Empire. Its first inhabitants.*

WHEN WE LEFT THE CITY OF SAMPITAI WE CONTINUED UP THE Batampina until we came to a town called Lichimpu, which has a population of ten or twelve thousand. It is encircled by a wall and a barbican with a moat; from what we were able to see it has good houses.

On the outside bank of the moat there was a large building with thirty furnaces along each inside wall. These furnaces smelt and purify an enormous amount of silver which is brought in small carts from Mount Tushenguim, five leagues away. The local Chinese told us that there were always more than a thousand men working in the silver mines which yield five thousand piculs of silver a year to the emperor. They told us other interesting details about the Tushenguim miners but I won't bother to mention them here for fear of being too long-winded.

When we left Lichimpu it was almost sunset and the following evening we anchored between two small cities that face each other across the river (which at this point is little more than a quarter of a league in width.) These two cities are called Pakan and Nakow, and both of them are very interesting, despite their small size, and they are well fortified with strong thick walls built of stone slabs. There were numerous pagodas covered in gold-leaf and adorned with weather-vanes and elaborately designed spires that must have cost a great deal of money. It was a beautiful scene that gave pleasure to the eye.

I will now relate what they told us there about the history of these two cities. I also heard this at different times afterwards and now you, my readers, can know about the origins of the Chinese empire, something that no writer in Christendom from ancient times up to the present day has ever written about.

In the thirteenth chapter of the first of the eighty 'Chronicles of the Kings of China' – which I heard read on many occasions – it is written that there used to be a kingdom known as Kwantipocow (judging by the record it would be situated around 62° north and on the same latitude as the coast of what we now call Germany.) The chronicles say that in the 639th year after the Flood there was a prince by the name of Turban, who was still unmarried but had fathered three children by a woman called Nankin, with whom he was deeply in love.

All of this scandalized his widowed mother, the queen, but Turban always made excuses whenever the royal counsellors pressed him to marry. The reasons he gave were unacceptable to his family and counsellors – indeed his excuses only spurred his mother on and rather than let the matter rest she encouraged the counsellors to press him all the more.

In the end, to avoid marrying against his own desires, Turban entered holy orders in the temple of a god called Gizom (this Gizom seems to have had an idolatrous sect among the ancient Romans, and to this day it survives in China, Japan, Cochinchina, Cambodia and Siam, and I actually saw for myself many of his temples in those lands.)

In his will Turban named his eldest son by Nankin as his appointed heir – but his widowed mother, who was fifty at the time, did not agree with the arrangement and said that if his last wish was to die in the religious life and leave the kingdom without a legitimate heir, then she herself would make good such a stain on the family's honour. Shortly afterwards she married one of her priests, a man called Silau, who was twenty-six years old, and in spite of a great deal of opposition, he took the solemn oath as king.

Turban was soon informed of what the queen had done and he realized that she had done it in defiance of the wishes expressed in his will and in order to exclude his own son from the succession. He promptly left his religious order and devoted all his energies and attention to returning to take control again of everything he had recently renounced.

His mother and her husband were afraid that if Turban succeeded it would finish with both their deaths: so they discreetly gathered a band of some thirty horsemen and eighty foot-soldiers and one night attacked the house where Turban was staying. They killed him and almost everyone in his company although Nankin and her three children and a few other members of the household escaped in a barge and fled downriver to a place some seventy leagues distant from the massacre; afterwards Nankin was joined there by some more supporters.

They made themselves secure on an island in the middle of the river and Nankin called the place Pilaunera, which means 'harvest of the poor'. She intended to live out her days there, working the land and supported by her followers, because at that time the land downriver from Pilaunera was still uninhabited (according to what it says in the same chapter of the chronicles.)

Nankin had lived for five years in this miserable poverty when the tyrant Silau, who was well aware how unpopular he was with his subjects, grew fearful that Turban's three sons, now that they were somewhat older, would try to take back everything he had usurped from their father; at the very least they could cause unrest and incite rebellion among the people, motivated by the rights they claimed to have to the kingdom. So Silau despatched a fleet of thirty rafts – said to be carrying one thousand, six hundred men – to track down Nankin and her followers.

Nankin received a warning about the force being sent against her and called her advisors together to discuss what action to take. It was agreed that the last thing they should do was wait there to meet the enemy fleet – Nankin herself was only a woman and her sons were still too young for leadership, while her followers were ill-nourished and poorly armed and would be heavily outnumbered and desperately short of everything that was needed to defend themselves against such a large force of well armed enemies.

Nankin ordered a head-count of all her followers and found that they didn't number more than thirteen hundred souls; of these only five hundred were men, the rest were women and children. For all these people they had just three small river-galleys and a small raft and these wouldn't carry more than a hundred people.

Nankin was well aware that these four boats could not possibly carry all of her followers and she could only wonder how to resolve such a great difficulty. The chronicles relate that she called her advisers together again and openly confessed her worries to them and asked them all for their opinions. The counsellors excused themselves from making a decision there and then, saying that in all truthfulness they felt that they were not wise enough to reach a decision so quickly about his dilemma. Instead, as they always did in times of peril, following their ancient customs and rites, they advised that lots should be drawn and whosoever was chosen would speak for all of them and reveal whatever thoughts God might inspire in his (or her) heart. In preparation for the drawing of lots there would be three days of fasting, weeping and repentance, so that all the people might plead as with one voice to the merciful Lord on High for relief and succour – for it was in his hands alone that their salvation surely lay.

Nankin and her family accepted this advice, which at that time seemed to be the best suggestion, and she issued a declaration that, on pain of death, nobody was to eat more than once in the next three days – so that their bodily abstinence would make their souls ready to receive God.

93 : *The fast is ended, the lots drawn.*

AFTER THE THREE DAYS OF FASTING AND PENANCE THE PEOPLE drew lots five times: on each occasion the lot fell to a seven year old boy called Silau – the very same name as the tyrant they all feared. This result left everyone very confused and saddened because it was checked and confirmed that the boy was the only one in the camp with that name.

However, after they had offered sacrifices to give thanks to God, with all the usual ceremonies using music and incense, they directed the boy to raise his hands to the heavens and to tell them what seemed to be the way out of their great peril and hardship. The story goes that the boy gazed at Nankin and said:

'O weak wretched woman! In your affliction and anguish you are sorely tried and bewildered by the meagre help afforded by human understanding – but thus it is that with sighs of humility you now submit yourself to the hand of the Lord on High! Now you must labour to tear your heart from out of the mists of the earth and truly fix your attention on the Heavens and there you will witness just how much the prayers of the innocent and the oppressed are worth to the Lord of Justice who created you: because at that very moment when you showed your weakness and powerlessness to him in all humility, at that very moment victory over the tyrant Silau was granted to you from on high, with this further great promise that the Lord of All sends to you through me, his worker-ant!

'He directs you to embark with your three sons and all your followers in the boats of your enemies. You will cross this land to the sounds of these waters, carefully keeping watch even by night, because before you reach the end of the river the Lord will show you a place where you will settle for a thousand years a royal house of such great renown that, until the ends of time, the mercy of the Lord will be praised in that land by the voices and the blood of foreign peoples, a sound as pleasing to his ears as the shouts of just and faithful children of a tender age!'

The chronicles relate that as soon as the boy had finished speaking he fell down dead, leaving Nankin and all her followers completely stunned.

This chronicle, that I heard read aloud on many occasions, goes on to state that on the fifth morning after the boy's prophecy Nankin's followers saw the enemy fleet of thirty rafts coming up the river in good order – but with not a soul to be seen aboard them! According to the chronicle, which the Chinese hold to be utterly truthful, this is what had happened: the fleet was proceeding as ordered mercilessly to execute Silau's cruel and devilish plan, but one night when they were anchored at a place called Catabasoy a black cloud appeared in the sky above the fleet. The cloud belched forth thunder-bolts and lightening and poured out a flood of torrential rain, rain that was so hot the men in the boats, who had all been awakened by the storm, jumped into the river to escape being scalded; but there was no escape and they all perished inside an hour because the scalding raindrops penetrated with an unbearable pain right through into the marrow of their bones and there was no clothing or anything else on earth that could protect them from that terrible rain.

When Nankin saw the empty boats she recognized it to be a great miracle. She received this gift from the hand of God with a flood of tears and gave Him abundant thanks for it. All her people duly set sail downstreram aboard the thirty rafts from the enemy fleet, as the boy had prophesied.

They travelled to the sounds of the rapid but favourable currents that carried Nankin and her people for forty-seven days to the site where the city of Peking now stands. It was there that Nankin went ashore intending to make her home, ensuring that she was as secure as possible with stockades and fortifications of loose stones because she still feared the tyrant Silau.

94 : *How the first four cities in China were founded. Some sights in Peking.*

FIVE DAYS AFTER NANKIN AND HER FOLLOWERS HAD LANDED IN this place she swore in her eldest son as prince of all her people. She did this to ease some of the fears she had always had for the succession and to free herself of the burden of leadership that she had endured for so long.

The very same afternoon that Nankin's son, Pekin, received the pledge of obedience from the few followers he had, he marked out a site where they were to build a town and make themselves secure against attack. He ordered the first trench to be dug as quickly as possible. When it was ready he re-emerged from his tent, accompanied by his mother – through whom everything was arranged – and his brothers and other leaders of the people.

This was his first formal appearance before his people as their prince. He was dressed in ceremonial robes and he walked with his party to the site, preceded by a servant carrying a foundation-stone that the prince had ordered to be cut. When the prince reached the spot where the first trench had been dug, he joyfully took the foundation-stone in his hands and fell to his knees. He raised the stone towards the heavens and proclaimed to the whole crowd gathered there:

'Brothers and comrades, to this foundation-stone of a new dynasty I give my own name: from this day forward it will be known as Peking. To this end I ask you, as comrades, and command you, as your king, to call this place by no other name so that until the end of time it will be fixed in the minds of our descendants that on the third day of the eighth moon in the 639th year after the Flood – when the Lord of All Creation demonstrated his righteous anger at the sins of men by flooding the earth – that on this day the young prince Peking started building his palace and gave his own name to it.

'Furthermore, in accordance with the prophecy revealed to us by the dead boy, Silau, this place will celebrate until the ends of time in the voices of strange peoples the paths of fearing the Lord and of pleasing Him with rightful sacrifice.'

To this very day the prince's exact words are engraved on a silver shield that hangs above the Pommicotau, one of the city's main gates; and to honour the memory of the boy Silau's prophecy there is always a guard of a captain and forty halber-diers posted at the gate – on all the other gates the guard is just four halberdiers, keeping watch on everything that enters or leaves the city.

The chronicles say the new king laid the foundation-stone for the city on the third of August, and ever since then, right down to the present day, the kings, and then the emperors, of China have followed the custom of appearing in public on that day every year. This royal procession is conducted with such majesty and such exotic, spectacular style that in all truth I declare anyone would be wary of trying to give an account of even the smallest part of it, never mind the procession in its entirety – so I don't want to start talking about this when I know very well that I wouldn't be able to do the subject full justice.

What the prince Pekin had said about 'the voices of strange peoples' when he laid the foundation-stone was taken by the Chinese to be an accurate prophecy, and his descendants passed a statute by which no foreigners – except for ambassadors and prisoners – were allowed to enter the kingdom, on pain of the severest penalties; so when the Chinese capture any foreigners they are compelled to banish them from one place to another – which is just what happened to the nine of us.

That is a brief account of how the city of Peking was founded and the Chinese empire populated by Prince Pekin, the eldest son of Nankin. Later Pekin's two younger brothers, Pakan and Nakow, founded two more cities, to which they also gave their own names; one also reads in the chronicles that Nankin herself founded and named Nanking, which today is the second city of the empire.

The chronicles tell us that the royal succession in the Chinese empire ran in an unbroken line from the time of Pekin down to a period that began in 1113, according to our European calendar. In a series of wars starting in that year the city of Peking was sacked and devastated twenty-six times by her enemies. However, by then Peking had a large population and the kings were very wealthy and the king Shishipan built a wall around the city over a period of twenty-three years; it is this wall and a second wall built eighty-two years later by his grandson Jumbilaytau that enclose Peking today.

As a matter of interest these two walls together run for a distance of sixty leagues, enclosing an area ten leagues long by five leagues wide. One reads in the chronicles that the two walls have sixteen hundred round bulwarks and two hundred and forty strongly fortified towers. These towers are tall, very spacious inside, and their spires decorated in many different colours make them most impressive. On every one of these towers there are golden lions standing on globes, which comprise the coat of arms of the Chinese emperor, giving us to understand that he is 'the lion crowned on the throne of the world.'

There is a wide moat girdling the outside walls, ten fathoms deep and forty fathoms wide. This moat is always crowded with boats using oars and with canvas shelters on the decks. These boats sell everything you could imagine, any sort of food and merchandise that you'd care to name.

According to what the Chinese told us, Peking has three hundred and sixty gates, with a guard of four halberdiers posted at every one, as I mentioned earlier, keeping a check of everything that passes through the gates. There are also several buildings, which the city has set aside as offices for anchacis and officials of justice; they also bring young children who have got lost there, so that the childrens' parents know where to come and find them again.

I will have more to say in due time about this remarkable city because what I have hurriedly mentioned here was only to give a brief account of the origins and foundation of this empire and of the founder of Peking, which is rightfully and truthfully the greatest city in the whole world – in its splendours, its government, its prosperity and wealth and in every other aspect you could mention.

I also wanted to give a brief account of the origins of Nanking, the second city of this great empire, and of these two other cities, Pakan and Nakow. The founders of these two last-named cities are buried inside magnificent, lavish temples, in sepulchres of green and white alabaster trimmed with gold that rest on the backs of four silver lions, surrounded by a great number of lamps and censers that burn a whole variety of perfumes and incense.

95 : *The Great Wall of China. The prison that serves this wall.*

NOW THAT I HAVE GIVEN AN ACCOUNT OF THE ORIGINS OF THE Chinese empire and described the walls of this great city of Peking, I think it is the right moment to deal as briefly as I can with another subject that is just as marvellous as either of those.

In the fifth book of the 'Catalogue of all Noteworthy Places in the Empire' we read that the king called Krisnagul Dakotay (who, by our reckoning, would have been reigning in A.D. 528.) was involved in a war with the Tartars over claims to the region of Shinshinpu, which borders on the kingdom of Laos. Krisnagul Dakotay defeated the Tartars in battle and was master of the day but the Tartars organized an alliance with six other kings and returned in greater strength eight years later to attack the Chinese empire. They captured thirty-two important positions, including the great city of Ponkeelor.

Krisnagul Dakotay feared that he wouldn't be able to defend the empire successfully and arranged a peace treaty with the Tartars: the Chinese had to withdraw their claim to the disputed territory and also had to give the Tartar two thousand piculs of silver to pay off all the foreign soldiers he had brought with him. After this treaty, the chronicles tell us, relations between the two kingdoms were calm and peaceful for the next fifty-two years.

However, after fifty-two years, the Chinese emperor grew fearful of the Tartars forming another hostile alliance and he determined to close the borders of the two empires with a great wall. He called all the peoples' representatives to the court and told them of his intention; they all thought it was an excellent plan – and a necessary one. To assist him in such an important undertaking they gave him ten thousand piculs of silver (that's fifteen million cruzados) and provided two hundred and fifty thousand men to work on the construction of the wall; thirty thousand of these were qualified supervisors and the rest were manual labourers.

When they had completed all the preparations for this remarkable enterprise they started on the work itself and in the next twenty-seven years the border between the Chinese and Tartar empires was closed from end to end – a distance of seventy jans (three hundred and fifteen leagues by our measurement.) It is said that seven hundred and fifty thousand men worked full time building the wall. A third of these were paid for by the common people, as I've already mentioned, a third by the priests and the island of Hainan, and a third by the emperor himself and the nobility and the chiangs and anchacis in the government service.

I saw this wall a few times myself and measured it: for the most part it is six fathoms high and forty palms thick; rubble is heaped up against the wall to a height of four fathoms in the manner of a mound; on the outer side the loose rubble is cemented with a bitumen-like mortar to form an escarpment that is twice as thick as the wall itself, making the wall so secure that a thousand basilisks wouldn't be able to tumble it.

Instead of towers or bulwarks the wall has fortified sentry-posts standing two storeys high, built on props of 'caubesy', which means 'iron wood', each prop being the girth of a hundred-and-fifty gallon wine cask and very tall as well. These sentry-posts look as if they are stronger than if they were made of stone and cement.

This wall, or 'chanfacau', as they call it, which means 'stout defence', follows a steady line until it runs into the cultivated lands in the mountains that lie in its path, where the jagged peaks form a natural barrier more secure than the wall itself. So the wall is built across every stretch of flat land, linking one mountain range to the next, and the mountains themselves serve as part of the defence.

There are no gateways anywhere in the whole three hundred and fifteen leagues' length of the wall apart from those built for the five great rivers of Tartary to pass through. These rivers descend with impetuous currents, cutting their way across more than five hundred leagues before they finally flow into the China sea and the Cochinchina sea. One of these rivers is more powerful than the others and makes its way into the kingdom of Sornau where it empties into the sea at the bar of Quy.

At each of these five river-gates both the Chinese emperor and the Great Tartar keep a garrison of soldiers. Each of the emperor's garrisons numbers seven thousand men: six thousand are infantry, a thousand are cavalry and they are all very well paid. Most of these soldiers are foreigners from Mongolia, Pancru, Tsien-pá, Khorasan and Jizar in Persia and others from the many regions and kingdoms that lie in the interior of Asia. The reason for the presence of so many foreigners is that, if truth be told, the Chinese themselves are not great warriors: they have little prac-tice in the arts of war and are a faint-hearted people with few weapons and no artillery at all.

There are three hundred and twenty command-posts of five hundred men each along the length of the wall, which makes a total of a hundred and sixty thousand soldiers – besides all the officers of justice, the upus or the personal guards of the anchacis and chiangs and all the other officials necessary for the government and welfare of the nation. The Chinese told us the total number permanently posted along the wall would be about two hundred thousand soldiers and officials. However, since the great majority of the garrison are convicted criminals condemned to guard duty on the Great Wall, the emperor is not obliged to give them any payment other than the food they eat.

The prison for these convicts in Peking is another building noteworthy in itself for the grandeur of its design. There are always upwards of three hundred thousand convicts on the waiting-list for guard and maintenance duty on the Great Wall. The vast majority of them are aged between eighteen and forty-five and they include a great number of nobles and highly esteemed men of great wealth who have had their sentences for serious crimes commuted to detention in this prison. The convicts wait to be taken from this prison to serve on the Great Wall as if it were a life sentence. They can appeal against their sentence, according to the statutes of war which are formulated and approved by the chiangs. In this and all other matters the chiangs have the same powers as the emperor himself, bearing the supreme authority of the whole empire. It is within the power and jurisdiction of these chiangs, who number twelve in all, to pay themselves a salary of up to a million cruzados, without anyone else being able to touch it.

97 : What we saw after leaving Junkinilau. Food production in China.

AFTER WE LEFT THE RUINS OF FIUNGANORSI WE CAME NEXT TO the great city of Junkinilau. It was very prosperous indeed and had everything in abundant supply. There were many distinguished-looking people, both on horseback and on foot, and in the harbour there was an enormous number of vessels, from small boats with oars up to big, sea-going junks.

We stopped over at Junkinilau for five days while our chifu conducted the funeral rites for his wife there. As an act of charity for the benefit of her soul he gave us all gifts of food and clothes; he also gave us a break from the punishment of our rowing-benches and let us go ashore at our leisure without having to wear our iron collars and manacles – all of which was a very great relief to us, of course.

We left Junkinilau and continued on our way upstream, all the time seeing on either bank countless imposing cities and towns and villages, all of them protected by thick, strong walls and with their citadels down by the water's edge. They had numerous towers and buildings belonging to their pagan sects, with bell-towers and spires covered in gold-leaf.

In the fields were such enormous numbers of cattle that in some cases the herds stretched for six and seven leagues at a time, while on the river itself there were so many boats that in some places, where they had gathered for a market-day in a town, they spread back so far along the river that you couldn't even see them all. Besides these market-days there were all the other smaller gatherings of three hundred up to a thousand sails that we came across at every turn in the river, massed along both banks and selling every variety of merchandise that you could name.

Many of the Chinese assured us that in China there are as many people living on the rivers as there are in the towns and the cities – and they added that if it wasn't for the immense organization and regulation of the empire's commercial life, and the laws and constraints that are placed upon the people in earning their livelihood, then without doubt the people would end up eating each other!

Every business or trade is divided into three or four branches – I'll give a few illustrations to show the way things are organized.

In the goose trade, for example, some men take the new-laid eggs and rear young geese for market; other men rear the geese to full-size then kill and sell them ready for cooking; others deal only in the feathers, skins and innards; yet others deal only in the eggs.

Now, a man who operates in one of these lines cannot operate in any of the others; the punishment for doing so is thirty lashes with no questions asked nor any opportunity to appeal or complain; neither is there any chance of bribery or influential connections being of any use to the culprit.

In the pig trade some men sell whole herds of live pigs; others kill them and sell the carcasses to the butchers; others slaughter the pigs and sell them in the markets as smoked bacon; some men sell only sucking-pigs while others deal in the innards, the fat, the feet and the blood.

Similarly in the fish trade: the man who sells fresh fish will not sell any salted fish and the man who sells salted fish will not sell any dried fish.

The production and sale of all food – meat, fish, fowl, fruit and vegetables – are regulated in this fashion. A man who is operating in one line of a trade – sucking-pigs, for example – cannot change to another – smoked salmon, say – unless he gets a licence from the local council; and he needs to have good reasons for wanting to change before he will receive such a licence.

There are men who earn their living selling live fish which they rear in big tanks and pools before loading them onto boats with watertight holds for bringing to market in distant regions.

As we made the one hundred and eighty league journey along this great river, the Batampina, from Nanking to Peking, we saw along the banks many sugar-mills and wine and oil presses that used every imaginable kind of vegetable and fruit. There are so many of these mills on either side of the river that they present a truly marvellous sight, standing one beside the other in rows that are two or three leagues long.

There are also great numbers of warehouses to be seen, storing an infinite variety of provisions; and there are just as great a number of very long buildings where they slaughter, salt, smoke and cure as many kinds of game and meat as are to be found on earth: mountains of pork, sucking-pig, bacon, goose, duck, crane, wild turkey, emu, venison, beef, buffalo, tapir, badger, horse, tiger, dog, fox – indeed the flesh of every kind of animal that breeds on earth.

We were all completely amazed by this sight as, indeed, who wouldn't be amazed by such novel, rare, almost unbelievable, marvels? We were to remark on many occasions afterwards that there couldn't possibly be enough people in the whole world to eat their way through that amount of food, even if they spent their entire lives eating!

Along the Batampina we also saw a great number of boats similar to foists, what the Chinese call 'panouras'. These boats have reed cages built onto them, fore and aft, and the cages are fitted inside with three or four shelves, with a space of two palms between each shelf. These cages serve as coops for the geese that the men sell along the river as they make their way upstream, using oars and sails.

This is the routine these boatmen follow when it is the birds' feeding-time: the panoura pulls into the riverbank and throws down a gangplank at a spot where the shore is very swampy or there are pools of water nearby. Then all the doors to the coops are opened and a man bangs four times on a drum. At the sound of the drum all the birds, numbering at least six or seven hundred, leave the boat with a tremendous screech and rush down the gang-plank in a great flock to throw themselves into the water in the fields. When their keeper thinks that the birds have had enough time to get a proper feed he beats the drum again and all the birds, with the same screeching as before, flock back up the gang-plank to the boat, each bird seeking out his very own perch in his very own coop; then the coops are closed again and the boat resumes its journey.

When these birds are ready to lay their eggs the boat pulls into the shore at a place where the land is dry but with plenty of greenery. The keeper then opens the coops and beats on the drum and all the birds leave the boats to go ashore and lay their eggs. After an hour or so (or as long as the keeper thinks the birds need) he beats on the drum again and the birds immediately rush back to the boat, without a single one, as I mentioned with regard to their feeding-time, trying to stay behind at liberty in the open country.

Once the birds are all settled down again in their coops the keeper and two or three of his helpers go ashore with baskets to gather the eggs, making their way to the places where the grass is by now speckled white with the freshly-laid eggs; and a day doesn't go by but they have ten or twelve baskets of eggs for sale.

When these traders have only a few geese left and want to replenish their stocks they go and buy the birds from men who make their living breeding and selling geese in bulk; as I've already said, no-one deals in anything other than the specific item covered by his trading-licence and these traders on the boats are not allowed to rear geese themselves. The people who breed the geese have big pools or ponds near their homes and there might be ten or twelve thousand young geese in one of these pools.

This is the method used by the breeders for hatching out the goose-eggs. They have long sheds housing ten, twenty or thirty manure-furnaces and they bury a batch of between two hundred

ILLUSTRATIONS

[1]

1 : LISBON c1520

Fernão Mendes Pinto, then a country boy about eleven years old, arrived in Lisbon in 1521 when this painting [1] was done. A great and bustling city, Lisbon was the entrepôt for trade from Africa and the Orient, and then onward throughout Europe.

[1] *Crónica de D. Afonso Henriques* by Duarte Galvão, c1520, Museu-Biblioteca Conde Castro, Guimarães, Cascais.

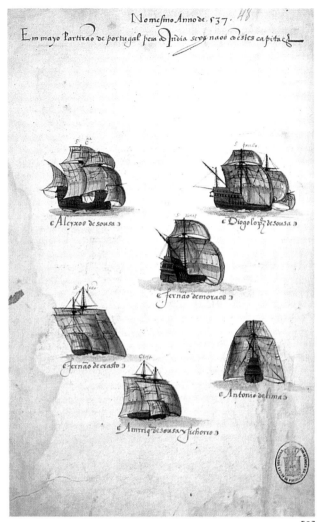

[2]

2 : THE JOURNEY TO INDIA, 1537

In 1537 Mendes Pinto joined the annual 'carreira da India' which plied between Lisbon and Goa. The recorded details for that year [2] show that his flotilla was unusually fortunate: no ships sank or were captured. (The record for 1500 shows that nine ships were lost of the twelve that sailed).

[2] Page for 1537, *Memória das Armadas*, Archivo nacional da Torre de Tombo, Lisboa – facsimile edition, 1979, Academia das Ciéncias, Lisboa.

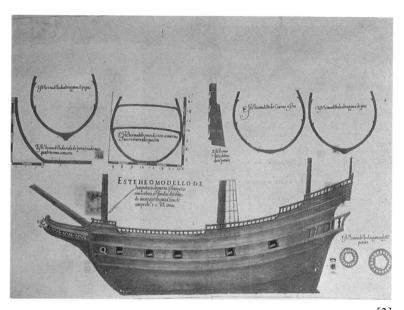

[3]

3–6 : PORTUGUESE NAUTICAL TECHNOLOGY

Portuguese shipwrights had devised the celebrated *caravel* – about 70 tons, shallow beam, lanteen sail – for Atlantic and African exploration; for the distant Indian trade they crafted the

[4]   [5]

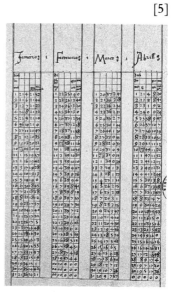

[6]

nau – 500–1500 tons, chiefly square-rigged [3]. The techniques of astro-navigation were Portuguese innovations, based on the nautical astrolabe [4] and sun declination tables, laboriously calculated, observed and compiled. [5] The German woodcut, [*above*] shows Portuguese navigators 'weighing the sun' [6]. These techniques allowed captains to fix their latitudes for the first time, and to sail confidently far from the sight of land.

[3] Plans from *Livro da Fábrica das Naus* by Fernando Oliviera, c1570. [4] Portuguese Astrolabe, 1555, Dundee Art Galleries and Museums. [5] Page from *Livro de Marinharia* by André Pires C16th. [6] Woodcut in *Warhaftig Historia* by Hans Staden, Magdebourg, 1557.

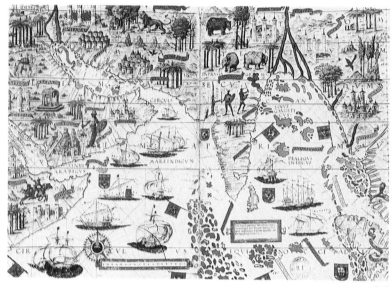

7–8 : PORTUGUESE MAP-MAKING
Techniques for fixing latitude, combined with the accumulation
of information from explorations and from the first known
organized surveys, enabled the Portuguese to construct relatively
credible maps. These were secret and closely protected, but
ingenious copiers smuggled them out and sold them to other
countries where they were greatly prized.

[8]

[7] From the so-called 'Atlas Miller' by Lopo Homen Reiners, 1519. [8] From the *Livro de Marinharia* by João de Lisboa, c1560, Archivo Nacional da Torre de Tombo, Lisboa.

[9]

9 : PRESTER JOHN

Muslim conquest in the 7th–8th centuries in the Middle East and
North Africa severed Christian contacts by land with the Far
East and Africa. Knowledge of early Christian kingdoms and
communities outside Europe passed into myth: somewhere there
was a great 'Prester John' who would one day help the
beleaguered Christians. From 1513 the Portuguese made effective contact with the Christian kingdom of Ethiopia. Mendes
Pinto took part in an embassy to the mother of 'Prester John'
who become an ally against the Grand Turk.

[9] From *Verdadeira Informação das Terras do Preste João* by P.
Francisco Alvares, 1540.

[10]

10 : TURKS ATTACK A PORTUGUESE FLOTILLA
From the 15th to the 17th centuries the Turks were the champions of Islam. No sooner had the Portuguese at last (1498) outflanked by sea the Muslim blockade of the land-routes to the East than the Turks over-ran Arabia, Syria, most of Persia and Egypt (1509–17) and threatened Portugal's tenuous lines of communication with India. Mendes Pinto fought at sea against the Turks, was captured and sold as a slave.

[10] Engraving from *Historiarum Orientalis Indiae* by Theodore de Bry, Frankfurt, 1598.

[11]

[12]

11–12 : IN THE PERSIAN GULF

From 1509 the Portuguese fleets were able to protect a growing trade with Persia, shown here being conducted agreeably alfresco [11]. The life of merchants in the fortified port of Ormuz could be agreeable too [12].

[11] Persian tile panel, C16th. Metropolitan Museum of Art, New York. [12] From the Portuguese codex, mid-C16th, Biblioteca Casanatense, Roma.

OCOVERNADOR AFFONCO DALBOQVERQVE SVCEDEO NA INDIA
A DOM·FRANCISCO·DA·LIME[...]   IDA·EM·NOVEM·BRO· DE
[...]609·TOMOV·D·AS·VEZES·[...]   [...]C·DADE·D·GOA·FA·SD·MALA
[...]·TE·ORVZ·E·FEZ·A·FORTALEZ[...]   A·E·CALECVTE·FOI·A·PERCIA·E·AO
[...]·STRETO·DE·ORMVZ·E·   MAR·ROXO

13–14 : THE FORTIFIED CENTRES   [13]
The great Albuquerque, [13] as military commander and then as

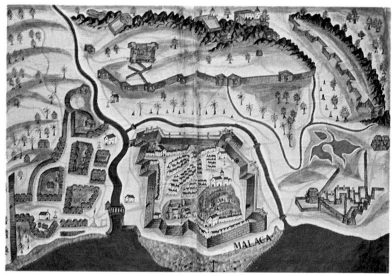

[14]

viceroy, established the Portuguese position in the East. Theirs was a trading, not a territorial, empire, based on their control of major sea-lanes from strategically-placed fortified centres at Moçambique, Ormuz, Goa, Diu, Cochin, Colombo, Malacca [14,] and later Macao. Within this framework, Portuguese traders like Mendes Pinto, as individuals or in 'factory' communities, spread throughout the East.

[13] Portrait in oil, anon, end C15th, Museu Nacional de Arte Antiga, Lisboa. [14] Engraving by Pedro Barreto Resende, from *Livro de Todas as Fortalezas, Cidades e Povações do Estado da India Oriental* by António Bocarro, 1635, Biblioteca Pública e Arquivo Distrital, Évora.

15–17 : PLANTS AND SPICES
Beyond Malacca lay the East Indies where the trade in spices was particularly important, especially in pepper, here shown being harvested [15]. The Portuguese brought to Europe knowledge of the rich botanical life of the East [16]. Valuable plants were transported and naturalized elsewhere (such as rice, sugar, tea

[15]

and many spices); a new pharmacopoeia became available through the publications of Cristóvão de Costa and Garcia de Orta [17] and exotic plants were cultivated in western gardens and glass-houses.

[15] From the *Livro das Maravilhas*, late C15th. [16] From Theodore de Bry, op. cit. 1598. [17] Title page, *Colóquios dos Simples e Drogas da India* by Garcia de Orta, 1563, Goa.

[16]   [17]

☞ **Coloquios dos fimples , e**
drogas he coufas mediçinais da India , e
afsi dalgũas frutas achadas nella onde fe
tratam algũas coufas tocantes amediçina,
pratica , e outras coufas boas , pera faber
côpoftos pello Doutor garçia dorta : fifico
del Rey noffo fenhor , viftos pello muyto
Reuerendo fenhor , ho liçençiado
Alexos diaz : falcam defenbar-
gador da cafa da fupricaçã
inquifidor neftas
partes.

¶ Com priuilegio do Conde vifo Rey.

Im preffo em Goa, por Ioannes
de endem as x. dias de
Abril de 1563. annos.

[18]

[19]

[20]

18–20 : FURTHER EAST

Mendes Pinto had several adventures in Pegu (Burma); the illustration shows a royal procession [18]. He traded in Java; there, as elsewhere in the East, Jesuits started schools. Young Javanese are here shown enjoying a form of football [19]. Mendes Pinto described the 'Juggernaut' in a festival in Laos, where worshippers cast themselves beneath the wheels of the enormous processional car [20].

[18, 19] Theodore de Bry, op. cit., 1598. [20] Portuguese codex, mid-C16th, Biblioteca Casanatense, Roma.

[21]

21–23 : AMONG THE CHINESE

The luxury of the Portuguese, especially in Goa, was notorious.
The illustration here [21] is from a celebrated book by Linscho-
ten, a Dutchman who sailed with the Portuguese; the book
stirred the Dutch (and the English) to oust the Portuguese from
their monopoly in oriental trade, which they steadily succeeded
in doing from 1630 onwards.

Portuguese free-booting enterprise met its match in the grandeur,
bureaucracy and exclusiveness of Chinese mandarins [22]. Not
till 1557, thirty years after trade began, were the Portuguese
allowed to establish a base, on the island of Macau [23]. Mendes
Pinto records the marvels of China, travelling the length of the
empire, from Canton to the Great Wall.

[22]
[23]

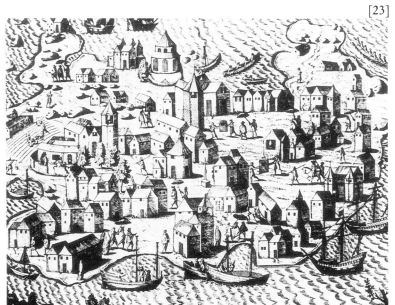

[21] From *Navigatio ae Itinerarium Johannis Hugonis Linscho-tani in Orientalem sive Lusitanorum Indiae*, 1599, the Hague.
[22,23] Theodore de Bry, op. cit., 1598.

24–28 : AMONG THE JAPANESE

After the Portuguese 'discovery' of Japan in 1543 (claimed by
Mendes Pinto) a rich trade developed with the largely indepen-
dent daimyos of the south-west. Here a Japanese screen painter
depicts the arrival of a Portuguese 'black ship' to trade at
Nagasaki [24]. Details from another screen [*overleaf*] show the
captain's procession [25], with gifts for the daimyo (including an
Arab horse), and a discussion in the Jesuit mission house [26].
Among items of trade highly valued in Japan (as in Europe) was
Chinese porcelain: the bowl shown here [28] was made for Pêro
de Faria, Captain of Malacca and Mendes Pinto's principal patron
in the East. Of all Portuguese imports, however, none was more

[24]

prized by the constantly warring daimyos than the musket. Mendes Pinto vividly describes its introduction. On the lacquered gunpowder-flask shown here [27] a Japanese craftsman had depicted a Portuguese merchant and his page.

[24] Screen by Kano Naizen, 1600–1610, Museu Nacional de Arte Antiga, Lisboa. [25,26] Two details from a screen attributed to Kano Domi, 1593–1600, Museu de Arte Antiga, Lisboa. [27] Lacquered gunpowder-flask, late C16th, Museu de Arte Antiga, Lisboa. [28] Chinese porcelain bowl, 1541, Museu Rainha D. Leonor, Beja.

[25]
[26]

[27]
[28]

29–32 : EVANGELIZING THE EAST

The Jesuits made a vigorous start with their mission to the East, begun only two years after their foundation. It was first led by Francis Xavier, 'Apostle of the Indies', and future saint. In eleven extraordinary years, he was said to have walked 100,000 miles and converted 300,000 souls [29]. Mendes Pinto admired him greatly and lent him money to build the first Christian church in

御寶前

願主
泉屋市兵衛

元和六庚申於生吉日

[30]

Japan. Progress there was especially encouraging: by 1622 there were some 250–300,000 converts [30]. [*continues overleaf*]

[29] Oil by André Reinoso, c1619, Santa Casa da Misericórdia de Lisboa – Museu de São Roque, (Photo: Philippe Boutefeu). [30] Japanese convert, 1621, Museu do Caramulo, Caramulo (Fundação Abel Lacerda).

In that year (1622) the Shogun Tokugawa, enforcing his newly-acquired absolute authority, began mass persecutions of the Christians, expelled the Jesuits and sealed Japan to all foreign contact – bar a limited trade through the Chinese and Dutch. 'Hidden Christianity' survived (20,000 declared themselves after Commodore Perry forced the opening of Japan in 1853), their faith sustained by devotional devices like the use of images of the female Buddhist goddess Kannon, as a simulacrum of the Virgin and Child [31].

[31]

[32]

Throughout the East, local artists added many works to Christian iconography, such as this touching bas-relief in ivory from India [32].

[31] Maria-Kannon from *Christianity and Japan* by Stuart Picken, Kodasha International, Tokyo, 1983, (Photo: International Press Service). [32] Virgin and Child, Indo-Portuguese, C17th, Museu do Caramulo, Caramulo (Fundação Abel Lacerda).

and five hundred eggs in the manure, sealing the furnaces to keep the manure warm. The eggs are left there until they are due to hatch: then a wounded, half-plucked capon is put into each of the furnaces and the doors closed again. Within two days the capon has dug all the eggs up out of the manure and they are then placed in prepared hatching-pits which have damp meal left inside them as food for the newly-hatched geese. For the first ten or twelve days the new geese are left to walk around at their leisure until they go and take the plunge into the pool of their own free will; then they are fatted up and reared for sale to the boat-traders, who take them and sell them in many different parts of the Chinese empire.

As I've already explained, the law prohibits these boat-traders, for example, from breeding their own geese for sale – and it is a law that is strictly enforced. If a man licensed to sell goose-eggs was caught selling hens' eggs he would be seized and given thirty lashes on the buttocks there and then, without having the chance to say anything at all in his defence. The only way to avoid punishment in this case would be for the trader to break the hens' eggs in half and pretend that they were sitting there ready for him to eat!

What is true of this one example applies in exactly the same way to every single trader, whatever he deals in: he is licensed to deal in one specific concern and, on pain of receiving thirty lashes, cannot step beyond that specification.

The men who sell live fish have to keep the fish in big tanks of water and fix a string through the fish's nose so that potential customers can pull a fish out of the tank to look at it without having to finger or dirty it. If one of these fish happens to die the trader has to cut it up and salt it straightaway, then sell it at the going rate for salted fish (which is a little cheaper than that for live fish.)

So it is that nobody breaks the rules and regulations laid down by the 'conchalis' of the crown, who are like our royal inspectors of weights and measures, knowing the severe, summary punishments for doing so; and in China the emperor himself is so respected, and the law so feared, that there isn't a single person in any walk of life who would dare to criticize or show disrespect to any official of justice, not even to an 'upu', who is the equivalent of our beadles and executioners.

99 : *The floating cities. Sights and customs elsewhere in China.*

ALL ALONG THE BATAMPINA RIVER WE SAW BARGES, LANTEAS and sampans loaded with every sort of food that the soil and the sea can provide – and in such vast amounts that I honestly admit I don't know how anybody could find the words to describe it all. My readers shouldn't for a moment imagine that I'm talking about quantities that would be called 'vast' in Europe – I'm talking about two or three hundred boatloads of any particular item!

This overwhelming abundance can be seen above all at the markets and fairs they have on their idols' feast-days when a mass of people are gathered together and everything that is on sale is exempt from all taxes and duties. Most of the temples are built on the river-banks so it is easier to bring the merchandise ashore – and the bigger the market, the richer and more prestigious that particular temple will be.

When the traders in their boats gather near a temple for one of these fairs they organize themselves into an enormous and impressive floating city, covering an area of perhaps more than a league by a third of a league and numbering more than twenty thousand boats, which doesn't even include the very small craft like gigs, canoes and dinghies; and all the buying and selling at the fair is done aboard this floating city.

By order of the Ay-tau of the Batampina – who is the most important of the ay-taus who govern the thirty-two provinces of the empire – sixty officials are appointed to supervise each floating city: thirty of them are from the provincial government and have the task of enforcing the laws of the province within the city and hearing any legal proceedings; the other thirty are there to protect the merchants who come from outside the province, to see that they are able to travel safely and without fear of robbers. Superior to these sixty officials there is a chiang, who in both civil and criminal cases has the absolute authority of the emperor, allowing of no appeal or complaint.

These fairs last for fifteen days, from the new moon to the full moon, and it is more exciting to see the organization, operation and grandeur of one of these floating cities than any number of fine cities built on the land.

In any one of these cities you'll find perhaps two thousand very long, straight thoroughfares or streets marked out between two lines of boats that usually have awnings and canopies of brightly coloured silk and lots of pennants, banners and flags fluttering in the breeze. The boats have brightly painted platforms where trading is done and you can buy anything you could possibly want there. On other boats you can find any of the tradesmen you would expect to find in a large town on dry land. The general public sail peacefully down these streets in small dinghies without any undue noise or fuss. If a thief happens to be discovered stealing something he is punished inside the hour in proportion to the gravity of the offence.

As soon as it is dark the streets are closed off with ropes thrown across from one line of boats to the other. Along each street ten or twelve lanterns are lit and hung from the tops of the masts so that everybody's comings and goings can be seen and, if necessary, a full report of everything that has happened during the night can be given to the chiang in the morning. And just let me remark here that the display of all these lanterns at night makes for the most beautiful and impressive sight that anyone could possibly imagine.

In each of these streets or thoroughfares there is an alarm bell and when the alarm on the chiang's boat is rung all the other bells are sounded in reply, producing such a blast of noise – but so tuneful and harmonious – that we were all stunned to hear it, a sound such as perhaps has never been imagined by men before!

In every one of these thoroughfares, even the poorest of them, there are oratories built on barges like galleys. These oratories are very well kept, with canopies of cloth of gold, and they serve as chapels to house different idols. Each chapel has its own priests to administer the sacrifices offered up by the ordinary people and they all make a comfortable living from the offerings and alms that they continually receive from the people.

Every reputable man and large trader on these imposing thoroughfares takes it in turn to lead a nightwatch made up of men from the neighbouring boats. These watches are in addition to the thirty officers appointed by the government who patrol the perimeter of the floating city in well-equipped boats to ensure that no thief will be able to slip away. These watches call out loud and clear as they make their rounds, so that everyone will know they are out and about.

Another remarkable thing we saw here was a street of more than a hundred boats, and every single one of them was laden with all kinds of wooden idols. These idols are sold to the public who take them as offerings to the pagodas. Besides the idols, they also sell wooden legs, arms and heads that sick people buy to offer up to the gods as part of their devotions.

There are other boats with awnings of silk where you can watch all sorts of plays or else enjoy a wide variety of games and sports, and many, many people go along to these boats to entertain themselves.

On other boats you can buy bills of exchange to transfer money from this world to the next – these ministers of Satan promise people high interest and big dividends on their money and assure them that without these bills of exchange they cannot hope to save their souls because God above is the mortal enemy of people who do not give alms to the pagodas. The priests preach so many lies and spin so many yarns about all this that the poor people very often go without food in order to give them something.

There are other vessels loaded down with piles of human skulls that people buy to bring as offerings to the graves of people who have just died. They believe that just as the dead person goes to the grave accompanied by those skulls, so his soul will go to the gates of heaven accompanied by the alms donated by the people to whom those skulls belonged. When the gatekeeper of Paradise sees the dead man approaching with so many servants in attendance, he will honour the dead man as a man who was the master of so many servants on earth; however, if the dead man appears at the gates poor and unaccompanied, the gatekeeper will not admit him. On account of this, the more skulls a man has at his grave, the more will he count himself to be blessed.

There are other boats which carry enormous numbers of live birds in cages. The bird-keepers play on musical instruments and call out in loud voices to the passers-by, 'Come and free these prisoners who are creatures of God just like yourselves!' So people hurry to give alms and purchase the birds of their choice – then throw the birds up into the air to let them fly away, while everybody stands shouting, '*Pichau pitanel catan vacashi!*' which means, 'Tell God above how we have thus served Him here below!'

There are men in other boats who have enormous tanks of water in which they keep large numbers of small freshwater fish, which have been caught with fine-mesh nets. There is the same routine here as for the birds: the men shout at passers-by to free the fish for the love of God because the fish are innocents who have never sinned against anybody. So people make a donation to the fish-keepers to obtain whichever fish they want, then they throw the fish back into the river, saying as they do so, 'Swim away there now and spread the word about the good I have done you as a service to God!'

The boats carrying these particular items for sale would number between at least one hundred and up to two hundred or more, besides many other boats loaded with other commodities in even greater quantities.

We also saw a great many barges bedecked in funerary colours and carrying biers, torches and vigil-candles; and there were women who act as professional mourners to bury the dead with as much ceremony as each person desires.

There are people called 'pitaleus' who keep all kinds of wild animals on very large barges. The animals include snakes, serpents, tigers, enormous lizards and many other kinds of beast. They are a marvellous but frightening sight and the pitaleus earn a living from putting the animals on show to the public, accompanied by music and dancing.

Then there are men who keep a great store of books that tell you everything you could want to know about the creation of the world (about which they tell countless lies) and the history, geography, laws and customs of every nation and kingdom on earth. Above all else, they tell the history of the kings of China: how many there have been and the achievements of each one, who founded the different cities and kingdoms in the empire and everything that happened during each reign. These men also write petitions and letters for people and give legal advice; from these and other related dealings they make a very good living.

Then there are bands of armed men who travel around in very light barges and who proclaim in loud voices to passers-by that if any man's honour has been insulted or injured by someone else he should come to their barge with his grievance and they will very soon see that his honour is satisfied.

There are barges that carry large numbers of old women who serve as midwives, giving homemade medicines to drug the babies and hasten or delay the birth. Other barges are full of nannies who look after not just waifs and strays but any other children too, for as long as the parents want.

We saw boats that were finely decorated, carrying upright men of great authority, accompanied by their stern, dignified wives. These were the match-makers and they also console women distressed by the death of their husbands or children and deal with other matters related to marriage.

Other boats carry large numbers of nurses who deliver enemas, many of whom are not at all unpleasant. In other boats there are lots of boys and girls who hire themselves for work to whoever needs them, with their certificates of trustworthiness.

There are other influential men, called 'mongilotus', who deal in out-of-court settlements, buying off criminal and civil lawsuits and buying up old contracts and titles to land and rights to outstanding debts, making settlements on whatever terms the parties involved can be persuaded to agree upon.

In other boats there are people who cure buboes with a sweat treatment, as well as treating wounds and severe fistulas.

To conclude then, so as not to delay any further by going into detail about everything to be found in these floating cities (if I did, I would never be able to finish my whole story) I will just say this: there isn't a thing on God's earth that you could ask for or desire that you will not be able to find in these cities and in far greater quantities than I have described. Here and now I do not want to mention any of the other towns, cities and regions of the Chinese empire because from what I've just told you about these floating cities you can judge for yourselves what the rest of the country is like.

Perhaps the main reason why the Chinese empire is so impressive, so wealthy and thriving is that it is criss-crossed by admirable waterways. Many of them are rivers created by Nature herself but many of them are canals that the kings, lords and commons ordered to be cut in olden days. As a result you can travel conveniently throughout the length and breadth of the empire and have regular contact with its farthest corners.

The narrowest rivers and canals have very high, wide bridges solidly built of stone in a style similar to our own. Some rivers are spanned by bridges made of a single section of stone stretching from one bank to the other; these stones might be eighty, ninety or a hundred palms in length and twenty or thirty palms in width. Such engineering deserves unqualified admiration and one can scarcely comprehend how they could cut such a large piece of stone from the quarry, never mind moving it from the quarry to the place where it rests.

The roads and streets of the biggest cities and smallest hamlets are all laid with large paving-stones of the highest quality. At the end of these roadways there are finely crafted arches with columns that display plaques with gold lettering singing the praises of the people who ordered the roads and arches to be built. On both sides of the street there are expensive stone benches where travellers and poor people are able to rest themselves and numerous fountains and springs of fresh water for people to quench their thirst.

In barren, sparsely populated districts they have unmarried women who give free board to poor people who have no money; and then there is this abuse and abomination – which they think of as a work of mercy: they leave the deceased in chapels for the repose of their souls while the dead person's lands, income and privileges are used to help the poor. The Chinese are convinced this evil is a good!

Other men who have died have left bequests to build shelters in the deserts and the wild moorlands. These are lit up at night with big, bright lights, so that travellers won't lose their way; and besides the shelters themselves, barrels of water are provided for the travellers to drink and refresh themselves. To make sure that such bequests are properly fulfilled, people are employed and very well paid to check that these shelters are in good order and arranged exactly as the benefactor wished them to be, for the good of his soul.

From the marvellous sights to be found in any single Chinese city you can well imagine what the impact of the whole empire would be like: but to make this absolutely clear I must state here – if my word is worthy of belief at all – that during the twenty-one years when the hard, merciless blows of Chance drove me all over Asia, as you can clearly see in this book of travels that I am writing, I saw in different countries the greatest possible abundance of every conceivable commodity, so many of which are simply not available in Europe, and yet in all truth I declare, even though I have not described to you each particular place I visited, that all the marvels of the rest of Asia put together cannot compare to the marvels of China alone.

This is true of all aspects of Chinese life and the gifts bestowed upon her by Nature, whether it is the warm and healthy climate, the dignified public life and well-ordered government, the prosperity or the grand scale and style they bring to everything they do. The crowning glory to all this is that there is such a great awareness of the obligations of justice and such an even-handed and excellent manner of government that every other nation should be jealous: for in the nation that lacks this one virtue all its other qualities, however noble and inspiring they may be, are obscured and tarnished.

From time to time I think about all these things that I saw in China. On the one hand it utterly amazes me to see Our Lord's generosity in sharing out the goods of this world among these people, while on the other hand it causes me the greatest pain to see how ungrateful they are for the great favours lavished on them, because they commit so many serious sins that continually insult Our Lord, whether in their bestial, diabolical idolatry or in the depravity of the sin against nature.

This last sin is not only permitted in public but is also taught by their priests to be a great virtue. You'll excuse me for not discussing this in any further detail because a Christian conscience will not suffer it, nor will common sense allow me to waste time and words on matters so depraved, inhuman and abominable.

100 : *We reach Peking and are put into prison.*

LEAVING THIS RARE AND REMARKABLE FLOATING CITY WE SAILED on until we finally reached the great city of Peking, where we had been sent to have our appeal case heard. It was a Tuesday, the 9th of October, 1541.

We were chained together in threes and taken to a prison called the Gofanchowserku. By way of a warm welcome we were each given thirty lashes as soon as we arrived and we suffered greatly from this whipping for several days afterwards.

The chifu in whose charge we had been brought to Peking

duly presented the records of our case, sealed with the twelve laquered signets just as it had been handed to him in Nanking, at the Pilanga, the appeal court. The twelve conchalis who were sitting on the bench to hear our case (the cases are allocated by a rotation system) promptly sent one of their number along to the prison where we were being held. He was accompanied by two court-clerks and six or seven constables that they call 'upus'. When he arrived, his threatening presence frightened us. He said:

'By the power and authority vested in me by the Ay-tau of the Batampina, President Supreme of the Council of Thirty-two who deal with strangers in our country, and in whose breast are enclosed the secrets of the Lion Crowned on the Throne of the World, I order you to tell me who you are, where you come from and if you have a true king, a king who serves God and fulfils his kingly duties by looking favourably on the poor and fully protecting them with his justice, so that the poor cry out in thanksgiving with raised hands and tearful eyes to the Lord of the Beautiful Visage, on whose holy feet the sandals are the glorified saints who reign in heaven with him!'

We answered him immediately:

'We are merchants from the kingdom of Siam who were sailing to Ning-po when we were shipwrecked in a fierce storm. We escaped with our lives but without so much as a thread to cover our bodies. Naked as we stood we set out on foot, begging from door to door, until we reached Taipur where the local chumbi, without any good reason, arrested us and sent us in chains to Nanking for trial. On the chumbi's word alone we were sentenced to be whipped and to have our thumbs cut off, without anyone having heard our defence at all.

'Then, with our attention fixed on heaven, we pleaded in tears to the Twenty-four of the Austere Life to show us compassion for the love of God, because we are poor and of no importance at all. In their holy zeal, the Twenty-Four immediately responded to our plea and arranged for our case to be called before the court of appeal in Peking.

'And now we plead with you, as we pleaded with the Twenty-Four, for the love of God to take note of our distress and see how unfairly we have been treated simply because we have no influence in the world nor anyone to say a single word on our behalf.'

The conchali remained silent for a little while before he

replied:

'You don't need to say anything more. The fact that you are poor is enough to ensure that the case will follow a different course to that which it has done so far. But I am empowered to grant you a period of five days, in accordance with the provisions of the Third Book, for your lawyers to prepare your defence. My personal advice is that you should petition the tanigores of the Fraternity of Mercy so that, in their dedication to the honour of God, they will try to alleviate your hardships.'

Then he gave us alms of a tael and said:

'Keep a close watch on this. Be warned that the other prisoners here are more interested in robbing their neighbour than in sharing what they have with those in need.'

Then he left us and went into another large building where there was a great number of prisoners. He heard appeal cases there for more than three hours, and confirmed the death-sentences on twenty-seven men who had been sentenced a few days earlier. All these men were whipped to death – a sight which so numbed and frightened us that we almost lost our senses.

The next day as soon as it was light they locked us all together into a long chain with iron collars round our necks and manacles on our hands. This was hardship enough in itself and we spent seven days in this torment lying one on top of the other in a corner, weeping wildly and bewailing our misfortunes, sick with fear of suffering the most painful deaths if what we had done in Calempluy should ever come to their attention.

Then, by the will of God, the four tanigores from the Fraternity of Mercy happened to pay a visit to the prison, which the Chinese call 'Kufilam Kuashi'. When the four men came in all the prisoners hurled themselves to the ground with a great thud, chanting as with one voice:

'Blessed be this day when God visits us through the hands of his servants!'

The tanigores responded in a restrained solemn manner:

'And may his divine and powerful hands, that shape the beauty of the night, hold you close to him as they hold those who always weep for the sufferings of the people!'

When they came to the corner where we were lying they asked us politely who we were and why we made greater lamentation over our imprisonment than the other prisoners. We

130

answered, weeping:

'We are just forlorn foreigners, so abandoned here that nobody in the whole country so much as knows our names! We beg you for the love of God to keep our case in mind. Everything we can tell you about our plight is in this letter we have brought to you from the fraternity of Ky Ay Hin in Nanking.'

Cristovão Borralho gave them the letter which they accepted with a further show of great courtesy. They said:

'Praised be the Creator of all things who choses so to use sinners in this world that, on the day to end all days, he will excuse them from paying the full retribution due for all their sins, and will reward them out of his holy treasure so much in excess of what they have merited, with riches as plentiful as the rain-drops that the clouds in the heavens pour down upon the face of the earth!'

One of the four put the letter into his breast-pocket and told us that when the letter had been presented to the Tribunal for the Relief of the Poor they would return and provide us with whatever we needed. Then they left us.

Three days passed and they returned on the fourth morning, bringing a scroll with a lot of questions written on it. We duly answered all the questions to their satisfaction. Then they sent for the clerk who was handling our appeal papers and questioned him in detail and asked his advice about the best way of obtaining justice for us. They made a list of things they should do to help our cause and told the clerk to leave the papers with them because they wanted to discuss the case at length with the lawyers. The next day they would return the papers to the clerk to bring to the chiang, as had been arranged.

101 : We remain in prison while our appeal is heard.

SO AS NOT TO DELAY MY STORY WITH A DETAILED ACCOUNT OF THE six and a half months we spent in prison, suffering no little hardship while we waited for our appeal to be heard, I will only briefly describe what happened to us during that time.

When the case came before the twelve conchalis (who are like our senior magistrates and appeal court judges) our two advocates from the Fraternity of Mercy took up their grave responsibilities to get the earlier proceedings annulled and the unjust sentence against us repealed. They petitioned the chiang, the president of the court, as follows:

'Your Honour, the accused cannot be condemned to a blood-punishment because there are no reliable witnesses who actually saw them robbing their fellow men nor were they found with any weapons on their persons, which is one of the offences required for a blood-punishment in the First Book of Laws. In point of fact they were discovered barefoot and naked like wretched waifs; and so they truly were. Their poverty and misery were more deserving of pious respect than the rigour with which the earlier ministers of the Arm of Wrath sentenced them to a whipping. God alone will be the infallible judge of their innocence or guilt.

'So it is in God's name that we ask Your Honour once, twice, three times over to bear in mind that he is a mere mortal, that his life will be over in a little while, that his life on earth is a gift from God for which he will have to render an account of all that has been said and asked of him, because by his own solemn oath he is obliged to fulfil his duties in the light of his unsullied judgement and pay no heed at all to the worldly considerations which only serve to knock the scales of justice off balance, the scales that God Himself has balanced according to the integrity of His divine justice.'

Our advocates had to send a copy of their petition to the prosecuting attorney, who made his own submission to the chiang as follows:

'Your Honour, I will prove the charges against the accused with eye-witnesses, both Chinese and foreign, and demonstrate that the accused are unashamed robbers, thieves of other people's property and not at all the merchants that they claim to be.

'If they were genuine merchants who came to trade on the Chinese coast, intending to pay all due taxes to the emperor, they would have put in at ports where there are royal customs-houses and not hopped from island to island like common pirates. Robbery and evil are abhorrent to God and that is why he permitted them to be ship-wrecked and then captured by the ministers of His justice.

'Now, in accordance with that same justice, they must taste

the fruit of their evil deeds – the death penalty, as specifically laid down for such crimes in the Second Book of Laws.

'While in some circumstances this law is such that the death sentence can be commuted, these circumstances do not exist in this case. We are dealing here with foreigners without any trace of religion or any clear knowledge of God, for love or fear of Whom they might desist from busying themselves with evil and perversity. This alone is reason enough that at the very least they should be sentenced to having their hands and noses chopped off and, furthermore, be sent for a life-sentence to Ponxilitau, which is the usual place to send criminals for such offences, as I will show from the many precedents for such convictions in the past.

'Thus I request your honour to accept the depositions which I hope to provide within the time allowed by the court.'

This submission was contested by our defence attorneys within the period allowed: they claimed the prosecutor's submission was highly defamatory and beyond what was permissible in a law court and they presented many other arguments in our favour.

The chiang promptly declared that he would accept the prosecution case if it could be proved with indisputable, God-fearing witnesses within the alloted period of six days. If the prosecutor failed to do so he would not be allowed any more time, even if he requested it, because the accusations were against poor people, who were often compelled by sheer necessity rather than common sinfulness to steal from other people in order to meet their needs.

The six days passed and the prosecutor didn't prove the least thing against us. He did request an extension of a further six days but the request was turned down because he was pressing a case against poor people for whom God seeks every dispensation.

Instead of an extension, he was directed to stop prolonging the case with false arguments and deliver his summing-up immediately to avoid delaying the course of justice any further. After his summing-up it would be decided if he had sufficient reason for requesting an extension. The chiang also ordered our own advocates to present themselves and plead their case on our behalf.

The prosecutor summarized his case against us on four points that were so defamatory and delivered in such discourteous language that the chiang was affronted and scandalized to hear it in a court of law. He was so upset by this bad example and contempt that he directed the prosecutor's words to be struck off the court record and issued the following statement:

'Before I refer to the case itself I announce a fine of twenty taels in silver on the prosecutor, the money to be used to help these foreigners. He hasn't proved the least of the accusations made against them. For this initial offence he is also suspended from his duties until the tu-tung rules on his behaviour; and let him be warned not to present his case so disrespectfully nor in such intemperate language again. For a second offence he will be punished in accordance with the ruling given by the chiangs who are admitted to the house of the Son of the Sun, the Lion Crowned on the Throne of the World. This matter is to be settled within the next three days, when this court will resume to hear the other arguments that both sides want to put forward.'

At dawn the following day the four tanigores from the fraternity who were visiting the prison that week sent for us to come to the infirmary where they were sharing out food among the sick. They told us what the chiangs had said and how they hoped for a favourable verdict. We threw ourselves at their feet, saying through our flooding tears:

'God will reward you for the great trouble you have gone to on our behalf! He will give you the eternal prize you seek!'

One of them replied:

'And may He preserve you all in the knowledge of His law, for in that knowledge lies the reward of all good men!'

Then he ordered two blankets to be given to each of us because we suffered very badly from the cold at night. He added:

'If there's anything that you need, simply ask us. God, our Master, is not used to being miserly in the giving of His alms.'

At that moment the clerk of the court arrived to notify us officially of the chiang's statement. He also gave us the fine of twenty taels of silver that had been imposed on the prosecutor and made us all sign a document that he had been to the prison.

We thanked him over and over again and told him to take as many of the twenty taels as he wanted; but he wouldn't take any of them, saying:

'I would not exchange for such a trifle the merit that I can earn with God on your behalf.'

134

102 : *We learn about justice in China.*

WE HEARD NOTHING MORE ABOUT OUR CASE FOR THE NEXT TWELVE days until the four tanigores from the fraternity came to the prison to visit the sick again. We begged them insistently that they should be trying to speak on our behalf to the chiang, who by that time had our case in chambers ready to deliver judgement. After all, we said, the fraternity was well aware of our poverty and distress.

But they were scandalized by our pleading and exclaimed:

'If you were natives of this country instead of foreigners the few words you have just spoken would be enough for us to scrub out the obligation that the fraternity has to you and never again involve it in your affairs! However, on account of your ignorance and stupidity we will pass over your folly this time – but you had better believe in all truth that whosoever is guilty of that sin, that man is unworthy to receive alms from God.'

We were taken aback by this answer and almost ashamed by the way it had been said but we asked their pardon, saying that our ignorance excused our behaviour before God and before them.

One of them looked at his companions and said:

'Perhaps these fellows are not so sinful in what they suggested just now, perhaps we are wrong to be scandalized by them because it could very well be that such behaviour is normal among their people. They are barbarians lacking the full knowledge of the truths of our religion, so it would not be at all remarkable if their own judges have so little integrity that it is necessary for the parties in a law-suit to pay more attention to obtaining personal favours than the actual rights and wrongs of the case.'

With this ringing in our ears we said to them:

'Brothers, you are guided by virtue in everything that you do, so we beg you to tell us why you were so scandalized by our request that to us seemed so necessary and appropriate to the miserable state you see us in here.'

The tanigore who seemed to have the most authority replied:

'It is indeed appropriate that you should remind us of the hardships you have suffered and that you should press us to make enquiries as soon as possible so that your liberty will be obtained that much the quicker; but it is not at all proper for you to ask us to speak to the judge with the aim of getting him to do what a man holding his office must never do. That would be to tempt him to sin against God and to go to hell in consequence, while we ourselves would be behaving like slaves of the devil rather than ministers of succour to the poor.

'And if you said that you are concerned about justice, then you will find it in the trial and judgement itself and not in what someone not directly involved in the case might have to say.

'Lawsuits are not properly judged on the strength of arguments repeated unnecessarily two and three times over, nor by libels and contradictions that are all out of order and introduced to confuse and distract the judge rather than to clarify and bring the course of justice to a satisfactory conclusion – these are all tricks invented by the wretches that some unfortunate litigants have to employ as advocates. No. A judge who is behaving as he should will settle disputes on the basis of definite proof and clear evidence from God-fearing witnesses and from them draw out a judgement by the light of reason.

'If justice is not administered like this in your homeland, my friends, then you should all live in great fear of the wrath of God because God above never closes his eyes to sleep, as earthly kings have to do, the kings who are as subject to all the worldly faults as any man among us, since they are men, just like us.

'So my advice to you, my friends, is that in your hardships you should try to fix your gaze humbly on the heavens because from there will come the verdict on your liberty and the pardon for any crimes you have committed; and we will assist you in this like true friends, if God is pleased to hear us.'

Then they gave us our usual ration of food and went off to visit the other prisoners in the infirmary; in this prison, there was always a great number of sick people for them to visit.

103 : *We hear judgement on our appeal. Ceremonies in the court-house.*

WE SPENT ANOTHER NINE DAYS WAITING FOR THE JUDGEMENT OF our appeal and we were more than a little fearful of the outcome. Then, on a Saturday morning, two court bailiffs came to the prison for us. They were accompanied by twenty constables called 'upus', who carried halberds and maces and wore helmets and suits of chain-mail. They were a chilling sight and their arrival worried and frightened us.

They locked all nine of us into one long iron chain and brought us to the Caladigan, which is the place where judgements are announced and sentences passed and carried out on the convicted.

As we were marched to the Caladigan we were all in such a state that I honestly don't think I would know how to describe our feelings at that time properly. As we moved along not one of us knew to what fate he was going, all we could do was submit to the will of the Lord Our God, whom we begged, weeping, by the wounds of His Holy Passion, to accept the sentence of the court upon us as a penance for our sins. Several times as we moved along, when fear portrayed to us clearer than ever the terrible sentence of a cruel death, we fell to our knees and clung to each other, and begged the Lord to show us his mercy, all of which greatly amazed the Chinese.

Racked with pain and enduring the mockery of crowds of boys we finally reached the outer courtyard of the Caladigan. Twenty-four executioners were waiting there (the Chinese call them 'Ministers of the Arm of Wrath') as well as many ordinary people who were gathered there to present petitions.

We waited there for a long time. Then a bell rang and doors set beneath a great stone arch were opened. This arch was decorated with numerous bas-reliefs and fine paintings and on top of the arch there was a silver statue of an enormous lion, standing on a large globe. This is the emblem of the Chinese emperors and it is usually put on the front of all the High Courts where chiangs (who are like our viceroys) sit.

As I said, the doors opened and everyone in the courtyard entered pell-mell into a great building similar to a church. The walls were covered from floor to ceiling with paintings depicting the unusual death-sentences carried out by terrifying executioners on convicted criminals, regardless of class. At the bottom of each picture was written: 'For such and such a crime, the penalty is death in this manner.' So in these horrifying paintings one could see the type of death sentence carried by different crimes and also be made aware of the utmost rigour with which the law applied these sentences.

At the far end of this building there was another, built across the first like a transept. It was far more elaborate and expensive than the first, covered in gold-leaf and providing a delightful feast for the eyes – but at that particular time we had no joy in anything on earth. In the middle of this transept there was a dais with seven steps leading up to it and enclosed by three rows of railings: one of iron, one of tin and one of blackwood. The railings were inlaid with mother-of-pearl and above the dais there was a canopy of white damask fringed with gold and green and large embroidered drapes of the same material.

Beneath this canopy, surrounded by pomp and majesty, the chiang was seated on an exquisite silver chair with a little table just in front of him. Three young boys were kneeling around him. They wore expensive robes and had golden chains around their necks. The boy in the middle looked after the pen the chiang used to sign documents, while the ones on either side took the petitions from the people and set them down on the little table for the chiang to deal with them.

On the right hand side of the chiang stood a small boy on a rostrum. He was ten or twelve years old, dressed in robes of white satin decorated with red roses and wearing a pearl necklace that wound three times around his neck. His hair was as long as a woman's, plaited and tied with a gold and crimson ribbon and adorned with expensive pearls. He wore sandals of green and gold, trimmed with large pearls. In his hand – as an emblem of what he represented – he carried a small bouquet of silken roses threaded with gold and sprinkled with very expensive pearls. He represented Mercy. This boy had such fine manners and was so handsome that the most beautiful woman would not have shown to advantage against him. He leaned against the chiang's chair, resting the arm that held the bouquet of roses.

On the chiang's left side there was another small boy, just as handsome and just as splendidly dressed, in crimson satin spotted with golden roses. The right-hand sleeve of his robe was turned up showing his forearm stained red with what looked like blood and in his right hand he held an unsheathed short sword, stained the same blood-red colour as his arm. He wore a tall crown like a mitre decorated all around with small blades like lancets. Although this boy was as finely mannered and as handsome as

138

the first, his blood-stained arm and sword made him a frightening sight. This second boy represented Justice.

The Chinese say that for a judge – who represents the emperor, who is, in turn, God's representative on earth – the two qualities of Mercy and Justice are equally essential and that the judge who is not familiar with both will come to be no more than a lawless tyrant and an usurper of the insignia he carries.

The chiang himself wore long, flowing robes of purple satin trimmed with green and gold and he wore something like a friar's scapular with a golden medal around his neck. Engraved on this medal was a hand holding a finely balanced set of scales with this inscription around the edge: 'The Lord on High has weight, measure and reckoning in His justice. So take care in all that you do, because if you should sin you will have to pay for it for all eternity.'

On his head the chiang wore a sort of beret woven of thick threads of gold, enamelled in green and purple. On the top of the beret was a small gold lion with its four feet resting on a golden globe. As I have explained elsewhere, the crowned lion signifies the Chinese emperor and the globe, the world, and these emblems declare the emperor to be 'the Lion Crowned upon the Throne of the World.' In his hand the chiang held a rod like a sceptre, made of the whitest ivory and about three palms long. On the first three of the seven steps up to the dais stood eight attendants holding silver maces; below them, kneeling on the floor in two rows, there were sixty fine-looking Moghuls holding halberds decorated with gold. Standing in front of these halberdiers, like captains of the guard, were two astonishing giants. They were very handsome and finely dressed with their shortswords slung around their shoulders and holding enormous halberds (the Chinese call these giants 'gigauhos').

On the floor at each side of the dais there was a very long table with twelve men sitting around it. Four of these men were district magistrates, two were clerks of the court, four were attorneys and the last two were High Court judges. All these officials were dressed in long white satin robes with very wide sleeves; these clothes symbolize the purity and the generosity of Justice. One of these tables dealt in criminal law, the other in civil law. These tables were covered in purple damask fringed and embroidered most attractively with gold. The chiang's table was made of silver and so was left uncovered; there was nothing on it except a small, round tray, holding an ink-well and some drying-salt, resting on a small, embroidered cushion.

In the first large building the twenty-four executioners – 'the Ministers of the Arm of Wrath' – were standing in line according to their rank. Everywhere else there was a multitude of petition-ers, the men standing, the women sitting on benches; and at the edge of the crowd close to the doors stood six attendants carrying copper maces.

I must say that when you see all this and the way it is pre-sented, it creates a sense of power and majesty, and the grave demeanour of the officials causes the utmost terror and awe in anybody who happens to see them.

At long last a bell was rung four times in quick succession and one of the High Court judges rose to his feet, bowed in respect to the chiang, and said in a loud voice so that everyone could hear him:

'Be silent and ready to listen in humility, or suffer the punish-ment decreed by the chiangs for disturbers of the silence of holy Justice!'

Then he sat down and another High Court judge stood up, came over from the table, bowed to the chiang and mounted the dais. He was handed a sheath of documents by an official and proceeded to announce in a loud voice the court's verdict in each case. This was attended by so many formalities that it took him more than an hour to finish.

When he came to our case we were all made to kneel down with our heads to the floor and our arms raised, like men at prayer, so that we should hear the judgement in this posture of humility. The High Court judge read out the judgement as follows:

'I, Pittu Dikalur, recently appointed as chiang of this sacred court for foreigners by the will of the Son of the Sun, the Lion Crowned on the Throne of the World, to whom are subject the sceptres and crowns of all the kings that reign on the earth, who are placed in homage at his feet by virtue of the grace and will of the Lord on High, now duly offer to all present my decision concerning the appeal of these nine foreigners that was forwarded to me at the request of the Twenty-four of the Austere Life in Nanking, by way of making a complaint about the treatment

140

these foreigners received from our courts.

'Under the solemn oath I swore when I took up this office to assist the Ay-tau of the Batampina, who presides over the thirty-two ay-taus who govern all the peoples of the empire, I now declare that on the ninth day of the seventh moon in the fifteenth year of the reign of the Son of the Sun, the charges brought against the foreigners by the Chumbi of Taipur were presented to me as follows:

'He accused the foreigners of being robbers and thieves. He claimed they had lived by robbery for a long time past, causing great offence to the Lord on High, Creator of All, and without the least fear of God they had bathed themselves in the blood of anyone who resisted them with good cause.

'For these crimes they were sentenced to a severe whipping and to having their fingers chopped off. The whipping was delivered straight away but the Advocates of God's Love for the Poor came to plead on the foreigners' behalf that they had been wrongly condemned since no proofs of any sort had been produced against them.

'The Advocates for the Poor requested that the case should be heard again calling witnesses who followed the ways of God and feared the righteous punishment of His holy justice, rather than the case being judged on the basis of unreliable misgivings.

'The High Court in Nanking replied to this first request that it was not right to strip Justice of her name.

'Then the Advocates for the Poor complained to the Twenty-four of the Austere Life – and with very good reason as one can see from the appeal that they lodged. The petition was promptly dealt with by the Twenty-four on account of the foreigners' wretched situation – they are impoverished and so far from home that no-one in China has ever even heard of their native country.

'The High Court responded to this cry for pity from the Twenty-four by referring the foreigners' case to this court.

'Here the case has proceeded smoothly and regularly. The prosecutor has proved none of his allegations but has merely asserted that the accused deserve the death penalty on the grounds of suspicion.

'However, to be pure and pleasing to God, sacred Justice cannot accept accusations from either party unless there is definite evidence to support the accusations; therefore I could not accept the prosecutor's libels because he had no proofs to offer. Then he chose to persist in asking for the death penalty without presenting either sufficient proof or justifiable grounds for such a sentence. He was fined twenty taels of silver for contempt; the fine was awarded to the accused to help them in their hardship. The prosecutor's allegations were struck off the court record because they were based on malicious intent and ill-will and had nothing to do with the concern for justice that is so pleasing to God, whose mercy always favours the weakest of the earth when they cry out to Him in their sorrow, which is one of the merciful consequences of His grandeur.

'I then contacted the tanigores of the Holy Fraternity who were to plead on behalf of the foreigners and they duly presented their case within the alloted time.

'Thus, having heard from both parties as required by the court, I ordered the hearing to be closed so that I could retire and make my judgement on the rights of the matter.

'So now, having heard and duly considered all the evidence without in the least being swayed from the demands of justice by any worldly concern, and acting in accordance with the precedents accepted by the twelve chiangs in the fifth book of The Will of the Son of the Sun – namely, that in such cases God's royal majesty leans towards the cry of the poor rather than the bellowing of the haughty – I direct that these nine foreigners be acquitted of all the charges brought against them.

'They are spared any criminal punishment but I do, however, sentence them to a year's labour in the work camps at Kuansi, where they will work to pay for their keep. When they have served eight months I direct the officials with responsibility for the foreigners to give them letters of safe passage so that they can return in peace to their native country or go wherever else they so choose.'

While the judgement was being read out all nine of us were kneeling down in front of the dais with our hands raised. There were lots of other points of ceremony that the court officials showed us as we went along and when the conchali had finished speaking we had to say in a loud voice for everyone to hear:

'The judgement of your untainted understanding upon us is confirmed, as well as your purity of heart that pleases the Son of the Sun!'

When we had said this, one of the officials at the tables stood up, bowed to the chiang, and said five times in a very loud voice to the great crowd of people gathered there:

'Is there anyone in the building or the city or the empire who has any objections to this judgement or any doubts about the release of the nine prisoners?'

There was no response from the crowd. The two boys who represented Justice and Mercy touched each other with the emblems they carried and chanted together:

'Let them be released and free in accordance with the just verdict that has been given!'

Then one of the upus struck a bell three times and the two court-bailiffs who had brought us there from the prison unlocked the chain that bound us all together and took the manacles from our hands, the shackles from our ankles and the collars from our necks; we were left standing there, free!

We gave great thanks to Our Lord Jesus Christ because all along it had seemed to us that we were going to suffer unjustly on account of some of the evil notions that the Chinese had about us.

We returned, unchained, to the prison, where a note was entered in the prison records, signed by the two court bailiffs and the nine of us, relieving the gaoler of any responsibility for us. We were now obliged to go and start our exile at Kuansi within the next two months; if we didn't comply we faced the penalty of being held prisoners at the emperor's pleasure, as laid down by their regulations.

We wanted to leave straight away and start begging through the city but the governor of the prison told us to wait until the following day when he would send us to the tanigores of the Fraternity of Mercy who would provide us with some alms.

104 : *Through the Fraternity of Mercy we receive further kindness.*

EARLY THE NEXT MORNING THE FOUR TANIGORES FROM THE Fraternity of Mercy made one of their regular visits to the prison infirmary. They were obviously very happy for us and congratulated us on the successful conclusion of our appeal. We thanked them profusely for their help and wept for joy without restraint.

The tanigores accepted our thanks and told us that we would not be worn out by our period of exile because we would not have to complete more than eight months of the year's sentence: the emperor had waived the other four months of the sentence as an act of charity for the love of God. This favour had been shown to us because of our poverty: if we had been rich and powerful we would certainly not have received the same treatment. The tanigores said they would go immediately and put this notice of remission with the documents concerning our sentence. They also said they would go and talk with a good man who had been posted as a commander and 'muntu' to Kuansi, the place of our exile. The man in question was a great and generous friend of the poor and would treat us well and see to it that we were paid for the work that we did during our exile.

They decided it would be best for us to go along with them to see the man because he might be prepared to take us into his care immediately and arrange for us to stay at an inn until we left, because we knew no-one at all in the whole country. He had done the same for many of the other people he was escorting to Kuansi.

We thanked them all over again for all their help, saying that God would reward them for the charity they had shown us on His behalf.

A short time later we all went to the home of the muntu. He came out to meet us on the terrace, leading his wife by the hand, either as a mark of great respect for us or else as a point of ceremony. As soon as he saw the tanigores he threw himself at their feet, saying:

'Masters and holy brothers! I have had my appointment confirmed and will accept it without any complaint whatsoever because this appointment has brought God's servants to my home which, you may be sure, is something I had never considered possible before because I felt myself to be so unworthy of such favour!'

When they had paid their respects to him with all due ceremony, the tanigores replied:

'May the Lord Our God, the inexhaustible fount of mercy, reward you with good in this life for the charity you have shown to the poor on His account. Believe this, dear brother, that the stoutest staff to support the soul and save it from falling no

144

matter how often it may stumble, the stoutest staff is the charity we show to our neighbours when that charity is untainted by any of the worldly considerations that besmirch the pure desire for good to which God's holy law obliges us.

'And so that you should deserve at the last to enjoy his divine smile and his sweet breath we have brought these nine poor unfortunates to you, perhaps the poorest to be found in the whole empire today. We ask you that in Kuansi you will do for them all that needs to be done for the sake of the Lord on High on whose behalf we ask this of you.'

The man and his wife replied so clearly and so memorably that we were all astonished to see the way they attributed everything to the source of all Good, as if they had received the light of the Faith or knowledge of our holy Christian religion.

Then the man and his wife and the tanigores all went into the house together while we were left outside. They talked among themselves for almost half-an-hour and then called us inside. The tanigores started talking to the man again about us, commending us into his care. He told us to write our names in a book that he had in front of him and said to us:

'I am not so good as to give you of my own property for the love of God, but neither am I so bad that through forgetfulness I should deny you the rewards of the labour to which the emperor has compelled you. So from today onwards you are free to earn your own living, although you may decide not to make use of the freedom, because I want this permission to be counted as alms from my hand. For the time being you can take shelter in my household, where I will provide you with all that you need.

'As for the rest, I don't want to make any promises because I feel such promises might tempt me to vain glory and the devil will be free to snatch my charity into his evil hands, as so very often happens with our frail natures.

'It is enough for the moment that you know I have completely taken you into my care for the sake of God and the holy brothers who spoke to me on your behalf.'

When he had finished the four tanigores took their leave of us, giving each man four taels and telling us:

'Don't forget to give thanks to God for the happy conclusion to this affair, because you would be guilty of a grave sin if you did not acknowledge so great a favour from him.'

So it was that we came to be sheltered in the home of this muntu, who was the best of company throughout the time that we stayed there with him.

When the period of two months' grace allowed by the court was over, we set out for Kuansi with this muntu to start our exile. The muntu always treated us very well and did many favours for us up until the time Kuansi was captured by the Tartars, who brought rampant misfortune, hardship and death to the city, as I will describe in detail further on.

105 : *About Peking, where the Emperor of China holds his court.*

BEFORE I GO ON TO TELL WHAT HAPPENED TO US AFTER WE SET OUT for Kuansi with this Chinese gentleman who had taken us into his care and given us high hopes of having our liberty within the next year, it seems to me to be the right time to give some information about the city of Peking which in all truth could be called the metropolis of the world.

I'll mention some of the things I noticed while I was in Peking: such as its prosperity, the system of government and the marvels to be seen there; the laws and the remarkable administration of justice; the admirable way in which they sustain the entire population; the way they reward the services of those who have been victorious in war, as laid down by the laws of the city; and other matters of a similar nature.

However I must admit to lacking something most important, namely the knowledge and wit to make plain the region in which this city is situated and the latitude in which it lies, both things that the scholars and the simply curious will be keen to know, as I am well aware.

However, as I am writing this book with no other purpose than to leave it for my children so that they can learn to read from the record of my hardships, it doesn't worry me too much that it is written so roughly because I think it's best simply to deal with these matters as best I can, and never mind long words and fancy phrases that would only serve to show up the limitations of my native wit. I'm afraid that if I tried writing in a cultivated style I would merely be caught out and people would be able to apply the well-known saying to me: 'So where did Pedro learn to speak Greek then?'

But in order to fulfil the promise made earlier I must do my best in this regard and tell you that the city of Peking, which is named after its founder, is situated in the latitude of 41° North. The city walls – as the Chinese told us themselves and as I later read in a little book called the *Akesendo* which describes the glories of the city, a copy of which I brought back with me to Portugal – run for a distance of thirty leagues, though some people declare that the distance is fifty leagues.

Now, since there is such a big difference between these two calculations, I would like to explain the cause of this dispute, going by what I saw and heard myself.

The way the city stands at the present time with all its fine buildings, the walls do indeed cover a distance of thirty leagues: there is an inner wall and an outer wall and both are solidly built and fortified with innumerable towers and bulwarks of a design similar to our own. But outside these walls that enclose the present-day city there is another longer wall, and the Chinese assert that in olden times the area between the two walls was covered with houses whereas nowadays there are numerous separate villages and hamlets surrounded by magnificent private estates.

Among these estates are sixteen hundred markedly better than the rest. These are the residences of the representatives of the sixteen hundred most important cities and towns in the thirty-two kingdoms of the empire. When the empire's parliament is summoned every three years all these representatives gather together in Peking to discuss the administration of the empire for the benefit of all, as I will describe in more detail later on.

Outside the walls of the present-day city there are the tombs of twenty-four thousand mandarins, covering an area of twenty-one square leagues. These tombs are built like little chapels that are covered in gold-leaf and set in little courtyards enclosed by railings of lathe-turned iron and brass; the gateways into the courtyards are costly, elaborate arches.

Near these tombs there are very large hostels surrounded by gardens and thick groves made up of all kinds of trees; all around the gardens and groves there are ornamental pools and fountains

147

and springs of water. The insides of the walls that enclose the gardens are covered with exquisite porcelain tiles. The spires on the towers along the walls have lions carrying golden banners; and in the corners of the gardens there are very tall minarets, painted in many different colours.

There are another five hundred hostels, called 'houses of the Son of the Sun', for all those who were maimed while fighting in the service of the emperor, and many others besides who have retired from the army because of sickness or age. Every single one of these old soldiers receives enough of a pension each month to support himself. The Chinese said the total number of these men is at least a hundred thousand, because they said there were two hundred men staying in each one of these hostels.

Elsewhere we saw a very long street of earthen houses where the twenty-four thousand oarsmen for the emperor's panouras are quartered. The fourteen thousand people who work in the royal kitchens live in another street of earthen houses that is more than a league in length.

In yet another street live an enormous number of prostitutes who are supported by a tribute paid by the women of the city. The women in this street are considered part of the court; many of them have fled from their husbands to live in this unhappy condition. If their husbands harm them in any way for having left, they are subject to a very heavy penalty because the women are living there under the protection of the tu-tung of the court, who is responsible for all matters concerning the royal household.

The minatos, that is, the laundry workers, who wash the clothes of the whole city also live inside the old walls. We were told there are over a hundred thousand people working as launderers because there is plenty of scope for them near the city with big rivers and streams and countless deep pools as well as reservoirs built of the strongest and best quality stone.

The *Akesendo* states that in the empty areas inside the old walls there are thirteen hundred impressive, costly houses and refectories for the male and female religious who follow the four largest religions of the thirty-two that are practised in the Chinese empire. They say that some of these religious houses have upwards of a thousand people behind their doors, besides all the people on the outside who supply them with everything

148

they need.

Something else we saw was a great number of estates with large, impressive buildings and big enclosures containing gardens and dense woods where you could find every kind of big- and small-game that you could name. These houses are like inns where there are always great crowds of people gathered to eat sumptuous banquets and watch plays, farces, bullfights and wrestling matches. Government officials like tu-tungs, chiangs, conchalis, ay-taus, chumbis, bracalans, muntus and lau-tis, and other people like lords, nobles, army officers and wealthy merchants and traders go there to lay on these banquets and entertainments for their friends and relatives. No expense is spared: the Masters of Ceremony carry silver maces, the serving platters are exquisite and all the plates are made of gold. In the rooms there are couches covered in cloth of silver with canopies of embroidered silk. All the service is provided by beautiful young maidens in expensive clothes.

Yet all this extravagance and much more besides in a similar incomparable style is considered nothing remarkable by the Chinese. They assured us that one of these banquets can last for a full ten days without a break and the cost of the abundance of food, the ostentation and ceremony of the presentation, all the attendants and servants, the music, fishing, hunting, sports, farces, plays and horse-racing can all mount up to twenty thousand taels.

These inns cost more than twenty-five thousand cruzados to build and they are financed by groups of wealthy merchants who invest their money in them as a business proposition. It is said their profits are much bigger than if they were to risk their money in sea-going trade.

When somebody wants to arrange a banquet he goes along to the 'xipatom' (the steward in charge of the inn) and says what he has in mind. The xipatom then shows the customer a book that lists and describes the menus and entertainments available at the various banquets, and the customer can choose the one he wants at his leisure.

This book of banquets is called the *Pinatoru* and I myself saw and heard it read several times. The first three chapters are an Introduction and describe the banquets to which a person would invite God Almighty. Next in importance are banquets for the

Emperor of China who the people say is present on earth as a special grace from Heaven to preside over all the kings of the earth. After the banquets for God and the emperor – and now dealing with ordinary human beings – the book describes the banquet appropriate for the tu-tungs, who are the ten supreme dignitaries in authority over the forty chiangs of the empire (who are like viceroys). The tu-tungs are called the 'splendours of the Sun' because just as the emperor himself is the 'Son of the Sun', so the tu-tungs who represent him are the splendour that proceeds from him, like the rays of light that come from the sun.

Before I leave these pagan barbarities that they are accustomed to, I will discuss in detail just one aspect of these banquets, namely the delicacies they say a man has to provide at a banquet for God Almighty, something I myself saw followed down to the last detail on some occasions – although for lack of the True Faith all their good works will benefit these people very little.

106 : *The procession of the Chiang of the Thirty-two Kingdoms.*

AS I MENTIONED IN THE LAST CHAPTER, THE FIRST BANQUET described in the *Pinatoru* is the one that a man provides for God Almighty. The introduction to the book observes:

'Every banquet involves a certain amount of expense but the actual amount depends on how much the host wants to spend; but while the banquet is paid for with the host's money he receives nothing more substantial in return for all the expense than the praise of flatterers and the gossip of good-for-nothings.

'Consider this, friend, and be advised rather to spend your wealth in providing a feast for God in the persons of the poor, and in secretly providing for the children of poor but virtuous parents, so that they will not suffer for the lack of those things which you have to excess.

'Bear in mind also the vile matter from which your father begot you, and the far viler matter in which your mother conceived you, and you will realize how much less you are worth than any wild beast without trace of reason and stirred only by the impulses of the evil flesh.

'However, since you wish to treat these mortal friends, who

tomorrow will be no more, as a good and faithful man you should invite God's poor to the banquet because God listens with compassion to their cries of need like a merciful father and promises them eternal content in the Palace of the Sun, where we believe His own will possess Him in great happiness for ever and ever.'

After these and many other noteworthy observations are read out to the client by a priest, as required by the rules of the house, the xipatom, the chief steward, goes through the book chapter by chapter with the client, beginning with the most luxurious banquets and ending with the most ordinary.

The xipatom has to know what class of people are being invited, how many of them there will be and for how long the feast is to last. For example, the banquet provided for emperors and tu-tungs involves so much pomp and ceremony and luxury, with an army of attendants serving a mountain of exquisite dishes and delicacies, besides all the entertainments and sports – none of which can be omitted – that the whole thing costs an awful lot of money.

Less expensive are the banquets appropriate for chiangs, aytaus, ponchacis, bracalans, anchacis, conchalis lau-tis, military officers and rich merchants. Banquets for anyone other than the emperor and the tu-tungs involve no more than the guests sitting themselves at the table and eating their fill at their leisure.

Fifty or sixty inns are kept busy providing these banquets, catering for every class and kind of people and served by a lower class of servant than those present at banquets for the emperor and tu-tungs.

There is just so much to see and be impressed by in these banqueting houses: the houses themselves and the way they are decorated and furnished; the kitchens, larders and slaughterhouses; the reception-rooms, sleeping quarters and sick-rooms; the courtyards and stables; the dining halls and private rooms with their expensive couches; the enormous service-sets laid out ready on the tables with all the chairs in place so that the guests have little more to do than walk in, sit down and start eating.

There are some banqueting houses where music is played on harps and violins accompanied by dulcimers, flutes, horns, sackbuts and many other sorts of instrument not to be found in Europe.

There is absolutely no shortage of anything at these banquets.

Very often there is a banquet arranged for women alone but the service is provided, as always, by women and beautiful young maidens in expensive clothes. Such is the beauty of these girls that frequently they are taken as brides by noblemen.

I will finish describing these banqueting houses by remarking that four per cent of the total cost of each banquet is used to provide food for the poor tables that are set up all over Peking. This four per cent is made up of two per cent from the Xipatom's fee and two per cent from the person who gave the banquet.

These poor tables are open to whoever wants to sit down at them. The four per cent levy also provides clean rooms and fresh, clean beds for the homeless for up to three days, except in the cases of pregnant women or people who are too sick to travel: these are given shelter for longer. In China attention is paid to whatever needs present themselves.

Something else we saw in this area inside the older, outer walls of the city was thirty-two enormous mansions with little more than the distance of a falcon-shot between them. These are the colleges for the thirty-two religions that are followed in the thirty-two kingdoms of the empire.

Judging by the vast numbers that we saw around these buildings there must have been more than ten thousand students in each; the *Akesendo* itself, the book which contains all the information about the city of Peking, estimates the total number of students to be around four hundred thousand.

There is another much larger and more impressive building situated at a distance from these colleges. All the successful graduates from the colleges, both to the priesthood and in Law and Government, go there to receive their qualifications.

A chiang attends this presentation ceremony and the principals of the colleges are subordinate to him; as a mark of supreme respect he is called the 'Xilaixitapu', which means, 'Lord High of all the Nobility'.

As the highest ranking personage there, the chiang is accompanied by a cortege as grandiose as that of any tu-tung: he has a guard of three hundred moghuls and twenty-four mace-bearers, then thirty-six women on white horses with silver harnesses and silken saddle-blankets, singing sweetly and playing delightfully on Chinese instruments.

Then come twenty sprightly horses with no riders but accompanied in excellent order by six halberdiers and four footmen. These horses wear blankets of lacework and cloth of silver, with neck trappings of the same materials and jingling silver mouth-pieces.

At the front of this grand procession march more than four hundred constables dragging long iron chains along the ground and making such a frightful noise that it would make anybody's hair stand on end.

Twelve men on horseback, called 'peretandas', carry sun-shades of crimson silk fixed on very large poles. Behind these peretandas come twelve men carrying banners of white damask with very long fringes and trimmings all in gold.

Last of all comes the chiang himself seated in a triumphal chariot, followed by sixty conchalis, chumbis and muntus, all of them walking with their gold swords of office at their shoulders.

The other lower-ranking officials – such as scribes, accountants, bailiffs and inspectors – walk ahead of this great throng, shouting at the tops of their voices to tell the ordinary people to go into their houses and leave the streets completely deserted.

At the very rear of this procession come the petitioners and pleaders, also walking.

On either side of the chiang or tu-tung (for both titles could apply to him) come two boys on horseback, both very finely dressed and carrying the emblems of justice and mercy just as I described them earlier: the boy on the left-hand, Mercy, is dressed in white; the boy on the right, Justice, is dressed in blood-red; and their mounts have saddle-blankets of the same colours, with reins and trimmings of gold and a net of silver filigree covering their haunches. Each of these boys is followed by another six boys of about fifteen years old, carrying silver maces.

There isn't a person alive who wouldn't be shaking from head to toe with fear at the sight of this procession – while at the same time marvelling at the grandeur and authority that it all represents.

So as not to cause any longer delay by discussing everything to be seen within the outer walls of Peking, I will resist describing in detail the many other things that we saw there, such as all the impressive buildings, the pagodas (which are their temples), the bridges supported on columns of very thick stone, the roadways covered with the finest quality flagstones, and the roads themselves: long and wide and well-made, lined on both sides with finely-wrought iron railings.

From what I have already described the reader should be able to judge for himself the quality of all the things that I have not described, because everything in the city is of the one, high standard.

Now I will discuss as briefly as I can some of the buildings I saw inside the city of Peking itself, above all the four that most impressed and fascinated me. I will also discuss other particular matters in the city that I think will be of interest to the readers.

107 : *More about Peking.*

I PROMISED TO TELL YOU MORE ABOUT PEKING, BUT EVERYTHING about the city is so remarkable that now I almost regret having made the promise – in all truth, I just don't know where to begin!

Now, the reader should not imagine that I am talking about a city like Rome, Constantinople, Venice, Paris, London, Seville, Lisbon or any other great city in Europe, no matter how famous and thriving it may be; nor should the reader bother to leave Europe and think of cities like Cairo in Egypt, Tauris in Persia, Amadabad in Cambay, Bisnaga in Narsinga, Gourou in Bengal, Avah in Chalu, Timplan in Calaminham, Martaban and Bagu in Pegu, Gimpel and Tinlau in Siammon, Ayuthia in Sornau, Passarvan and Demak on the island of Java, Panguor in the Ryukyus, Uzangui in the Great Cochim, Lansam in Tartary or Kyoto in Japan, which are all capital cities of great kingdoms.

No, I would dare to declare that not one of these great cities has anything to compare to the most insignificant aspect of life in Peking, much less anything to compare with the grandeur and luxury to be found everywhere in the city, whether we're talking about the superb architecture, the boundless wealth or the overwhelming abundance of all the necessities of life. Then there's the people themselves, the trading, the ships coming and going, all of them impossible to count; the judicial system, the system of government, the stability at the imperial court; the authority of the tu-tungs, chiangs, anchacis, ay-taus, ponchacis and bracalans, who all have charge of very large kingdoms and provinces, and command enormous incomes. These officials are normally resident in Peking; occasionally they themselves have to visit their provinces and kingdoms on important business and in such cases their deputies remain in Peking.

However, I will leave all that aside for the time being and discuss it in detail later. Let me start now by repeating that the city walls of Peking have a circumference of thirty leagues, which does not include everything enclosed by the outer walls I have already mentioned briefly (very briefly indeed when compared to everything that could be mentioned!).

These two walls around the city are very stout and built of the best stonework; there are three hundred and sixty gates in each wall, fortified with two very tall towers, drawbridges and living-quarters for the guards. At each of these gates there is a guard of four halberdiers and a scribe who keeps a record of everyone who enters and leaves the city through that gate.

By a ruling of the tu-tung each gate is dedicated to one of the saints so that on every day of the year one of the gates celebrates with great solemnity the feast day of its own particular patron, after whom the gate is also named.

The Chinese told us there are three thousand eight hundred pagodas inside the walls of this great city, and people are there all day long sacrificing an enormous number of birds and wild animals. They say these are more acceptable to God as sacrifices than domestic animals that people have reared in their homes: the priests give many justifications for this practice and so persuade the people to accept this superstition as an article of faith.

Many of these pagodas are very luxurious, particularly those belonging to the sects of Shaka, Amida, Gizom and Canom, which are the four oldest of the thirty-six religions which flourish in this diabolical labyrinth where Satan sometimes shows himself in various guises to make them believe all the more in these illusions and falsehoods.

The main thoroughfares of the city are very long and wide and lined with impressive buildings of one or two storeys; there are railings of bronze and iron along either side of the street, with entries leading off to the sidestreets. At the end of each street there are expensive gates set in arches, the gates are closed at night and there are alarm bells hanging from the high point of every arch. Each street has its own guard of an officer and troopers who are obliged every ten days to present a report to the city council of everything that has happened in that particular street so that the ponchacis and chiangs can be informed if justice requires it.

The *Akesendo*, which I have cited so many times, also states that this great city has a hundred and twenty canals built by the emperors and their people in ancient times. These canals are three fathoms deep and twelve fathoms wide and they criss-cross the whole city. The canals are spanned by numerous stoutly built stone bridges with tall columns at either end and comfortable benches for passers-by to sit down and rest themselves. The people of Peking say they have eighteen hundred bridges crossing their hundred and twenty canals, every one of them built to the same high standard in terms of design, materials and maintenance.

The *Akesendo* also tells us that there are a hundred and twenty impressive squares in the city, every one of which hosts a market each month – which works out at four markets in the city on every single day of the year!

We ourselves went to ten or twelve of these markets during the two months we were at liberty in the city. There was an infinite number of traders there, on foot and on horseback, using box stalls like travelling salesmen and selling as many different articles as you could put a name to; there were also the customary tent-stalls of the rich merchants, set up and arranged in very good order in their allotted streets, selling such quantities of silk, lace, canvas, clothes of cotton and linen, marten and musk and ermines, delicate porcelain, gold- and silver-plate, seed-pearls and pearls, gold-dust and gold-bullion – just so much that the nine of us walked around as if in a daze.

And if you want me to talk about all the iron, steel, lead, copper, tin, brass, coral, red marble, crystal, fire-stone, quicksilver, vermilion, ivory, cloves, nutmeg, mace, ginger, cinnamon, pepper, tarmarind, aniseed, borax, indigo, honey, wax, sandalwood, sugar, preserves, dried fruit, flour, rice, meat, game and vegetables – well, all these things were to be had in such abundance that I feel as if there are not enough words in the dictionary to name them all!

The Chinese told us that Peking has one hundred and sixty ordinary slaughterhouses, each one of which contains a hundred butcher's shops serving as many different meats as are to be found on God's earth. These people eat every kind of meat there is: lamb, mutton, goat, pork, horse, buffalo, deer, tiger, lion, dog, mule, donkey, zebra, tapir, otter, badger – indeed the flesh of any animal that you could name.

In every one of these butcher's shops the price of each meat is fixed and, besides the weighing scales the butcher uses to weigh the meat himself, at each door there are scales provided by the city council where the meat can be re-weighed just to make sure the people are not being cheated.

As well as these slaughterhouses there is not a street in the city which doesn't have five or six houses where all kinds of animals are slaughtered and good quality meat sold; and then there are many taverns where the food is cooked to perfection in the cleanest of conditions.

Then there are the butchers' arcades selling smoked meats, bacon, pork, game and beef in such quantities it would be best not to try and estimate how much – but I mention it so that everyone will see with what generosity the Lord Our God has shared out with these benighted people the fruits of the earth he created . For which generosity, let his name be praised for ever.

112 : *Care for the homeless and handicapped.*

MOST OF THE TIME THE EMPEROR OF CHINA HOLDS COURT IN Peking, which he solemnly swears to do at his coronation service when the Sceptre of All Government is placed in his hand, a ceremony I will talk about a little later on.

In certain districts of the city there are streets set apart for buildings that the Chinese call 'laginampur', which means, 'schools for the poor.' In these schools, which are supervised by the City Council, all the abandoned children who do not know their fathers are taught religion, reading and writing and skilled trades up until such times as they are able to earn a living with their own hands. There are at least two hundred of these schools in the city, perhaps as many as five hundred.

There are an equal number of homes, also under the supervision of the City Council, where poor women act as nursemaids to all the abandoned children who do not know who or where their fathers and mothers are. Before a child is accepted into one of these homes the courts carry out a detailed investigation of the case; if they trace the child's father or mother the parents are severely punished and exiled to barren, disease-ridden regions of the empire.

After being reared the children are allocated to one of the 'laginampur' to receive their education and training. If a child suffers from some disability and is not able to learn a skill or trade, then he is trained to earn his living in some other way, depending on the needs and the ability of each child. For example, if the children are blind they are allocated in groups of three to mill-owners: two of them to grind and the third to winnow.

This is how the Council is able to provide for all the disabled people the city has in its charge: no merchant or tradesman can do business legally without a licence from the Council and when someone applies for a trading licence it is quickly granted but carries an obligation to support one or more of the disabled people who have been trained in that particular trade or line of business. So the man's business not only supports the man himself but also brings relief to the poor and crippled.

The Chinese say that this arrangement is a work of charity demanded by God, one that is very pleasing for him, and one that will lessen the punishment due to us for our sins.

In the example of the blind people, the miller has to feed and clothe the three of them and pay them seven cruzados a year, so that when they die they will have something to leave behind to save their souls from perishing in the deep fiery pit on account of their poverty, which is the fate of the poor according to the fourth precept of the goddess Amida.

This Amida was the goddess from whom these benighted people originally derived their superstitions and false teachings, apparently about six hundred and thirty six years after the Flood. The cult of Amida, along with all the others – thirty-two of them as far as I know – that are to be found in this barbaric country, originated in Pegu and then through its priests and monks spread from there through all the mainland kingdoms of Siam, Cambodia, Tsien-pá, Laos, Gucos, Pafuas, Chien-mai, the Uzangui Empire, Cochinchina and then across to the archipelago of Hainan, the Ryukyus and Japan, so that this scabies has infected and corrupted as much of the world as the damned sect of Mohammed.

The disabled who do not have the use of their feet can earn their livelihood and avoid starvation by working for ropemakers, making hempen ropes and big fruit baskets and other similar work that can be done with the hands.

The poor people who do not have the use of their hands are given big baskets that are fixed round their shoulders, and they earn money carrying meat, fish, vegetables and other goods home from the markets for people who cannot carry it themselves or do not have any servants to carry it for them.

The people who have no use of either their hands or their feet and are completely unable to earn a living for themselves are placed in big houses like monasteries where a great number of professional mourners offer up prayers for the dead. Half of all the donations the mourners receive from bereaved families is given to these cripples, while the other half is given to the clergy.

People who cannot speak are housed in another building like a hospital and to support themselves they receive all the fines imposed on female hawkers and loose women who have disgraced themselves in public.

For prostitutes who fall victim to some incurable disease in their old age there are nursing homes where they are generously provided for by other prostitutes. All these women pay a monthly levy towards the upkeep of these homes because later on in life any one of them could suffer from the same sickness; then the other women will support them just as they supported the sick older women when they had their health. There are men in every part of the city who collect this levy once every month and they receive a good salary for doing this job.

In other buildings like monasteries there is an enormous number of little orphan girls who are fed, clothed and sheltered at the expense of women who have forfeited property after being charged with adultery by their husbands. The reasoning behind this is that the woman's adultery has shown she would abandon her child along with her husband, so it is only justice that while she is punished another orphan should find shelter.

There are other districts of the city where the City Council supervises the care of honest poor men, paid for by fines levied on attorneys who pursue claims that have absolutely no basis in justice, and judges swayed by favouritism or bribery who do not conduct the affairs of the court in the manner that justice demands.

So you can see that the Chinese are very well organized in making provision for the old and the infirm.

113 : *Granaries for the poor: the king who began this provision.*

SOMETHING ELSE MY READERS SHOULD DEFINITELY KNOW about is the amazing lengths – involving immense organization – that this pagan Emperor of China goes to in order to keep every part of the empire supplied with food, so that the poor will not suffer from a lack of the necessities of life.

I will repeat to you what I had read out to me several times from the Chinese chronicles concerning these provisions for the poor, which are an example of both charity and good government to the Christian kingdoms of Europe.

These chronicles, written down in Chinese characters, tell us that an emperor called Chou Xi Rang, the great-grandfather of the present emperor, had lost his sight after a serious illness. This Chou Xi Rang was cherished by all his subjects on account of his dignity and the gentle manner with which he fulfilled his duties.

The emperor desired to render some supremely pleasing service to God and so one day he convened the representatives of the people and decreed that granaries for corn and rice were to be established in all the towns and cities of the empire for the relief of the poor. These granaries would provide food for the poor to live on and avoid starvation in those years when, as occasionally happens, blight or drought stop the earth from yielding up a harvest.

To pay for all these granaries the emperor himself would give up a tenth part of the royal taxes; and he ordered that a general proclamation be made about this decree in the chief towns of every district in the empire.

The chronicles go on to relate how this proclamation was brought to the emperor for him to sign with a gold signet ring that he used on account of his blindness. As soon as he had set his seal on the proclamation God restored his sight completely and he was able to see for the remaining fourteen years of his life.

If this story is true it would seem that Our Lord wanted to

160

show us just how pleasing to Him is charity to the poor, even among infidels who have no knowledge of Him.

From that time onwards right down to the present day there has always been a great number of these granaries throughout the empire – fourteen thousand of them in all, we were told.

This is how the government organizes a steady supply of fresh grain: as soon as the first crop indicates that the harvest is safe and assured the grain in the stores is divided among all the people in the district, shared out according to the needs of each person as a loan in kind for a period of two months. At the end of the two months everyone hands back as much of the new crop as they had received of the old, plus an additional six per cent to cover any loss or wastage. In this way the amount of grain in storage never diminishes.

In the years when there is a poor harvest the grain is shared out among the people without any consideration for profit or gain. Where people do not have the means to return the amount of grain they receive, the loss is made good out of the land-taxes that are paid to the emperor – that is the alms pledged by Chou Xi Rang in his decree, and there is a copy of the proclamation in every council chamber in the empire so that the officials in charge of the granaries have to take note of it.

The rest of the royal income from taxes in the empire – which comes to an enormous amount of piculs of silver – is divided into three portions: one third pays for the upkeep of the royal household and the government of the empire; one third pays for the defence of the empire, stocking arsenals and supplying the army and navy; and one third is deposited in the royal treasury in Peking. In ordinary circumstances the emperor is not allowed to touch this money because it is allocated for the defence of the country during the frequent wars that the Chinese have with the Tartars, the King of Cochin and the kings of the other countries that share a border with the Chinese empire.

This money stored in the treasury is called 'Chidampur', which means 'Walls of the Kingdom', because the Chinese say that while that treasure is there, ready for use to relieve any hardship which the empire might face, the emperor will not impose any extraordinary tax or tribute on the poor; and the poor, in return, will not resent their emperor as happens in other lands where such generous, sensible provisions have not been made.

So it can be seen that in the Chinese empire there is excellent organization and prompt execution of whatever needs to be done in any situation.

Francis Xavier, the blessed priest and scholar and Light of the Orient in his own time, whose virtue and holiness have made him so well-known throughout the world that I need not discuss him any further here, Francis Xavier himself, when he travelled in China, was astonished by the high degree of organization and the many other praiseworthy things that he saw there.

Indeed, Francis was so impressed that he said if God saw fit to bring him back to Portugal, the favour he would wish for our own king would be for him to study the laws and statutes by which the Chinese live in peace and war. Francis firmly believed that their laws were far superior to those of the Romans in their Golden Age or any of the other nations mentioned by the ancient historians.

114 : *The greatness of the Chinese Empire. Religious sects.*

NOW, I CONFESS I'M AFRAID THAT BY GOING INTO DETAIL ABOUT all the strange and remarkable things we saw in Peking I could be stirring a few doubts about their authenticity in the minds of my readers. So to avoid providing further material for the begrudgers and cynics who measure everything by the little they know and can understand with their narrow, coarsened intellects, and who pass judgement on the veracity of things that I saw with my own two eyes, I will refrain from describing many things that would probably be of interest and entertainment to the fair-minded among my readers, the ones that have wide sympathies and do not measure life in other lands solely in terms of the mediocrity and vulgarity of their own immediate surroundings.

I know these readers, with their generous spirits and the natural curiosity of true intelligence, would very much enjoy hearing about everything I saw. Yet I can hardly be too critical of anyone who has his doubts about the truth of what I describe because, to be quite honest, very often I myself feel dazed when I think of the wonders of Peking – I who was there and saw them with my own two eyes!

For instance, it is hard to imagine the size of this pagan emperor's household and the imperial service, or the great pomp and ceremony surrounding the highest officials of justice and government, or the fear and reverence that the common people have for all these officials, or the extravagant luxury of their idolatrous temples. Quite simply, unless you've been there it's hard to grasp the scale and quality of anything in the city of Peking.

Consider this for a start: the city of Minapau stands inside the actual perimeters of the emperor's palace estates and Minapau alone has a population of a hundred thousand eunuchs, thirty thousand women and twelve thousand guards, who all receive large salaries and pensions from the emperor. There are also twelve tu-tungs, the highest ranking officials in the empire, who are known to the ordinary people as 'the Rays of the Sun', because the emperor himself is the 'Son of the Sun' and these tu-tungs represent the king's person in all matters.

Next in rank below the tu-tungs are forty chiangs, who are like viceroys, and then there is a host of other lower ranking officials called anchacis, ay-taus, ponchacis, lau-tis and chumbis who have similar duties to our council chairmen, governors, aldermen, admirals and commanders-in-chief.

In the court city of Minapau there are more than five hundred of these officials and every one of them has an entourage of at least two hundred people. To increase the spectacle, these entourages are mostly made up of foreigners from many different countries, the greater part of them being Moghuls, Persians, Khorasans, Malays, Calaminhans, Tartars, Cochins and some Burmese from Chalay and Toungoo.

The Chinese themselves are not physically impressive but are weak and fit for very little; however, they are very able and enterprising in all areas of agriculture and engineering and they are very imaginative architects and the inventors of many intricate, ingenious objects. The Chinese women are very pale and chaste in behaviour and actually more inclined to all sorts of work than the Chinese men.

The land itself is very fertile, so rich and abundant in everything that, to be honest, I don't know how to describe it. I don't think anyone has enough imagination to grasp – let alone enough words to describe – all the fruits of the earth God has chosen to grant to these idolatrous people who insult his name and show their ingratitude for all the favours shown them by believing that it is on the merits of their emperor alone that the earth produces such abundance rather than through Divine Providence and the love of that Lord for whom all things are possible.

Their ignorance and incredulity give rise to the great folly and profusion of superstition that exists among them, involving many abuses and diabolical rituals, including sacrifices using human blood, offered up with a mass of incense.

Some people offer bribes to their priests in order to secure great wealth for themselves in this life and an infinite amount of gold in the next. In return for these bribes the priests issue the people with certificates called 'cuchimiocos': these are like credit notes, so that when a man dies he will be repaid a hundredfold in heaven what he gave the priest on earth, as if the bribe was an investment in heaven. These wretches are so taken in by this ruse that very often they forego food and the necessities of life to give something to these priests of Satan, convinced that they have a good bargain.

There are priests belonging to another sect, called Naustolins, who preach the opposite to this and solemnly assure their congregations that there's nothing more to life than living and dying like an animal, so they should enjoy their worldly goods while they can because they'd be fools to worry about anything that comes afterwards.

There is another sect, called Tri Mi Chow, who believe that for as long as a man is alive on this earth he will spend as long a time again buried beneath the earth, after which through the petitions of the priests he will return to life again with his soul in the body of a week-old baby, where he will live until he has enough strength to go and look for his old body that was left behind in the tomb; from there he will carry it up to the Heaven of the Moon and sleep there for many, many years until he is transformed into a star and remains fixed and shining in the heavens forever and ever.

Another sect, called Gizom, believe that only the birds and the beasts – on account of the penance they did through their sufferings in this life –will enjoy peace in Heaven. As for man, who spends his life in subjection to the flesh, robbing and killing and committing every other sort of sin, there is no way at all for him to be saved unless at the point of death he bequeathes whatever wealth he has to the pagoda and the priests who will pray on his behalf.

The whole basis of all these devilish sects is the tyranny and self-interest of the bonzes who preach these falsehoods to the people and spare no rhetoric in asserting them to be true – and their poor followers, believing in all these things, give everything they can spare to the priests to make themselves safe from all the terrors they are threatened with unless they do just that!

I don't want to discuss any more than these few sects nor deal with all the other abuses of religion to be found in the Chinese empire because I would never get finished if I were to discuss them all; but from the few that I have described the reader can easily imagine what all the others are like because they are all cast from similar moulds.

So I will leave these great evils and ignorance to Divine Providence and the mercy of the One who alone is competent to impose the necessary correction. From now on I will do no more than describe the further hardships we endured in our exile in the city of Kuansi until we were captured by the Tartars, which was in the year of Our Lord, 1544.

115 : *We are taken to Kuansi to serve our exile.*

AFTER WE HAD SPENT TWO AND A HALF MONTHS AT LIBERTY IN THE city of Peking, we were taken to Kuansi to start serving our year's banishment on a Saturday, the 13th of January, 1544.

When we arrived there the chiang ordered us to be brought before him. After he had asked us a few questions, he decided that we should serve our sentence in the personal guard of eighty halberdiers allowed him by the emperor. We considered this to be no small favour from the hands of Our Lord because not only would it be easy work but there would be good food and better pay and more freedom to come and go than we could have expected.

We had been settled in for almost a month, all of us happy to be enjoying better treatment than we could have hoped for and each man happy to share the little he had with his eight companions,

when the devil saw the true brotherly spirit that existed amongst
us and quickly acted to destroy it. He sowed the seeds of an
argument between two men that grew to harm all nine of us. This
dispute was born of a certain vanity that exists among the Portuguese, something that I can't explain other than by our having
low boiling points in matters of honour.

This was the point of honour at stake: two of our number
happened to start arguing about which family enjoyed higher
standing in the King of Portugal's household, the Madureiras or
the Fonsecas. One word led to another until the two were arguing
like drunken fishwives:

'Who do you think you're talking to?'

'Just who do you think you are?'

And probably neither of them owned much more than the
clothes he was wearing!

They were both in such a rage that finally one of them clouted
the other man around the head and in reply had his cheek slashed
open with a knife. Then the first man grabbed a halberd and
sliced off the other man's arm and in the meantime the other
seven of us had started fighting among ourselves to settle this
miserable argument. By the time the chiang himself arrived to see
what was going on seven of us were badly wounded. The chiang
ordered us all to be seized and given thirty lashes immediately.
The whipping was more painful even than the wounds we had
received in the brawl. We were taken away and thrown in a
dungeon where we spent forty-six troubled days with chains
round our hands, feet and necks.

This whole affair was duly put in the hands of the Public
Prosecutor who prepared a libellous case against us. One of the
articles of his case, which he backed up with seventeen witnesses,
was that we were people without knowledge or fear of God: we
did no more than offer lip-service to God, which any wild beast
at all could do if it knew how to talk. The Prosecutor's submission concluded as follows:

'That men of the same race from the same country, who speak
the same language and are subject to the same king and the same
religion, that such men fight and kill each other so mercilessly
without any good reason whatsoever is something that can only
be understood if they are slaves of the Voracious Serpent from
the House of Hell – which these men obviously are, to judge by

their words and deeds that bear the hallmark of the Serpent herself.

'So, in accordance with the law of the third book of "The Linch-Pins of The Will of The Son of the Sun", *Nileterau* by name, the court should isolate these men from any contact with our people, as if they had a contagious disease, and banish them to the mountains of Chabaki, Sumbor or Lamau, the usual place of exile for such criminals, where at night-time they can hear the roaring of the wild animals in the forest, who are of the one family and the one vile nature as themselves.'

One morning we were taken from our dungeon to the Pitau Caladan, the court where the anchaci sits in awesome majesty, surrounded by a host of legal officials and administrators of justice and a multitude of petitioners and spectators from different places. Here they gave us another thirty lashes each. After they announced our sentence we were taken to another prison where things were a little bit easier than before but where we spent our time cursing the Madureiras and the Fonsecas and, above all, the devil himself who had ensnared us in this mess.

We were in this second prison for almost two months and recovered from our wounds and the whippings although we suffered greatly from both hunger and thirst.

Finally, Our Lord saw fit that the chiang should have mercy on us. There is a special day when the Chinese give generous alms for the benefit of the souls of the dead: it was on this day that the chiang reviewed our sentence again.

The chiang took into consideration the fact that we were foreigners, people from a land so remote and distant that up until then no-one in China had ever been there nor even seen it mentioned in any book or manuscript, so there was no-one in the whole empire who could speak our language. He also bore in mind that most of the time we had to endure the misery of grinding poverty, which was sufficient to distract the good and the meek from the paths of righteousness, never mind people like ourselves who had no forebearance in their adversities; it seemed clear that the discord among us was due to the effects of our wretched poverty rather than to our malicious characters, as the Public Prosecutor had alleged. Lastly, he took into account the shortage of exiles available to serve the empire or the officials of justice in some basic way (a necessity to which the Chinese had to resort.)

In the light of all this the chiang decreed, as an act of charity done in the name of the emperor, that the due penalty for our offence had been satisfied by the sixty lashes we had already received; however, we were to remain as prisoners in Kuansi until the tu-tung saw fit to decree otherwise and if any one of us, at any time in the future, should start a brawl in the street, or draw blood from any person at all, that man would be whipped to death the very same day.

This sentence was read out to us shortly afterwards. We were sorrowful enough when we heard it, thinking on the wretched situation we now found ourselves in, although we knew it to be better than the earlier sentence we had received.

After the sentence was announced we were chained together in threes and taken from the prison to an iron foundry where we were put to work and suffered abundant hardship and deprivation for the next five months, with no clothes on our bodies nor beds to lie on, weak with hunger and eaten alive by lice, until finally we all fell sick with a feverish stupor. Since the sickness was contagious they threw us out of the iron foundry to go and beg for food and shelter until we were fit again. They opened our cells and let us go free.

For more than four months we had to go from house to house, sick as we were, begging for food, clothing and shelter. We rarely received anything because there was widespread drought in the country at the time, but we were forced to live in peace with each other and we reached an agreement solemnly sworn to by each one of us. We vowed that henceforth we would live in peace and harmony with each other like the Christians we were; and each man in turn would act as leader for a month, everyone else obeying him as if he were truly in command and responsible for the rest of us; no-one was to act just to suit himself or do anything without the leader's permission. This agreement was written down like a set of rules to govern ourselves by. In this way we lived in peace with each other as Our Lord wanted us to, even though we suffered great hardship and lacked the necessities of life.

116 : *We discover a Portuguese living in Kuansi.*

SO WE LIVED FOR THE TIME BEING IN PEACE AND HARMONY WITH each other, following the rules we had agreed upon. Our leader for the first month, Cristovão Borralho, saw how necessary it was to use every available means of earning our livelihood. He organised us into pairs each week, one pair to beg for alms in the city, another pair to find water and do the cooking, and the others gathering firewood to sell or to use ourselves.

One particular day it was my duty to go and gather firewood with a man called Gaspar de Meireles. We got up in the morning and left the house to go to the forest. This Meireles was a musician. He could sing and play the mandolin delightfully, talents that are greatly admired among the Chinese because they spend much of their time feasting and enjoying the pleasures of the senses. They loved Meireles' singing and playing and he was very often called upon to perform for them and always received enough money to buy food for all the rest of us.

Now, as we were walking through the city on our way to the forest on the morning in question, we happened to meet a large funeral procession. There was a big crowd of people laughing and singing as they escorted the body. In the middle of the crowd there was a large group of musicians, singing and playing on their Chinese instruments. The leader of these musicians recognised Gaspar de Meireles as they passed us in the street. This man caught hold of Meireles and pushed a mandolin into his hand, saying:

'I beg you to sing as loud as you can so that the deceased can hear you! Believe me, he is a very sad man who longs to be with his wife and children whom he loved so much!'

Gaspar de Meireles made excuses but the musicians' leader wouldn't listen to them; he started to get angry and said to Meireles:

'If you don't give this poor man the benefit of the talents that God has given you, then I will no longer think of you as a saintly man, as we have all regarded you up until now, but rather believe that the excellence of your music is a mark of an inhabitant of the House of Hell. Originally they too had the ability and character to sing so sweetly, although now they weep and moan in the Lake of the Night like starved dogs gnashing their teeth and, drenched in the slabber of their hatred for men, one can see the froth of their wickedness in the insults they offer to the One who lives and reigns in the highest heavens!'

Then ten or twelve men grabbed hold of Gaspar de Meireles and as good as forced him to start playing as they carried him away down the street with them to the place where the body was going to be cremated, which is the custom among these pagan sects.

So, with my companion taken away by force, I walked on alone to the forest to gather a bundle of firewood for my day's work.

That evening, when I was walking back into the city with my bundle on my shoulders, an old man came out in the road in front of me. He was by himself and was dressed in black damask robes trimmed with lambs' wool. As soon as he saw me he stopped and waited for me by a track leading down from the road and away into the forest. When he saw that I wasn't looking at him as I approached, he started clearing his throat loudly to attract my attention. I looked up when I heard him spitting and saw him waving at me as if he wanted me to come over to him. This took me by surprise and I said to him in Chinese:

'Potau quinay?' ('Did you call me?')

The man didn't say anything but from the nods and waves of him I understood him to mean, 'Yes.'

Then the thought came into my head that he could be the leader of thieves who wanted to steal my bundle of firewood, which sometimes happens there. I set my bundle down on the ground so that I would be able to defend myself. I had a piece of wood in my hand that I used as a walking-stick, and I strode purposefully towards the old man. When he saw that I was following him he walked hurriedly further along the track, which convinced me that he was, indeed, a thief. I turned and walked back to my bundle of firewood and lifted it onto my shoulders as quickly as I was able. I was planning to get back to the main highway where there would be lots of people heading towards the city. However, the man saw what I was planning to do and started spitting again, louder than before. I turned to look at him again; he was kneeling down with his hands raised to heaven and I could see he was wearing a silver cross of almost a palm's length.

By now I was so puzzled and astonished that I just stood there staring at him, wondering who on earth he could be; and all the while the man kept nodding and making pleading gestures for me to go over to him.

Finally, I decided to go and find out who he was and what he wanted. I made my way along the track towards him, with my stick at the ready. I still didn't think he was anything other than a Chinese but when I reached him he threw himself at my feet and cried out in Portuguese amid a flood of sobs and tears:

'Blessed and praised be the sweet name of Our Lord Jesus Christ! After so many years and so long an exile He has allowed me to set eyes on a fellow Christian who professes the faith of my God nailed on the Cross!'

What I'd just heard was so rare and so unexpected that I was utterly startled. I pulled away from him and shouted at him like a man in shock:

'I adjure you in the name of Our Lord Jesus Christ to tell me who you are!'

He replied, weeping harder than ever:

'Brother, I am a poor Portuguese Christian by the name of Vasco Calvo. I am a brother of Diogo Calvo who was the master of the carrack belonging to Dom Nuno Manuel of Alcouchete. It is now twenty-seven years since I was first held captive here with Tomé Pires, who was sent from Goa by Governor Lopo Soares as an ambassador to the Emperor of China, a mission which ended disastrously, with the connivance of a Portuguese commander.'

I had calmed down by now and helped the old man up from the ground where he had been lying, crying like a child. I was weeping as much as he was but I asked him to sit down so that we could talk; this took a bit of persuasion because he wanted to bring me to his house straightaway. Eventually we sat down and he started telling me all his troubles and the whole story of his life from the day he had left Portugal until he met me there in that forest outside Kuansi. Among other things he told me about the deaths of Tomé Pires, the envoy to China, and the other Portuguese who had been left in Canton by Fernão Peres de Andrade to go to the Chinese Emperor. What he told me differs greatly from what our historians have written about the affair.

We spent the rest of the daylight there exchanging stories about our hardships and then walked into the city together. He brought me to his house and then asked me to go and bring all my companions to see him.

I went back to the hovel where we were living and found everybody there waiting for me. I told them whom I had met and they were all as amazed as you would expect them to be. We all headed off immediately to see Vasco Calvo. He was waiting for us eagerly, with the table laid ready for a feast, and when he welcomed us everybody's eyes were full of tears.

He brought us to another room to meet his wife and children, two little boys and two young daughters. His wife welcomed us as if she was the mother or sister of all nine of us.

After talking for a long time we finally sat down to eat and Vasco Calvo himself came round with the water to wash our hands. Even while we were at the table eating, everyone's eyes were still full of tears. When we had finished eating, Calvo's wife excused herself with great courtesy and prepared to offer thanksgiving to God in a true Christian manner. They always said Grace in secret because they were somewhat wary of the pagan Chinese and some of the strict relations that she had.

She took a key out from her sleeve and opened a little door in a small, well-designed oratory that included an altar with a silver cross, two silver candlesticks and a silver vigil-lamp. The woman and her four children knelt down with their hands joined and said these prayers in fluent Portuguese:

'O, one true God, we sinners stand before your cross to profess as dutiful Christians our faith in the most holy Trinity, the Father, the Son and the Holy Spirit, three Persons in One God. We promise to live and die as true Christians in your most holy Catholic faith, professing and believing about your Holy Will everything held and taught by our Holy Mother, the Roman Church. And our souls, redeemed by your precious blood, we offer to you as a token and a tribute, pledging to serve You all our lives, and at the hour of our death to surrender our souls to you as to our Lord and God, Whose they are by virtue of both creation and redemption.'

Then they said an Our Father, a Hail Mary, the Credo and the Salve Regina, all spoken in beautiful Portuguese.

The sight of these innocent little children professing their faith and saying their prayers in such a remote godless land made every single one of us weep unashamedly.

By now it was more than three o'clock in the morning and we walked back to our own house, as astonished by everything we had seen as we had every reason to be.

117 : *The Tartars storm Kuansi. The aftermath.*

WE SERVED EIGHT AND A HALF MONTHS OF OUR SENTENCE IN Kuansi, suffering more than enough hardship and deprivation because we had nothing more to live on than handfuls of scraps that we were able to beg around the streets and houses.

Then, on Wednesday, the thirteenth of July, 1544, not long after midnight, the city erupted into such a tumult of shouting, bells ringing and widespread panic that we thought the last day had arrived.

We hurried to the house of Vasco Calvo and asked him what was happening. He told us, with his eyes full of tears, that news had reached the city that the Tartars were laying seige to Peking with the largest army that had ever been assembled since the time of Adam.

This host was reported to include the armies of twenty-seven kings who had allied themselves with the Tartars and to number one million, eight hundred thousand men. There were six hundred thousand horsemen who had travelled overland from Lansam, Fanstir and Mekuy with eighty thousand mules to carry their provisions and baggage; and one million, two hundred thousand foot soldiers who had been ferried in sixteen thousand boats down the Batampina to Peking.

The Emperor of China himself didn't dare offer resistance to such an overwhelming force and had withdrawn to Nanking. As for Kuansi, at that very moment a Tartar warlord with seventy thousand horsemen was camping no more than a league and a half away in the forest at Manicataran, ready to advance on the city in less than two hours.

The news of the Tartars' approach scared us out of our wits. We clung to each other, trembling and jabbering senselessly, but we managed to ask Vasco Calvo if there was anything we could do to save ourselves. He replied, very wearily:

'Right now, my friends, the only way we'd be safe would be to find ourselves on the road between Loura and Curuche, at the foot of a mountain where I spent many an hour in my youth. But, since that cannot be, we must commend ourselves into the safe keeping of the Lord Our God.

'Let me tell you that less than an hour ago I had a thousand taels of silver to give to the man who could take my wife and children to safety – but it was to no avail. The city gates were already closed on the orders of the chiang and the walls manned by a mass of people, with other troops held in reserve at strategic points to go wherever they are needed most.'

We spent the rest of that unhappy night tormented by fear and sorrow. We weren't able to talk about what lay ahead nor discuss what we should do; we just lay there, racked by terror and moaning and weeping over our hopeless fate.

At daybreak, before the sun was above the horizon, the Tartars came into view of the city and a menacing, chilling sight they were. The horde was divided into seven large forces, carrying countless battle-flags of green and white quarters, the colours of the Tartar king. To the beating of a mass of drums the Tartars advanced to the great pagoda of Politau Namejan which stood a little way outside the city walls. At the front of the army were hundreds of light horsemen with their lances at the ready, weaving in and out among the seven divisions and the baggage that came in the vanguard.

The Tartars reached the pagoda in the formation I have described and halted there for half an hour. Then, to the sound of the war-pipes and drums that were played without ceasing, they re-organized themselves into one enormous crescent shape that encircled the city.

They advanced slowly to little more than a musket-shot's distance from the walls and then hurled themselves forward with such a shattering roar that it seemed the heavens were crashing down to earth. They reached the walls and set up more than two thousand scaling-ladders: they were attacking at every point along the walls and stormed up the ladders fearlessly.

For a while the defenders resisted but it wasn't enough to drive the Tartars back. They broke down the four main gates with battering-rams and quickly killed the chiang and great numbers of mandarins and nobles who tried to block their entry. That was the end of the resistance. The barbarians poured into the wretched city from every direction, killing all the inhabitants they could get their hands on. They spared no-one and it is estimated that more than sixty thousand people were slaughtered in Kuansi, including many women and beautiful young maidens, the daughters of lords and wealthy merchants.

When the killing was finished the city was set alight. All the houses and luxurious temples were knocked to the ground so there weren't two stones left sitting one on top of the other.

The Tartars camped at Kuansi for seven days and then returned to the main army at Peking. They took away an incalculable amount of gold and silver but didn't have the pack-animals to carry anything else. All their other loot from the ruined city was burned before they left, to stop the Chinese being able to make use of it.

☐The Tartars took the Portuguese with them to rejoin the main army, which abandoned the siege of Peking on 17th October 1544, according to Pinto. They took the Portuguese to Tuymicão, where their king was holding court, and he gave them freedom to leave. Pinto gives the date for their leaving Tuymicão as 9th May 1544 (which is inconsistent with his previous date). He and his companions travelled to 'Lechune' which has been identified as Llasa in Tibet. There he describes a heathen pope – the Dalai Llama. They attended a service taken by the Dalai Llama where one of the Portuguese, Vicente Morosa, showed mock devotion in so ardent a manner that he set the whole congregation laughing.

The Portuguese continued their journey, now by river, with a Tartar ambassador, to Cochinchina. There, Pinto describes the suicide on a funeral pyre of the wife of a deceased nobleman, and the triumphant return from the wars of the Cochinese king.

By now, Pinto and his companions had travelled the length of China, from north to south. They looked for a ship to take them down river to Macao, on the coast, where they might find passage to Malacca.☐

132 : We sail for Malacca, but a storm drives us onto the southern part of Japan.

MY READERS CAN READILY IMAGINE OUR RELIEF AND HAPPINESS at putting so much hardship and ill fortune behind us. We finally left Huzamguee on the 12th of January in a boat for the Chinese coast where we thought we could find a Portuguese ship that would take us back to Malacca.

We sailed down a great freshwater river that was more than a league wide. The twists and turns of the river were so great that our compass readings changed from hour to hour.

We followed this river for seven days, seeing impressive towns and cities all around us. From what we could see they must have belonged to very prosperous people indeed. All the buildings were extravagantly designed and decorated, whether they were private houses or pagodas with their spires covered in gold-leaf; and the harbours of the towns were jammed tight with boats too numerous to count, carrying and selling enormous quantities of every sort of provisions and merchandise.

We stopped for twelve days at Quanjiparu, an imposing city with a population of fifteen to twenty thousand people. The 'Noodelum', who was escorting us to the coast on the orders of the King of Tartary, traded with the local people for silver and pearls. He told us he had made fourteen hundred per cent profit on his dealing and added that if a man had salt to trade, he shouldn't be content with less than three thousand per cent profit on his outlay! We were told that the King of Quanjiparu has an annual income from his silver-mines of two thousand five hundred piculs – and he has many other sources of income besides these mines. The only defence this city has is a brick wall eight palms wide and a moat five fathoms wide and seven palms deep. The inhabitants are weak and defenceless: there's no artillery, not enough weapons even to hinder five hundred decent soldiers from capturing the city.

We left Quanjiparu on a Tuesday morning and held our course downstream for another thirteen days until we reached the Chinese port of Sanchan, the island where the blessed Francis Xavier died in 1552, as I will describe later.

There were no ships in Sanchan bound for Malacca – the last had left nine days before we arrived – so we sailed on to Lampakow, seven leagues further along the coast, where there were two junks from the Malayan peninsula at anchor, one from Patani and one from Lugor.

However, a characteristic of the Portuguese is that we are very fond of our own opinions, and while we waited in Lampakow there was such a dispute among us – when it would have served us best to have agreed amicably – that we were close to killing each other. I'm too ashamed now to give the details of what happened other than to say that the noodelum who had escorted us from Huzamguee was shocked by our savagery and would have nothing more to do with us. When he left he wouldn't even take the letters and gifts we wanted to give him for the king. He said he would rather have his head chopped off when he returned than insult the king by bringing him anything from the likes of us. The captains of the two junks wanted nothing to do with us either and they set sail without us.

We spent a further nine days on that little island, in bad humour and at odds with each other, forced to live out in the open country where we were prey to all sorts of dangers. I doubt very much if we could have escaped alive from there if the Lord Our God had not remembered us.

We had been stranded in Sanchan for seventeen days altogether, enduring great misery and hunger, when a Chinese pirate dropped anchor there. This pirate was called Samipocheca and he had just been heavily defeated by the Ay-tau of Chenchow, whose fleet had destroyed twenty-six of the pirate's ships. He had escaped with just two junks and most of the men in these were badly wounded, so he was compelled to stop over in Sanchan for twenty days until all the wounded could recover.

The eight of us were prisoners of necessity: we agreed to sail with this pirate, for him to take us along wherever he happened to be going, until such times as God should better our situation by sending another, safer vessel in which we could get to Malacca.

After twenty days we ourselves had still to make peace with each other after our dispute but the wounded pirates had all recovered. Thus we were still at odds with each other when we set sail with these pirates: three of us sailed with Samipocheca; the other five were in the second junk captained by his cousin.

We left Sanchan to sail to Lailu, which is seven leagues from Chenchow and eighty leagues from Sanchan. We followed the coast of Lamau with favourable winds for nine days and were lying off the mouth of a river five leagues below Chabakee when we were attacked by seven large pirate ships.

The battle raged from six until ten o'clock in the morning . The air between the ships was filled with javelins and cannon-shot until finally three boats were in flames: two of the enemy and our junk with the five Portuguese aboard her. We weren't fit to help them because by this time nearly everybody on our own junk had been wounded. In the afternoon a breeze from off the sea revived us and it pleased God that we were able to disengage and make good our escape from the pirates.

We sailed on for another three days, half wrecked as we were, until a storm from off the land blew us off course so violently that we were driven out to sea and lost sight of the coast during the night. We weren't able to get back on course and were forced to go and seek shelter on the island of Ryukyu where Samipocheca was well known to the people and to the king himself.

With this intention we sailed on through the archipelago towards Ryukyu, but our pilot had been killed in the recent battle and we were troubled by head-winds and contrary currents. We had to tack from one course to another in quick succession for twenty-three difficult days until it pleased Our Lord that we should sight land.

We had sailed in close to the shore looking for a good anchorage or harbour when we caught sight of a large fire almost on the horizon away to the south. We thought it must be a village where we would be able to buy water, which we needed badly. We sailed round and anchored off the island in seventy fathoms. Two small boats carrying six men presently came out from the shore and pulled alongside. After exchanging greetings and courtesies with us they asked us where we were from. Samipocheca said:

'We are merchants from China carrying a cargo to trade with you, if you grant us permission.'

One of the men replied:

'The "Natoken", the lord of the island of Tanegashima, will be happy to grant you a trading licence if you are ready to pay the customary duties required in Japan, which is the great kingdom you see stretching away before you here.'

The man proceeded to tell us everything we needed to know and showed us the best place to anchor.

We eagerly hauled in the anchor and used the longboat to tow the junk to an anchorage away to the south where there was a large town called Miojima. A lot of prahus quickly came out from the shore with food and drink for us to buy.

133 : *We go ashore and meet the Natoken of Tanegashima.*

WE HADN'T BEEN ANCHORED IN THIS INLET FOR MORE THAN TWO hours when the natoken, the ruler of the island, came out to our junk accompanied by a large group of merchants and nobles who had big chests full of silver to trade with us.

After we had exchanged the customary courtesies and the natoken had assured himself that he would be safe, he pulled alongside. When he saw the three of us and knew by our beards and complexions that we were not Chinese, he asked who we were and where we came from. Samipocheca, the pirate captain, answered him:

'Your Excellency, these men come from a place called Malacca where they arrived many years ago from another distant country called Portugal. We ourselves have heard it said several times that the King of Portugal reigns in majesty at the ends of the earth.'

The natoken was amazed to hear this and he said to the people standing beside him:

'May I be struck dead if these aren't the "Tenjiku-jiu" about whom it is prophesied in our chronicles that, "flying over the waters they will master the people of all the lands where God has created the riches of the world." So we have had good luck if they have come here today with peaceful intentions!'

Through his interpreter, a Chinese woman from Ryukyu, the natoken asked Samipocheca where he had met us and why he had brought us with him to Japan. Samipocheca replied:

'These men are indeed honest merchants. I found them stranded in Lampakow and took them aboard as an act of charity, as I usually do when I find people in such circumstances, in the hope that God will thus spare my ships from the unforeseeable hazards that stalk the seas and ruin so many poor sailors.'

The natoken was satisfied with this explanation and he promptly climbed aboard our junk with a few people chosen from the large number he had brought along with him. He walked all around the junk, inspecting it from poop to prow, then sat down on a chair beside the canvas shelter amidships and started asking us a lot of detailed questions.

We tailored our answers to suit what we reckoned he would like to hear and he seemed very well satisfied with them. He sat there talking with us for a long time and showed himself to be an intelligent, open-minded man. He took his leave of us and Samipocheca but didn't pay much heed to anybody else. Before he left to go ashore he said to us:

'Tomorrow you must come to see me at my palace and bring me news of that wide world you have travelled across. Believe me, that is a gift more to my taste than any other merchandise you have with you!'

Early the next morning the natoken sent a prahu out to our junk with a load of provisions, including grapes, pears, melons and every sort of vegetable that grows on Tanegashima – at the sight of which we gave thanks to Our Lord Jesus Christ.

Samipocheca sent some expensive cloth and Chinese jewellery back to the natoken and he told the master of the prahu that as soon as he had the junk fully secured against the weather he would go ashore to see the natoken and bring samples of the merchandise that he had for trade.

The following morning we went ashore with Samipocheca and ten or twelve Chinese, the ones he thought had most dignity of bearing. He wanted to put on an impressive show for this first visit to the natoken, for such an occasion always brings out the vanity in these people.

We reached the natoken's palace and were warmly welcomed by him. Samipocheca presented him with an expensive gift and then showed him samples of all the different goods that he had to offer for trade. The natoken was suitably impressed and ordered the leading merchants on the island to come to the palace to settle the prices with Samipocheca. When that was done it was arranged that the cargo would be unloaded next day and brought to a house where Samipocheca and his crew could stay until they returned to China.

With all the trading arrangements completed, the natoken turned to us again and started asking us all sorts of detailed questions. Our answers still had more to do with keeping him intrigued and entertained than with telling him the truth. At least that was the case with a few of the answers where a bit of embroidery was necessary so as not to destroy the high opinion he had formed of our dear country.

He said that the Chinese had told him Portugal was much larger and much richer than the whole of the Chinese empire. We said, yes, that was probably the case. He had also been told that the King of Portugal had conquered, by sea, the larger part of the world; we said that was true as well. As well as all this, he had been reliably informed that the King of Portugal had so much gold and silver it filled more than two thousand treasuries from floor to roof. We said that we couldn't be quite sure of the actual number because the kingdom of Portugal was so enormous and so wealthy that it was impossible to be absolutely precise about the numbers involved. We spent more than two hours answering these and other similar questions. Then he said to his attendants:

'There's not a king on this earth who could be called fortunate unless he's a vassal of such a master as the King of Portugal obviously is!'

Samipocheca and his men took their leave of the natoken but he asked us to stay with him that night because he still had lots of questions for us about the outside world, which he was very eager to hear about. In the morning he would arrange a house for us to stay in while we were there, one of the best houses in the city.

We willingly obliged and he sent us to stay with a very rich merchant who took great care of us that night and indeed throughout the twelve days that we stayed with him.

134 : *Diogo Zeimoto fires a musket, with unexpected consequences.*

EARLY THE FOLLOWING DAY SAMIPOCHECA UNLOADED ALL HIS merchandise as arranged and stored it in some suitable houses given to him for that purpose. He sold his entire cargo in three days, due as much to the small quantity as to the demand for it on the island. The pirate made so much profit that he fully recovered the value of everything he had lost with the twenty-six boats the Chinese fleet had destroyed. He told us afterwards that the Japanese merchants had quickly paid whatever price he asked for his goods, so that the cargo worth two thousand five hundred taels had earned him more than thirty thousand taels.

We three Portuguese took no part in all this because we had nothing to sell; instead we spent our time hunting and fishing and walking around looking at the magnificent temples built for their idols. The bonzes, or priests, in the temples made us feel very welcome; the Japanese seem naturally friendly and sociable.

In the midst of all this idleness, one of my companions, Diogo Zeimoto, went hunting with his musket several times to amuse himself. He enjoyed hunting and was quite a good shot. One particular day Zeimoto went to a marsh where there were all sorts of birds and he shot twenty-six wild duck.

The Japanese had never seen a musket fired before and the news quickly reached the natoken who, at the time, was inspecting some foreign horses that he had bought. He was astonished by the reports and immediately sent word for Zeimoto to come to see him.

When the natoken saw Zeimoto approaching with his musket over his shoulder and followed by two Chinese weighed down with game he got very excited, as I noticed he did with anything he liked. Until that day no-one in Japan had ever seen a musket or knew anything about gunpowder. They didn't know what Zeimoto was up to and agreed among themselves that it must be sorcery. Zeimoto saw how astonished they all were and how fascinated the natoken was; he fired off three shots right in front of them and killed a kite and two turtle doves.

Anyway, this affair is something that is hard to credit and so as not to waste words in exaggeration and to excuse myself from telling everything in detail, I will say no more than to tell you that the natoken brought Zeimoto up behind him on the horse he was riding, surrounded by a large crowd of people; and four footmen, with iron staffs in their hands, walked ahead shouting out to the crowd, which by this time was impossible to count:

'The natoken, Prince of Tanegashima and the lord of our lives, desires and demands that all here present, and everybody else who lives on this island should honour and revere this Tenjiku-jiu from the ends of the earth, because from this day onwards the natoken takes him into his household as well as the two torch-bearers who have come here with him. Anyone who does not willingly comply with this will have his head chopped off.'

And all the people replied in a tremendous roar:

'Thus let it be done forever!'

When they arrived in the palace courtyard amid all this pomp and hubbub, with myself and Cristovão Borralho left standing a good way behind, they dismounted and the natoken took

Zeimoto's hand and led him into a dining hall where they sat down at a table to eat, and that night Zeimoto slept at the palace, which was the greatest honour of all. From that day on Zeimoto enjoyed the natoken's great favour and the other two of us benefited as well to some degree on Zeimoto's account.

Zeimoto understood that there was no better way to repay the natoken in some part for these honours, nor any greater pleasure to bring him than to give him the musket; so one day, when he came back from hunting with a vast amount of pigeons and turtle doves, Zeimoto offered the musket to the natoken. He accepted it as if it was a pearl of great price and declared to Zeimoto that he valued it more than all the treasure in China. He ordered Zeimoto to be given a thousand taels of silver and begged Zeimoto to teach him how to make gunpowder, without which the musket was just a useless piece of metal. Zeimoto promised that day to teach him and he kept his promise.

From that time on the natoken's whole pleasure and amusement was practising with his musket. His family and the court saw that nothing pleased him more than this and they ordered other muskets in the same style to be made. This was soon done and so keen was the curiosity and the demand for these muskets that when we left Tanegashima five and a half months later there were more than six hundred muskets on the island.

On my last visit to Japan in 1556, when I was sent there with a gift for the Daimyo of Bungo by the viceroy Dom Afonso de Noronha, I was told by some merchants that in the city of Funai alone, the capital of Bungo, there were more than three thousand muskets. I was amazed to hear this since such rapid growth in the use of muskets didn't seem possible, but these merchants – who were respectable, honest men – told me emphatically that in the whole of Japan there were more than three hundred thousand muskets; and they themselves in six trips had brought twenty-five thousand over to sell in the Ryukyu islands.

So, beginning with that one musket that Diogo Zeimoto gave to the natoken in 1542 as a token of friendship to repay the honours and favours he had received, from that solitary musket Japan has become so flooded with them that now the remotest village or hamlet has upwards of a hundred muskets, and in the cities and large towns you're talking about thousands of them.

From this you can see just how enterprising the Japanese are, with a temperament inclined towards the arts of war, in which they take more delight than any other race on earth.

135 : *I am sent to meet the Daimyo of Bungo.*

WE HAD BEEN ON TANEGASHIMA FOR TWENTY-THREE DAYS, content to pass the time at our leisure and enjoying lots of fishing and hunting (two activities which are very popular in Japan) when a trading-ship from Bungo arrived in Miajima. There were a lot of merchants on board and when they came ashore they went directly to the natoken to present gifts to him, which is the custom among them.

One of these merchants was an old man with fine manners whom all the others treated with deference. This man knelt in front of the natoken and handed him a letter, an expensive dagger embellished with gold and a little box full of fans. The natoken graciously accepted the gifts with all due respect and then the two men chatted for a good while, the natoken asking a few questions about private matters; then he read the letter and was lost in thought for a while afterwards.

Eventually he excused the old man and ordered his servants to give his visitor an honourable welcome. Then he called the three of us over to him and gestured for our interpreter, who was standing a little further away, to come forward as well. He said to us through our interpreter:

'My dear friends, I beg you to listen to this letter I have just received from the Daimyo of Bungo, my lord and uncle, and afterwards I will tell you what I want you to do for me.'

He gave the letter to one of his stewards and told him to read it aloud to us. The letter was as follows:

'To Huskaran-goshu, Natoken of Tanegashima, my own right eye, seated in equality beside me with each of my own loved ones; I, Origami-du, as much your father for the true love I bear you in my bowels as the man from whom you took your being and your name; I – Daimyo of Bungo and Fakatawa, lord of the palaces of Fianjima, Tosa and Bandu, supreme master of the island kingdoms of Goto and Shamanashiki – I wish you to know, my son, addressing these words to you from my own mouth, that in the last few days men have arrived here from

184

Tanegashima who tell me that you have three Tenjiku-jius from the ends of the earth staying in your city, people well suited to the Japanese, wearing silk and carrying swords, not like ordinary merchants concerned with buying and selling but like men of honour who seek to gild their names for honour's sake.

'These men also told me that the Tenjiku-jius have talked to you at length about the wide world far beyond our shores, swearing to you that there exists a land much larger than Japan, inhabited by small, black people – all of which I find incredible. So I beg you as if you were my own son to see your way to sending one of the Tenjiku-jius back to Bungo with Finjandono whom I have sent to visit my daughter. I cannot come myself because, as you know, my long sickness and low spirits have drained me, overwhelmed as I am by pain and sadness and tedium.

'And if the Tenjiku-jius have any reservations about making this journey you can reassure them, on your honour and mine, that whoever comes will soon return safely to you. So act like a son who wants to please his father and make me happy with a visit from one of these men to satisfy my curiosity. All the rest of what I have to say about this will be said to you by Finjandono, through whom I beg you to share with me all your good news about yourself and my daughter because I know her to be the eyelid of my right eye, the sight of whom brightens my face with joy. From Origami-du at the palace of Funai, at the seventh mamoco of the moon.'

After the letter had been read out the natoken said to us:

'This Daimyo of Bungo is my uncle and my lord. He is my mother's brother but he is better than a father to me. I call him that because he is the father of my wife, for whose sake he loves me every bit as much as his own children. For my part, on account of all the love I owe him in return, I declare to you that I am so keen to do his will that I would gladly give up most of my lands if God would change me into one of you, so that I could go to see him and bring him this great pleasure which I know, owing to his ill-health, he will value more than all the treasures of China.

'Now that I have explained to you what he is asking, I beg you with all my heart to comply with his wish for one of you to go and see him in Bungo, this lord who is both my master and my uncle. One of you two must go because Zeimoto to whom I gave the name and rank of blood-relation, must remain here until he has finished teaching me how to shoot as well as himself.'

Cristovão Borralho and myself replied:

'Your Highness, may we kiss your hand in gratitude for the favour you show us in wishing to make use of us; and since you have indicated this to be your pleasure, decide now which one of us you want to go to Bungo, so that whoever is chosen can go and get ready at once.'

The natoken was quiet and thoughtful for a little while as he made his choice. Then he pointed to me and said:

'You go. You're more cheerful and less serious than Borralho and that's more agreeable to us Japanese and more of a tonic to a sick man. This air of carrying the world's troubles on his shoulders that your friend has would only make a sick man feel sicker and more miserable than ever!'

Then he chatted and joked with us about the journey to Bungo until Finjandono returned, the sort of pleasantries that come easily to the Japanese. The natoken handed me over into Finjandono's care, telling him over and over again that my personal safety was of the utmost importance. I was very pleased to hear all this and it calmed some of the fears I had felt earlier due to my lack of familiarity with these people; and the natoken ordered two hundred taels to be given to me for the journey, while I got myself ready to set out as quickly as I could.

Finjandono and myself left Tanegashima in a boat called a funce that uses oars. We went ashore every day and so were able to enjoy fresh food and drink. The first day we anchored at a place called Hiamangu; then, running ahead of favourable monsoons, we stopped off at the picturesque city of Kangashima, next at a beautiful place called Tanora, then on to Minato and Fiunga before we reached the fortress of Osaki, seven leagues from the Daimyo of Bungo's palace at Funai. We stopped over at Osaki for two days because its commander who was Finjandono's son-in-law, was very ill. We left the boat there and travelled overland to the royal palace.

We arrived at the palace at noon but the daimyo wasn't able to see us straightaway; instead we were taken to the royal apartments where we were warmly received by the daimyo's wife and her children. They made me in particular feel very welcome. We ate and rested after the rigours of the journey. Then Finjandono put on his court clothes and, accompanied by some of his family rode on horseback to the palace, bringing me along with him.

The daimyo, who had been advised of our arrival, sent one of his young sons down into the palace courtyard to meet us. This boy was nine or ten years old and was accompanied by members of the nobility. He was very expensively dressed, and two footmen carrying maces walked ahead of him. He took Finjandono by the hand and said to him with a bright cheerful face:

'Finjandono, may your arrival in the household of my lord the daimyo be such an honour and joy to you that your children merit, simply for being your children, to sit at the table with me at my birthday party!'

Finjandono replied, from where he had prostrated himself on the ground:

'My lord, may the inhabitants of heaven from whom you learned to be so good, reply on my behalf or give me the tongue of a ray of the sun in order to thank you with joyous music for the honour that you do me now through your majesty, because without inspiration I shall sin in speaking, like the ingrates who skulk in the deepest lake of the Dark Cave of the House of Hell.'

With this, Finjandono tried to grab the dagger the boy had in his belt in order to kiss it but the boy wouldn't permit it. Instead, he took the old man's hand and, accompanied by all the nobles who had come down to the courtyard with him he led Finjandono to the room where the daimyo was waiting.

Although the daimyo was lying sick in his bed he received Finjandono with another ceremony full of courtesies, which I excuse myself from describing for fear of making the whole episode too long-winded. The daimyo read the letter that Finjandono had brought from the natoken and then asked a lot of questions about his daughter. Then he told Finjandono to call me over (up until then I had been standing a short distance away). Finjandono duly presented me to the daimyo, who made me very welcome and said to me:

'May your arrival in this land, of which I am the lord, be as pleasing to me as rain from heaven on our rice-fields in a dry season!'

I was a bit unnerved by such a novel greeting and said nothing to the daimyo in reply. The daimyo looked around at all the courtiers who were there and said:

'I think the stranger is alarmed. It could be because he's not used to seeing so many people. We'll leave all this for another day until he feels more at home and won't find everything as strange as he does now.'

Then I spoke up and said to my interpreter:

'What Your Highness said about my being alarmed is true, I confess. However, it is not the crowd of people that perturbs me because at other times and in other places I have seen much larger crowds of people.

'No, what perturbs me is to simply find myself standing before Your Highness. This alone is enough to leave me speechless for a hundred, yes, for a thousand years, if I were able to live that long!

'The crowd standing here are mere men like myself, but Your Highness was cut from a grain so superior to all others that God immediately desired that you should be a lord and the rest of us should be your slaves, and that I myself should be a mere ant in comparison to your grandeur, an ant too small for Your Highness even to notice, a tiny ant who doesn't even know how to answer your questions properly!'

When courtiers heard these boorish inanities they clapped their hands in astonishment and said to the daimyo:

'Does Your Highness hear now how he can talk? The man can't be a merchant who wastes himself in buying and selling, he must be a bonze who preaches to the people in the temple or else a man born to be a pirate!'

The daimyo replied:

'You are right and I agree with everything you say. But now that we've settled that he's not suffering from timidity let's get on and ask him a few questions. I don't want anyone else to say anything, I want to be the one who asks the questions. Believe me, I'm looking forward very much to talking to this man – so much so indeed that I might even take a bite to eat in a little while because at the moment I don't feel sick at all.'

His wife and her daughters were standing beside the bed when he said this and they were so overjoyed that they fell to their knees and raised their hands to heaven, thanking God for this favour he had shown them.

136 : *The Daimyo of Bungo's son has an accident which places my own life in danger.*

THE DAIMYO TOLD ME TO COME OVER TO THE COUCH WHERE he was lying, sick and racked by gout, and then said to me:

'Please don't be annoyed because you've been left standing there. I really am so glad to see you and to have the chance of talking to you. But first I want you to tell me if you know of any remedy found there in your land at the ends of the earth that could cure this crippling illness and melancholy. It's almost two months now since I ate a proper meal!'

I said to him:

'Your Excellency must understand that I'm not a doctor and know nothing about medicine, but on board our junk back in Tanegashima there is a potion that has cured complaints much more serious than the one afflicting you. If you treated yourself with that potion I'm sure you would very soon be restored to complete health.'

The daimyo was greatly pleased to hear this and he gave orders there and then for the potion to be brought from our junk in Tanegashima. Once he started taking the cure he was restored to full health in thirty days, after being confined to bed for the previous two years, unable to move or control his arms.

After my arrival in Funai I spent the next twenty days at my leisure. I had to answer all the questions put to me by the daimyo. his family and the courtiers. They were all like people who had never heard of anywhere else in the world save Japan but I won't bother to give an account of my answers to all their questions because they bore little resemblance to reality and I would only be filling pages to induce tedium rather than enjoyment.

I also went to see and enjoy their public festivals, their temples, their military training and the ships of the fleet. Fishing and hunting are great favourites with them, especially hunting with falcons and goshawks; sometimes I spent the day out hunting with my musket and bagged lots of doves, pigeons and partridges which are all plentiful in the region. My musket was as great a novelty in Funai as it had been in Tanegashima. The people had never seen a musket before in their lives and it would be hard to exaggerate their fascination with it.

Now, the daimyo was very fond of his second son, Arikandono, who was sixteen or seventeen years old. Arikandono had asked me several times to teach him how to shoot but I had always excused myself by telling him that I wouldn't be staying in Funai long enough for him to learn how to shoot properly. He wasn't satisfied with this and complained to his father, who, to keep his son happy, begged me to let Arikandono have a couple of shots with the musket just to satisfy his curiosity. I said to the daimyo:

'Your Excellency, I will give him two shots, four shots, a hundred, a thousand – just as many as Your Excellency commands.'

I said this when the boy was sitting at the dinner table with his father and his practice was bound to be left until after the siesta, but in the end he wasn't able to use the musket at all that day because in the evening he went with his mother to an important pagoda where celebrations were being held for the daimyo's return to good health.

The next day, which was a Saturday and the eve of the feast of Our Lady of the Snows, Arikandono and two young courtiers came to the house where I was staying, during the siesta. I was having my nap on a mat when they came in and spotted my musket hanging on the back of the door. Arikandono didn't wake me up but decided to take a couple of shots first because, as he said afterwards, he thought these wouldn't count as the shots I had promised to him.

He told one of his companions quietly to light the musket-fuse and took the musket down from the door. He had seen me load the musket a few times but he didn't know the right amount of gunpowder to use. He filled more than two palms-lengths of the barrel with gunpowder and then loaded the musket ball. He brought the musket to his shoulder and aimed it at an orange-tree in the yard. Of course when he lit the musket it exploded and almost blew off the thumb on his right hand. He fell to the ground as if he was dead and his two companions ran back to the palace, shouting in panic as they ran through the streets:

'Arikandono is dead! The foreigner's musket has killed the daimyo's son! Arikandono has been killed! The foreigner has killed the daimyo's son!'

Their shouting caused so much alarm among the townspeople that everybody came out onto the streets and surrounded my house brandishing weapons and shouting for my blood. I was inside in God alone knows what state of mind because I had been startled from my sleep by the explosion and the uproar and found Arikandono lying motionless on the floor beside me soaked in blood. I knelt down and embraced him, so stunned and beside myself with fear that I couldn't even remember where I was.

By this time the daimyo had arrived, slumped in a chair carried by four men on their shoulders, and so shocked that he didn't have the colour of a living man at all. His wife walked behind him with her two daughters, each of them supported by a lady-in-waiting on either side. They were bare-headed and surrounded by a crowd of lords and ladies. All of them looked to be in a state of shock.

The daimyo's party came into the yard and saw Arikandono lying there as if he was dead. I was embracing him and we were both covered in blood. It looked to all of them as if I had killed him. Two men rushed forward with their daggers drawn to kill me on the spot but the daimyo shouted out sternly:

'*Ta wa ta*! Question him before you kill him! I suspect there may be a plot behind this. It could be this man is in the pay of the families of the traitors I sentenced the other day.'

Then the daimyo closely questioned the two young courtiers who had come with Arikandono. They told him my musket was bewitched; that was why it had killed Arikandono. When they heard this, the people standing around shouted at the daimyho:

'What more does Your Excellency need to hear! Put him to a slow death by torture without any more delay!'

Then the crowd went to find Yurubaka, my interpreter, who had ran away from the house in fright. They brought him back like a prisoner and stood him in front of the daimyo and all the judges. They made all sorts of threats about what would happen to him if he didn't accurately translate everything I said. Yurubaka was trembling and weeping and promised he would do just as they asked.

Then they sent for three scribes and five executioners who arrived with their swords drawn. I had my hands tied by now and was made to kneel down in front of the judges. The President of the Court, the bonze Askeran Teijo, had his arms tucked up in his sleeves and held a dagger stained with the blood of Arikandono himself. He said to me:

'I adjure you, as the son of the Fiend that you are, and guilty of this heinous crime worthy of the inhabitants of the House of Hell thrown into the Deep Cave at the centre of the earth, to tell us here and now in a loud voice that everyone can hear the reason why you cast spells on your musket to kill this innocent boy, who is as dear to us all as the hair on our heads.'

I was so beside myself that I didn't say anything in reply; they could have killed me and I wouldn't have realised what was happening. However, the bonze spoke again with a furious, outraged expression on his face:

'If you don't answer me I will have you condemned to the death of blood, fire, water and air! Your body will be thrown to the winds in pieces as light as the feathers of a bird!'

Then he gave me a hard cuff around my head to bring me to my senses. He asked me again:

'Speak up! Tell me if you were paid to do this. How much did they pay you? Who are they and where are they from?'

By now I had come round a little and I answered him:

'God knows the truth of the matter and he will be my judge.'

The bonze wasn't satisfied with this and made more threats against me, painting many more scenes of the terror and horrors that lay ahead of me. This went on for more than three hours until, thanks be to God, Arikandono started to come round.

When Arikandono saw his mother and father drenched in tears beside him he cried out:

'Mother! Father! I beg you to stop crying and don't blame anyone for what has happened! I alone am to blame and this man is completely innocent. So I beg you from the bottom of my heart and by this very blood I have spilt to order his release before I die of shame!'

The daimyo immediately ordered the executioners to untie my hands.

At that moment four bonzes arrived to tend Arikandono's wounds. When they saw the state he was in, with the severed thumb hanging loose, they made such a fuss that Arikandono cried out again:

'Get these devils out of my sight and bring me someone who won't keep asking me how I feel! God has seen fit that this should happen to me and it's as simple as that!'

These four were dismissed and others were brought in but

they told the daimyo that they didn't dare try to cure his son's wounds. The daimyo was left saddened and disconsolate. He asked the advice of the people around him and they told him he should send for a bronze called Taisho, a very famous healer amongst them. At the time he was in the city of Fakatawa, seventy leagues away.

When he heard what they were saying, Arikandono called out, wounded as he was:

'What can I say about that advice you've given my father – while I lie here injured with the blood pouring out of me! I would have recovered already if my wounds had been staunched but you want me to wait while you send someone on a hundred-and-forty league round trip to bring back a decrepit old man who won't be here for another month at the earliest!

'Apologize to the foreigner and calm him down. Then clear out of this house and let him cure me as best he can. I would rather be killed by this poor soul who has wept so much for me than by the Bonze of Fakatawa, ninety-two years old and unable to see his hand in front of his face!'

137 : *The conclusion of this episode with the daimyo's son. We sail to Ning-po where our discovery of Japan causes great excitement.*

THE DISCONSOLATE DAIMYO, WHO WAS SO ALARMED TO SEE THE state his son was in, now turned his face towards me and said to me with great meekness:

'I beg you to see if you can help me now. You see the danger my son is in. Please believe me that if you are able to help him I will regard you as dearly as another son and give you anything you ask of me. Just bring him back to health for me!'

I said to him:

'First may I ask Your Excellency to dismiss this crowd because all this hullaballoo is making me nervous; then I will take a look at your son's wounds and if I think I am able to cure them I will gladly do so.'

The daimyo ordered the crowd to leave. When they were gone I went over to Arikandono and had a fresh look at his injuries. There were two wounds, the partially severed thumb on his right hand and a large but superficial wound on his forehead.

Then Our Lord renewed my energy and I told the daimyo that he shouldn't exhaust himself with worry because I trusted that God would restore his son to full health in less than a month.

I started preparing to treat his wounds but the daimyo was reprimanded by the bonzes for allowing me to proceed:

'Your Excellency, your son will die tonight without fail. It would be better for you to have this man's head chopped off instead of allowing him another opportunity to kill your son! And if that happens, as it is only too obvious that it will, his death will become a scandal and Your Excellency will be held in the utmost contempt by your own family and subjects.'

The daimyo wavered:

'Yes you're right. Now I beg you to tell me what I should do!'

'You should send for the bonze Taisho and listen to his counsels and no-one else's. He is the holiest man in Japan and he alone will be able to cure your son's hand, just as he has cured so many other people. We ourselves have seen him do it!'

The daimyo was all set to follow this perverse advice from these slaves of the Fiend when Arikandono stirred and began to complain that his wounds were hurting him badly. He said:

'I don't care who you get or where he comes from but get someone who can help me with these pains!'

The daimyo turned to his advisers again and implored them to help decide what to do. On the one hand there was the advice of the bonzes, on the other hand his son was lying there in mortal danger. His advisers told him they thought it would be better for his son to be treated as quickly as possible rather than wait until the bonze Taisho arrived from Fakatawa. The daimyo accepted their counsels as the best advice and thanked them gratefully. Then he turned to me and speaking humbly again promised to make me very rich if I returned his son to health. I told him with my eyes full of tears that I would look after his son as well as I was able.

I commended myself into God's hands and put a bold face on it, as they say, because I saw there was no alternative: if I didn't cure his son the daimyo would chop my head off!

I prepared everything I needed and soon started treating Arikandono's hand, which was the more dangerous wound. I put six stitches into his thumb although I'd guess a proper surgeon would have used fewer than that; I also put five stitches in the smaller wound on his forehead and put two egg poultices on them and bandaged them neatly as I had seen done on several occasions during my time in the Orient.

I took the stitches out five days later. I continued the treatment and it pleased God that inside twenty days the daimyo's son was fully restored to health, save for a slight loss of feeling in his thumb.

From that time on the daimyo and his courtiers always welcomed and honoured me. The daimyo's wife and her daughters gave me many gifts of silken clothes, the courtiers gave me swords and fans and the daimyo himself gave me six hundred taels, so that in the end my healing of Arikandono left me with fifteen hundred cruzados more than I had brought to Japan.

One day I received a letter from Zeimoto and Borralho, my Portuguese companions back in Tanegashima. They said that Samipocheca, the Chinese pirate with whom we had come to Japan, was making preparations to return to China. I told the daimyo and asked for his permission to go back to Tanegashima, which he readily granted. He was still thanking me gratefully and generously for the recovery of his son and ordered a funce to be made ready for me as quickly as possible, equipped with everything I might need. I set sail from Funai on a Saturday morning, accompanied by twenty of the daimyo's servants and a courtier who was in command of the funce.

We reached Tanegashima at sunset on the following Friday and I was welcomed with great joy by Borralho and Zeimoto. We spent another fifteen days in Tanegashima while Samipocheca's preparations were completed and then finally set sail for Ning-po, a port on the Chinese coast I have often mentioned before, where the Portuguese had a trading settlement at this time.

We were able to keep to our course and, thanks be to God, we arrived back in Ning-po without mishap. We were very well received by the Portuguese there who found it a great novelty to see us at the mercy of the Chinese. They asked us where we had come from and where we had joined the pirate-ship. We told them everything that had happened to us, giving them a complete account of our voyage and how we had discovered this new kingdom of Japan; we also mentioned the great quantities of silver to be found there and the great demand for Chinese goods there.

Everybody was so excited by these reports that they couldn't contain themselves. They quickly organized a service and procession to give thanks to Our Lord for such a great favour shown to them. The procession went from the main church, Our Lady of the Immaculate Conception, to the chapel of Saint James on the outskirts of the town, where mass was celebrated and a sermon delivered.

Once this pious, holy work was over, greed quickly took control of the hearts of most of the men in the town. Such was the rivalry to be the first man to sail back to Japan that they split up and formed into armed gangs gathering up all the merchandise in the town.

When the local Chinese traders saw such an extraordinary display of umbridled greed, the price of a picul of silk rose from forty taels to one hundred and sixty in just eight days! So then they took the goods by force or in bad faith.

Driven by this thirst and desire for profit it took just a fortnight for all nine junks in the harbour at the time to be loaded and made ready to sail – but some of them were so badly organized and so badly equipped that they had no ship's master other than the actual owners of the junks who knew nothing about navigation or pilotage at all.

I was aboard one of these junks when they set out all together one Sunday morning, sailing against headwinds, against the monsoon, against the tides and against all common sense. We behaved as if we had completely forgotten the dangers of the sea, so arrogant and blind that we couldn't see how there would be any obstacles blocking our path to riches in Japan.

Our junks sailed recklessly throughout the day between the islands off Liampu and the mainland. Then, at midnight, a squall of rain and wind overwhelmed us and drove all our junks onto the shoals of Gotom, situated at 38° north. Miraculously, two junks escaped but the other seven were completely wrecked without a single survivor. About six hundred people were killed on those shoals, including one hundred and twenty rich and respected Portuguese, besides the loss of more than three hundred thousand cruzados of merchandise.

The two junks that survived this disaster held their course and sailed together for the Ryukyu islands. However, we arrived there at a conjunction of the moon and we were caught by such contrary winds from the north-east that our two junks were driven apart and we never saw each other again. When it was almost evening, the wind drove us west-nor'-west and the seas became so rough and mountainous that we were stunned by the sight of them.

Our captain was a courageous nobleman by the name of Gaspar de Mello. He saw that our steering was already gone and that there were nine palms of water in the hold amidships. After discussing it with his officers he decided to chop down both masts to try and steady the ship.

We cut the masts down with as much care as possible but we still weren't able to stop the mainmast from falling on top of fourteen men, including five Portuguese, crushing them to death and spattering their brains and guts all over the place. It was a pitiful sight to see and so disheartened the rest of us that we were like men in a stupor.

The storm got steadily worse and we let ourselves drift on the crashing seas, our souls in torment, until it was almost sunset and the junk began to break up altogether.

Gaspar de Mello and everyone else on board saw the miserable end to which our sins had brought us, and we sought refuge before an image of Our Lady. We begged her with tears and cries of anguish to intercede for us with her blessed Son to obtain pardon for our sins – because there wasn't one left among us who had any further regard for this life.

That was how we spent most of the night. The junk was half swamped and we drifted until the first watch, then we ran aground on a sandbank which ripped the boat to pieces. Sixty-two people were killed, some of them drowned, the others crushed beneath the keel, as sorrowful and frightening a sight as any decent Christian could imagine.

No more than twenty-four of us, as well as a few women, survived this wretched shipwreck. At daybreak we recognized from the landmarks of the Fire Island and the Taydakan mountains that we were on Okinawa, the largest of the Ryukyu islands.

☐When the Portuguese got ashore they were arrested for piracy. They claimed they were traders not robbers, but the Chinese authorities argued that their Portuguese compatriots had seized Malacca – an act of conquest that had nothing to do with trading. The testimony of a Chinese pirate (who accused the Portuguese of undermining the country by their actions, influence and religion) weighed heavily against them. They were sentenced to death.

The women of the Ryukyu islands were deeply moved by the misfortune of the Portuguese. One of them had given shelter to the wife of the Portuguese pilot. When this wife heard of her husband's sentence, she scratched her face with her nails. Her despair so impressed the lady of the house that she and the other women appealed to the dowager queen. Together they submitted a petition to the king, who granted the Portuguese their freedom.

Pinto reached Ning-po safely and from there sailed to Malacca, where Pêro de Faria was still in command. As Faria wanted to help Pinto, he offered him a voyage to Martaban in Burma where the Portuguese had lucrative trade agreements. Pinto arrived on 26th March 1545. Pinto's mission was to urge the Portuguese trading in Martaban to return to Malacca without delay for Malacca was again threatened by the Achinese.☐

148 : *The situation I found in Martaban.*

IT WAS WELL AFTER MIDNIGHT WHEN WE ANCHORED OFF THE mouth of the Salween river, planning to continue upriver to Martaban in the morning. When we had settled down we heard the sound of heavy cannon-fire from time to time throughout the night, which puzzled us and made us wonder whether we should go any further.

At daybreak the captain called us all together for a meeting, which was the usual routine in these situations. The captain said that since every man had to risk his neck, every man should have his say about the risks he ran.

The captain started by mentioning the gunfire we had heard during the night and his doubts about sailing on up the river to Martaban. After several other opinions had been voiced it was decided that we would go ahead and see for ourselves just what was going on.

We hoisted sail and coasted up-river, helped by the wind and the tide. When we doubled the Moonay Point we came into full view of Martaban and saw the city was under siege. There was an enormous army that stretched almost as far as the eye could see, while on the river itself there was a huge armada of galleys and sailing-vessels.

We were immediately on our guard and wondered what the exact situation was, but we sailed on into the harbour nevertheless and dropped anchor for all to see. We hoisted our flag and made the usual salutes as a sign of good intentions and a pinnace quickly came out from the shore with refreshments for us.

There were six Portuguese in the pinnace. We were greatly relieved to see them and gave them a warm welcome when they came aboard our junk. They explained the situation to us: the King of the Burmese had already sacked the Talaing capital of Pegu and was now laying seige to Martaban. We told them we planned to set sail again for Bengal that very night but they strongly advised us against such a move: the Burmese fleet numbered at least two hundred ships, including a hundred galleys manned by foreigners, and some of these would undoubtedly be fit to overtake and capture us.

They told me to go back ashore with them instead, to see João Caeiro who was commander of the Portuguese in the king's army. Caeiro would explain everything to me and could best advise me what we should do. They said Caeiro was a great friend of Pêro de Faria, the commander in Malacca, and they had often heard Caeiro praising his fine character and his noble background. I would also be able to meet Lanzarote Guerreiro and the other captains I had letters for; and between one thing and another we could decide what action would be of most service to God and our master, the King of Portugal.

This advice sounded good enough and I went ashore with them to meet João Caeiro. I was warmly welcomed in their camp by Caeiro and his men, who numbered seven hundred in all, every one of them looking well and prosperous. I brought the orders and letters that I had been given by Pêro de Faria in Malacca and discussed them with Caeiro. He duly approached the four captains I had been sent to locate and they all said that they were more than ready to return to Malacca to serve their master, the King of Portugal, as the need arose. However, they pointed out that Pêro de Faria's letters had all been written when

Malacca was threatened by an Achin force of one hundred and thirty ships under the command of Bijasura, the King of Padir and Lord High Admiral of the Achin fleet; but this fleet had since been defeated off Tenassirim by the local people with a loss of seventy vessels and five thousand men – so for the time being the Achin threat had been removed and there was no need for the captains to return to Malacca; indeed, by all accounts the Achins had been so badly defeated that it would take them more than ten years to recover fully.

This was their main reason for not returning, but they gave many others as well, and it was finally agreed that they could remain at Martaban; however, I insisted that João Caeiro write me a full report of our meeting. I had nothing more to do in Martaban and I was determined that as soon as I had Caeiro's report to cover myself I would return to Malacca.

So I stayed in the camp with João Caeiro, firmly intending to leave as soon as I was ready – but I was to be there for another forty-six days and to see the conclusion of the siege of Martaban. I will say a little about this episode, because I think anyone with natural curiosity will very much enjoy hearing about the outcome of the siege and the fate of Saw Binnya, the King of Martaban.

The siege had already lasted for six months and thirteen days when I arrived. There had been five major assaults using more than three thousand scaling-ladders but the defenders had always fought courageously and had shown themselves to be men of tremendous spirit. However, there was no hope of relief for them from anywhere else and their casualties were slowly diminishing their numbers. The Burmese army simply outnumbered them far too heavily. Saw Binnya was so short of men and essentials that he declared there were no more than five thousand men left in the entire city: the other one hundred and thirty thousand were already dead, killed by hunger or cold steel.

Saw Binnya discussed the situation with his generals and advisers, and it was agreed that he should try to tempt the King of the Burmese' self interest. Saw Binnya set about this straightaway and told the King that if he lifted the siege he would receive thirty thousand bissas of silver (which is a conto in gold) before he withdrew and a further sixty thousand cruzados in tribute every year.

The king's reply was that he wouldn't deal with Saw Binnya at all until he had surrendered unconditionally.

Saw Binnya approached the king a second time. If he was allowed to leave Martaban aboard two ships with his wife, children and personal treasure, and sail into exile to the Sornau, King of Siam, he would hand over the city and everything in it; but, again, the King of the Burmese, whose name was Tabin Shew-ti, wouldn't accept any conditions.

Saw Binnya made a third offer: if the Burmese army withdrew to Tagala, six leagues away, so that Saw Binnya and his family and household could leave the city in peace, the king could take the city itself and the entire kingdom with its vast accumulated treasure, or else receive three contos in gold; but again, the offer was refused.

Now Saw Binnya despaired of ever being able to come to a peaceful settlement with his cruel enemy, but he kept turning over in his mind the possibilities of escape from Tabin Shew-ti's hands. Finally, he decided to seek the help of the Portuguese: they seemed to be his last chance of saving himself from this mortal danger.

The negotiations were conducted in secret between João Caeiro and Paulo de Seixas, a native of Obidos, who was in the service of Saw Binnya. One night Seixas disguised himself as a native of Pegu and went to Caeiro's tent with a letter from Saw Binnya. He offered Caeiro half his treasure to come in four ships and take his wife and children to safety. The letter ran as follows:

'To the courageous and steadfast captain of the Portuguese, favourite of the great King at the ends of the earth, the Strong Lion with the stunning roar who wears a crown of majesty in the palace of the sun:

'I, the unfortunate Saw Binnya, who was a prince but am prince no longer of this unfortunate, beleagured city, now make it known to you, through these words uttered in the steadfast truth of my faith, that from this hour onwards I subject myself as a vassal to the great King of Portugal, to be sovereign master of myself and my children, with due recognition of such privileges and handsome tribute as he ordains.

'So I ask you, on behalf of your king, to come without delay as soon as Paulo de Seixas gives you this letter and anchor your ships alongside the Temple quays. You will find me there waiting for you so that without more ado I can surrender myself into your trust with all the precious stones and gold I can bring. Half of this treasure I will gladly hand over to the King of Portugal. The only condition is that he permits me, with whatever fortune is left to me, to raise an army of two thousand Portuguese from either the Indian colonies or Portugal itself. I promise to pay them very well and to use them only to repossess this city that my disastrous ill-fortune now forces me to surrender.

'As for yourself and your men who help me to escape, I promise by our holy laws to reward you all so generously that you will have absolutely no grounds for complaint.

'Time is short and doesn't allow this letter to be any longer than it is, but Paulo de Seixas, who is delivering it to you, will guarantee and explain everything that he has seen for himself and that I have told him.'

When Caeiro had read the letter he called a secret meeting of the most trustworthy and capable men in his command. He read them the letter and then told them himself just how important and advantageous Saw Binnya's offer was to the interests of God and the king. Then he turned to Paulo de Seixas and asked him under oath if Saw Binnya's treasure was truly as fabulous as it was rumoured to be. Seixas replied:

'On my oath, I cannot tell you just how great this treasure is. What I can tell you is that no fewer than five times I have seen with my own eyes a huge building the size of a church stacked from floor to ceiling with gold bars and ingots, enough to fill the holds of two large carracks; and I've also seen twenty-six sealed sea-chests where Saw Binnya stores the treasure of Brisagusan, who was once the King of Pegu. Saw Binnya told me the treasure includes one hundred and thirty thousand bissas of gold which amounts to sixty-five contos in gold.

'Then there's the silver bars that I saw at the shrine of Kai Adoka, the God of Storms. I couldn't say exactly how much that would be worth but there was so much of it that I would say that four big carracks wouldn't hold it all.

'On another occasion he showed me a statue of Kai Frigau that had been taken from Degum: it was made of solid gold and covered in gems – such a remarkable piece of work that its equal couldn't be found anywhere on earth! That statue alone is surely priceless!'

Everything that Paulo de Seixas had said he had sworn on oath to be true but Caeiro's men were so amazed that most of them thought it couldn't possibly be true. They told Seixas to leave the tent while they discussed Saw Binnya's proposition among themselves.

The upshot was that, for our sins, they decided to do nothing. There were so many different opinions and viewpoints expressed at that meeting that the Tower of Babel itself didn't hear such discord! The main reason, so I was told, was the jealousy of six or seven men who wanted to behave like noblemen in front of everyone else. These men thought that if God saw fit for this plan to succeed then João Caeiro, whom they had a grudge against, would reap such fame and honour that the King of Portugal would think nothing of making him a marquis or, at the very least, appointing him as viceroy of India.

To conceal their own timidity and malice, these agents of the devil pointed out various insurmountable obstacles to Saw Binnya's plan, and expressed concern about their own wealth and their own necks if the King of the Burmese discovered what Caeiro was up to. In the end they flatly refused to have anything to do with the escape plan. Indeed, they said they would reveal the whole plot to the king if Caeiro insisted in pursuing it, which is what he himself wanted to do. Thus, Caeiro was forced into concealing his support for the plan because he feared that if he tried to compel the others to follow him they would betray him to the King of the Burmese, as they had threatened to do, without regard for God's wrath or the contempt of all honourable men.

149 : *Saw Binnya's decision.*

WHEN JOÃO CAEIRO SAW THERE WAS NO POINT IN PERSISTING ANY longer because he was never going to persuade the others to accept Saw Binnya's plan, which is what he himself wanted to do, he wrote a letter to Saw Binnya offering all sorts of excuses why he couldn't help him. He gave the letter to Paulo de Seixas who left immediately to go back into Martaban; by this time it was three o'clock in the morning.

Seixas found Saw Binnya waiting at the Temple quays he had mentioned in his plea for help to Caeiro. They say that when Saw

Binnya had read the letter and realized that he wasn't going to be rescued by us – as he had convinced himself he would be – he was so overcome by grief and sorrow that he fell to the ground like a man struck dead and just lay there. When he came round again he started beating his head with his own fists, lamenting his unhappy fate and crying out between his sobs and tears:

'Ah, these Portuguese! These bloody Portuguese! How badly they have repaid the luckless wretch that I am! How badly they have repaid everything I did for them on so many occasions! I thought I had earned the treasure of their friendship and had them as loyal subjects to help me in just such an extremity as this! I wanted no more than life itself for my children, and looked to enrich their own king and have them with me in Martaban where the least of them would have had power and influence! And it would have pleased the Lord who lives and reigns in the beauty of his heavens if they had proved worthy of him by doing me this favour, to which my sins were the obstacle, because they would have spread his holy law through me and I would have been saved by the promises of his revealed truth.'

When he had calmed down a bit he gave Paulo de Seixas permission to leave Martaban with the native girl who was the mother of Seixas' two children. He took two bracelets off his own arm and gave them to Seixas as payment for his services during the seige but he said to Seixas before they parted:

'I beg you to remember me not for the trifles I give you now but for everything I have done for you in the past. And don't forget to tell your Portuguese friends how hurt I am by their ingratitude, which I am determined to denounce before God on the day of reckoning and accuse them of criminal behaviour!'

Paulo de Seixas left the city that same night with his two little children and their mother, a beautiful girl of great dignity whom he later married in Coromandel, where he also sold Saw Binnya's two bracelets for thirty-six thousand cruzados to Miguel Ferreira, Simão de Brito and Pêro de Bruges, who were traders in gems; later Trimillah, the Rajah of Narsinga, bought the bracelets for eighty thousand cruzados.

Five days after Paulo de Seixas' meeting with Caeiro, Saw Binnya realized that he had absolutely no hope of help at all, and he discussed with his ministers the evils and misfortunes that were mounting up daily.

They agreed that they should slaughter every living being in the city who was unable to fight: all this blood would be offered as a sacrifice to Kai Nivandul, the god of war; all the treasure in the city would be thrown into the sea so that Tabin Shwe-ti, the King of the Burmese, would not be able to take it for himself; and, finally, they would set fire to the city. Anyone left who was fit to carry arms would dedicate themselves as *amoks*, working themselves up into a frenzy before hurling themselves at the enemy to die fighting to the last man.

Saw Binnya approved of this as the best course of action left open to him. He wanted the plan to be carried out quickly and ordered buildings in the city to be knocked down and as much firewood as possible to be gathered up. However, that same night two of his three senior commanders, dreading what was going to happen the next day, deserted to the Burmese camp with four thousand men.

This disloyalty and desertion was such a blow to the morale of the people who remained in Martaban that no-one wanted to muster when the alarm bells rang or to mount sentry duty on the stockades. Instead they told Saw Binnya that if he couldn't come to some arrangement with Tabin Shwe-ti they would simply open the city to the Burmese because it was much better to die fighting than to stay stuck there, dying one at a time like sick cattle.

In order to quell this mounting unrest Saw Binnya told them he would do as they asked. He ordered a count to be taken of the people who were fit to fight and found that they didn't number more than two thousand men – and these were all so depressed they didn't have the heart to fight off a crowd of old women.

Saw Binnya was at the end of his tether and he discussed the hopeless situation with his wife. By this time there was no-one else left to offer advice or speak honestly to him. As the last resort he decided to surrender then and there and let Tabin Shwe-ti do with him as he pleased.

At six o'clock the next morning a white truce-flag was hoisted on the walls of the city. Another was quickly hoisted in the Burmese camp in acknowledgement, and Smim Prum, the Burmese commander in the field, sent a horseman to the bulwark where Saw Binnya's flag was flying. They shouted down to him from the walls that Saw Binnya wanted to send a letter to the king and wanted safe conduct for his messenger. Smim Prum duly sent two Burmese noblemen on horses into the city with guarantees written on a sheet of beaten gold bearing the king's seal.

These two Burmese noblemen remained in Martaban as hostages and Saw Binnya sent one of his relations with a letter to the king. This man was like a monk; he was eighty years old and considered among the Talaings to be a holy man. This is what the letter said:

'Your Highness, our love for our children runs so powerfully through our frail bodies that there isn't a parent among us who wouldn't descend a thousand times into the deepest lake in the House of Hell for the sake of his children, never mind commending ourselves into the hands of the One who treats us all with so much clemency.

'This past night I have agreed with my wife and children to forget any consideration which might clash with their good, for I consider this good to be more important than all others. The excuses in my own defence that I could offer I do not wish to avail myself of; I simply prostrate myself at your feet, my Lord, so that the mercy you show towards me and my family will earn you even greater merit in the eyes of God.

'Your Highness should order possession to be taken of me right now, along with my wife and my little children, as well as the city, the entire kingdom and all its treasure because, from this moment on, I have surrendered them all to you, as to their rightful and natural king and master, while I lie prostrate before you and beg you to allow myself and my family to embrace poverty and end our days in the religious life, where we will always weep in severe penance for the guilt of our past crimes.

'As master of the larger part of the earth and the islands of the sea Your Highness could make me rich with honours and worldly estates but I renounce them all as I prostrate myself before you to make a solemn perpetual oath, witnessed by the God above all gods who moves the clouds in the heavens with the smooth movement of his powerful hand, that we will never, so long as we live, leave the religious order you direct us to join: and may it be in a place where we lack everything so that thus starved of the lure of earthly promises our penance will be all the more acceptable to the One who forgives all things.

'This holy brother, abbot of the golden pagoda of the holy

206

Kai, whose authority and austere life bring with them the weight of my own person, will relate at your feet whatever else you need to know about my surrender. My confidence in him will calm all the discordant voices that are ceaselessly battling for supremacy in my soul.'

Tabin Shwe-ti read this letter and promptly replied with a letter full of pledges and promises that everything in the past was as good as forgotten already and that he would settle Saw Binnya with such a large wealthy estate that he would be more than happy for the rest of his days – but the king did not fulfil the least of these promises, as I will explain presently.

That day passed with everybody full of excitement at the prospect of Martaban's surrender. Early the next morning the Burmese army appeared in formation around Tabin Shwe-ti's camp quarters: he had eighty-six ornate camp tents, each of them set between thirty war-elephants drawn up in two lines as if they were going into battle, their war-howdahs bedecked with flags, and coloured trappings on their broad foreheads. There were two thousand, five hundred and eighty elephants in all; there were also twelve thousand Burmese troopers on horses wearing rich harnesses and trappings. These horsemen were positioned around the camp in four lines and they were all wearing cuirasses and greaves and coats of chain-mail and carrying lances, short-swords and small gilded shields.

Outside the horsemen there were four lines of Burmese foot-soldiers, numbering more than twenty thousand. Everybody else belonging to the king's army, who were far too numerous to count, were massed outside these lines behind their different officers, with an enormous number of flags and guidons and a tumult of various musical instruments that made such a noise when they were played all together that, besides striking mortal fear and astonishment into us, they made it impossible for any two people to hear or understand each other.

Around the edges of the whole array a host of other horsemen rode up and down with lances in their hands, roaring and shouting at the soldiers to keep them in proper order.

The King of the Burmese was putting on this magnificent display to celebrate the surrender of Saw Binnya, so he had also ordered all his foreign officers and their men to arm and dress themselves for this victory parade. They were positioned in two long lines to form a passage for Saw Binnya to walk along from the city gates to the king's pavilion, a distance of two thirds of a league.

There were thirty-six thousand men from forty-two different nations in these two lines: Portuguese, Greeks, Venetians, Janissaries and Turks, Jews, Armenians, Tartars, Moghuls, Abyssinians, Persians, Malabaris, Achins, Javanese, Mois, Siamese, Arakanese, Bengalis, Gujeratis, Karens and many more from Savady, Toungoo, Borneo, Mindanao, Calaminhan, Indraguiri and a host of other places that I had never even heard of before.

These foreigners all lined up in the order directed by Smim Prum, the king's commander in the field. He placed the Portuguese immediately outside the city gates, where Saw Binnya would be coming out. Next to the Portuguese were the Armenians, then the Janissaries and the Turks and then all the rest of them in the order that pleased Smim Prum, so that all the foreign soldiers were lined up from the gates of Martaban to the king's pavilion, where his own Burmese bodyguards were on duty.

150 : *The surrender. Humiliation of the Portuguese mercenaries.*

AT ALMOST ONE O'CLOCK IN THE AFTERNOON A CANNON FIRED A single shot: this was the signal for the gates of Martaban to be opened and the surrender to begin.

First to come out through the gates was the guard Tabin Shwe-ti had ordered to be put on Saw Binnya the day before. It comprised four thousand Siamese and Burmese soldiers armed with muskets, halberds or spears, and three hundred war-elephants. This guard was under the command of an uncle of the king, a Burmese called Monpakassar, the governor of the city of Malitay in the kingdom of Chalu.

Ten or twelve paces behind the elephants came a large group of distinguished noblemen the king had sent to accompany Saw Binnya to the royal pavilion. Leading this group were the Shere Khan of Malacoo and another lord, whose title I don't know, riding beside each other on elephants wearing harnesses and trappings of gold and collars decorated with jewels. Behind these two, and also mounted on elephants, came Binnya Kendo, lord of Cosmim, a notable city in the kingdom of Pegu, and the Mangibray Dakosain; then came Binnya Brahja and Chowmalakur; Nhay Vagaroo and Smim Ansedah; Smim Catan and Smim Guarain, son of Mankamichow, king of Yangomah; Binnya Lah and Binnya Chak; the Rajah of Savady, brother of the King of Berdiu, and Binnya Basoy; the lord Kutalanhammidoo and the Monteo of Negrais; the Shere Khan of Kulaam, and Dambambu, lord of Merguim; and many, many more whose names and titles I can't remember. A further eight or ten paces behind all these lords came the Rolim of Mounay, the senior religious figure in the whole of Burma and considered by the king himself to be a holy man. He alone was allowed to walk alongside Saw Binnya as his guardian and intermediary with Tabin Schwe-ti.

Directly behind the rolim, on three palanquins, came Saw Binnya's wife, Nhay Kanatoo, and their four little children, two boys and two girls aged between four and seven. His wife was the daughter of the late King of Pegu who had also been defeated and deposed by Tabin Shwe-ti. Thirty or forty young noblewomen walked alongside the three palanquins. These women were beautiful but their heads were bowed and they were weeping their eyes out in fear and humiliation, and they leant on one another for support.

On either side of the palanquins and the weeping women walked a line of 'talagrepos', who are like our Capuchin friars. They were all old men, barefooted and bareheaded, praying on beads as they walked along, trying to comfort and encourage the women and reviving them with water when they fainted, which happened time and time again. It was such a pitiful scene that there wasn't a man present who wasn't struck dumb with pain and sorrow.

Behind this inconsolable group came another guard, this time of foot-soldiers; last of all came another troop of about five hundred Burmese horsemen.

Saw Binnya himself was mounted on a small elephant as a sign of the poverty and disdain for worldly things he had embraced in accordance with the life of a religious that he now wanted to lead. There was no other display of rank or power and he was dressed for mourning in a long black velvet cabaia; his hair, eyebrows and beard were completely shaved off and around his neck he wore a cord of very old leather; and it was like this that Saw Binnya, Viceroy of Martaban, went to surrender to the King of the Burmese.

Saw Binnya's face was marked by such sorrow that nobody who saw him could hold back their tears. He was seventy-two years old, handsome and well-built with a severe, serious face and eyes that were now weary and sorrowful – but he still had the bearing of a magnanimous prince.

In the courtyard just inside the city gates a large crowd of women and children and a few old men had gathered to see Saw Binnya before he left the city. When they saw the state he was in they cried out so loudly six or seven times that the earth seemed to shake. Then they started weeping and wailing and scratching their faces with their own fingernails, and lifting stones to beat themselves on the head so savagely that most of them were soaked in their own blood. Such was the horror and the pity for anyone witnessing all this that even the Burmese guards – Saw Binnya's enemies and men hard-hearted by nature – even they were moved to weeping like children.

At this moment Saw Binnya's wife fainted, revived and then fainted again, as did some of the noblewomen around her palanquin. Saw Binnya had to climb down from his elephant to go over to revive and console her. When he saw her lying on the ground as if she was dead, with their four little children embracing her, he fell to his knees and raised his eyes towards heaven and said through his flooding tears:

'O sublime power of the divine all-powerful God! Who can comprehend the workings of your divine justice that has no regard for the innocence of these who have never sinned? You give vent to your wrath in ways far beyond the limits of our understanding. However, Lord, my God, let me not forget who you are, nor who I am!'

Then he fell face down on the ground beside his wife and that enormous crowd let out such a chilling moan that I could never find words to describe the way it made me feel. When Saw Binnya came round again he asked for water to sprinkle on his wife's face to revive her. Then he took her in his arms and stayed there comforting her for a long time, consoling her not like the pagan he was but like a conscientious Catholic. He stayed there

210

with her for almost half an hour until his guards made him climb up onto his elephant again and they continued along that sad path to Tabin Shwe-ti's pavilion.

Saw Binnya was still distraught with grief but as soon as he came out through the gates and started to pass between the two lines of foreign soldiers he looked up and noticed the seven hundred Portuguese lined up on either side of him. They were dressed for the victory parade in cuirasses, with plumed berets perched on their heads and each man had his musket at his shoulder; João Caeiro was standing halfway along the line, dressed in crimson satin and carrying a golden two-handed sword, calling his men to attention.

When Saw Binnya caught sight of Caeiro – and Caeiro recognised him too – he turned his head away and let himself fall forward with his face on the elephant's neck. He didn't want to go any further. He said to all those around him with his eyes full of tears:

'Brothers and friends, I declare to you in all truth that this sacrifice allotted to me by God in his justice is less painful and humiliating for me to endure than to have in my sight people as ungrateful and malicious as these Portuguese. Kill me here and now or else get these people out of my sight. I will not take another step until they are gone.'

And then he turned away so that he wouldn't have to see us. He wanted to show how grievously disappointed he was with us – and it's obvious, from the scene in Caeiro's tent I described earlier, that Saw Binnya had more than enough reason to spurn us.

When the captain of the Burmese guards saw that Saw Binnya had stopped and heard why he was refusing to go any further, although he didn't know Saw Binnya's reasons for complaining about us, he turned around on his elephant and said sternly to João Caeiro:

'Get out of the way quickly! It's forbidden for evil people like you to tread on earth that could bear fruit. God forgive the man who put the idea into the king's head that you could be of some use to him! Shave off those beards so that you won't be able to fool anyone and leave us to get some use out of you as women in return for our money!'

Then all the Burmese guards started to turn on us and pushed us roughly out of our lines, swearing at us and insulting us.

In all honesty I have to say that I have never felt so ashamed in all my life of being Portuguese as I did then.

Once we had been pushed aside, Saw Binnya continued on his way to the king's tent. Tabin Shwe-ti was waiting for him, surrounded by regal pomp and accompanied by a large group of noblemen, including fifteen 'binnyas', who are like dukes, and another six or seven men of even greater rank and authority.

When Saw Binnya entered the royal pavilion he threw himself at the king's feet and lay there prostate on the ground like a man too stunned to utter a single word. The Rolim of Mounay, who had come in with Saw Binnya, revived him and then, as an acceptable intermediary because of his religious orders, he spoke on Saw Binnya's behalf to the king:

'Your Highness, your heart must be moved to pity, whatever crime has been committed. Bear in mind that what is most acceptable to God, what most inclines him to acts of mercy, is just such an act of mercy as is now open to you. Imitate God in this clemency that everyone desires, although no-one opens their mouth to call out for it, and you can take it as a certainty that God will remain so indebted to you that when He comes to judge you at the hour of your death He will place his all-powerful hand on your head and excuse you from any blame for your sins.'

The rolim went on to say many other things to move the king to pity, who did indeed promise completely to pardon Saw Binnya. The rolim and all the other lords who were there were delighted to hear this and praised the king lavishly: they thought he would keep the promises he had just made in front of everyone.

By now it was almost dark and the king dismissed everybody. The wretched Saw Binnya was handed over to a Burmese captain by the name of Smim Kumidau; his wife and children and all the other noblewomen were put in the care of Smim Ansedah, an old and respected man whom Tabin Shwe-ti trusted greatly and whose own wife was there in the camp as well.

151 : *Martaban sacked.*

IT WAS ALMOST DARK WHEN THE FORMALITIES OF THE SURRENDER were concluded and Tabin Shwe-ti was afraid that his soldiers would leave the camp and start looting the city as they pleased, so he ordered guards under Burmese officers to be posted at each of the twenty-four city gates with the strictest orders to allow no-one to enter the city, not even the foreign mercenaries who had been promised a completely free hand with their looting.

These precautions had nothing to do with scruples about his soldiers looting: Tabin Shwe-ti was concerned about saving all of Saw Binnya's personal treasure for himself. For the next two days he had no dealings at all with his captives while he gathered up the treasure. There was rumoured to be so much of it that a thousand men did well to have it gathered up in those two days.

But on the third morning after the surrender Tabin Shwe-ti went up onto Baydam Hill, which was the distance of two falconet-shots from Martaban's walls. He ordered the guards to withdraw from the gates and then the sad city of Martaban was given over to the king's army. A bombard fired a single shot as a signal for the sack to begin and the people charged forward so ferociously that in the struggle to get through the gates more than three hundred people are said to have been suffocated, trampled on or crushed to death.

The soldiers were too numerous to count and from many different nations; most of them were complete strangers to the laws of God and good government, and they were all so blinded and maddened by the prospect of loot that any one of them would have thought nothing of killing a hundred men for the sake of a cruzado – indeed on six or seven occasions it was necessary for the king himself to intervene to restore some degree of order to the riot and uproar that had engulfed the city. The sack lasted for three and a half days. Such was the savagery, the greed and the thirst for loot among those fierce and ruthless soldiers that the city was ransacked from top to bottom and there wasn't a single thing left in it that would have been of use to anyone.

In another formal proclamation, heralded by trumpets, Tabin Shwe-ti ordered Saw Binnya's houses to be knocked down. These were all impressive buildings that had cost a great deal of money to build. Another thirty or forty houses belonging to the leading families in the city were also torn down, along with all the wharves, pagodas and shrines. Many people believe that more than ten contos of gold were destroyed inside those sumptuously designed and decorated temple buildings.

Nor was Tabin Shwe-ti content with this. He ordered fires to be started in more than a hundred places where buildings were still standing. These fires were fanned by the wind and spread with such ferocity that in a single night the entire city was burned down, and even the city walls, with their blockhouses and bulwarks, cracked and crumbled, right down to their foundations in places.

The total cost of Tabin Shwe-ti's dreadful vengeance on Martaban has been estimated at a hundred and sixty thousand people dead from hunger or cold steel and as many again taken prisoner; one hundred and forty thousand buildings and sixteen hundred temples burned down; some sixty thousand statues, most of which were covered in gold, destroyed in the burning temples; three thousand elephants eaten during the siege; and the capture of six thousand bronze and iron artillery pieces. Tabin Shwe-ti's soldiers looted one hundred thousand quintals of pepper and almost as many quintals of medicines, sandalwood, benjoim, sealing wax, nutmeg, rosewood, camphor, silk and many other different sorts of expensive merchandise; above all they seized an incalculable amount of clothes that had been brought there in more than a hundred big ships from all over the Orient – Cambay, Atjeh, Melindi, Ceylon, the Straits of Mecca, Ryukyu and China.

No-one can say for sure how much gold, silver and precious stones were taken from the city because that's something people usually conceal or lie about, but what Tabin Shwe-ti alone took for himself from Saw Binnya's treasury was declared to be worth more than a hundred contos in gold, and our own king lost a half of that because João Caeiro didn't accept Saw Binnya's offer, perhaps on account of our sins, or else simply through the weakness and jealousy of mean-spirited men.

The next morning, with Martaban looted, burned and levelled, twenty-one gallows were erected on the hill of Baydam from where the king had viewed the sack of the city. Twenty of these gallows were the same size and design but the last one was smaller and stood on stone pillars enclosed by railings of black wood. A canopy with golden fringes was raised over it and it was guarded by a hundred Burmese horsemen. The gallows and the horsemen were enclosed by earthworks and lots of black flags sprinkled with blood were flying from the top of the earthen parapet.

No-one knew what was going on so six of us decided to go and find out. As we walked towards the hill we could see the trappings of death all around us. Then we heard a great hubbub in the camp which puzzled us even more. We hadn't yet discovered what the disturbance was about when we saw a large number of horsemen inside the king's stockade. They carried lances and were forming themselves into two lines to make a long wide passageway. They called out loudly for all to hear:

'On pain of death, let no-one be seen here with weapons nor be heard to utter a word of what is in their hearts!'

A good distance away from these soldiers Smim Prum, the king's commander, was approaching with a hundred war-elephants and a mass of soldiers. Behind these came fifteen hundred Burmese horsemen in lines of four ranks, with six men in each rank. These were under the command of Talan Hajibru, the Viceroy of Toungoo.

Next came Chow Saru Siammon with three thousand Siamese carrying muskets and lances. They weren't in formation but all together in a crowd, and in their midst was a large group of women – a hundred and forty of them I was told – tied together in groups of four. They were accompanied by monks of the Austere Life, who encouraged the women in the face of the death they now had to endure.

Behind these women, surrounded by twelve footmen carrying maces of silver, came Nhy Canatoo, Saw Binnya's wife. Her four little children were there too, carried by men on horseback.

These poor creatures were the wives and daughters of the officers who had led the defence of the city for Saw Binnya. This was a means of revenge for this Burmese tyrant who wanted to unleash the anger and the malice he had always felt towards women. Most of the unfortunate victims were aged between seventeen and twenty-five years old. They were all fair-skinned with their hair in golden tresses and they were all very beautiful. As they walked along they were so helpless and so distracted by fear that they collapsed on the ground every time they heard an official call out. They were then revived by other women who were helping them along, but the miserable noblewomen took little heed of any encouragement and consolation because by now they were so beside themselves that they didn't even seem to hear what the monks said to them, although very occasionally they raised their hands to heaven.

Behind Nhy Canatoo came another sixty monks walking in two lines, reading from their prayer-books. Their faces were lowered and they were weeping without restraint. From time to time some of them chanted, in the manner of a litany:

'O Lord, who are sufficient unto yourself, justify our deeds so that they may be acceptable to your divine justice.'

And others responded, also in tears:

'Thus as it pleases you, O Lord, thus let it be, so that we may not lose the rich gifts of your promises.'

Behind these monks came a procession of more than three hundred boys, naked from the waist down. They were holding white candles and had hempen ropes around their necks. They were chanting another moving litany:

'Merciful Lord, hear the voice of our pleading, and grant pardon to these captives, so that they can happily enjoy the riches of your favour!'

And they walked along in this fashion saying other similar things on behalf of the victims.

Behind these boys came another guard of Burmese soldiers, carrying lances and bows and a few muskets. Last of all came another hundred battle-elephants, like those at the head of the whole procession.

The total number of people involved in this procession as officials, guards or representatives of justice, amounted to ten thousand on foot and two thousand on horseback, besides the two hundred war-elephants and not to mention all the onlookers, Oriental and European alike, who were simply too numerous to count.

152 : *The executions.*

THIS UNHAPPY PROCESSION MADE ITS WAY THROUGH THE MIDDLE of the camp towards the place where all these women were going to suffer. They only reached the gallows with a great deal of difficulty because, since they were women, they were frail in both body and spirit, as well as most of them being young and very delicate, so they stumbled and fell with every step they took.

216

When they finally reached the gallows the royal stewards, who were on horseback, started proclaiming the sentences at the tops of their voices again:

'Let the peoples of the earth hear and see the justice that has been decreed for these criminals by the living God, the Lord of all truth, the sovereign Lord of us all, whose desire and pleasure it is that these one hundred and forty women should die, yielded up to the element of air, because their husbands and fathers followed their advice and rebelled with the rest of the people in Martaban and killed twelve thousand Burmese soldiers from the Kingdom of Toungoo in the course of the siege.'

Then a bell rang and the whole rabble of officials and guards gave out such a roar that it would have scared the wits out of you just to hear it. The heartless executioners were now ready to begin carrying out these severe sentences, while the wretched victims clung to each other, the tears pouring down their cheeks.

The women all looked towards Nhy Canatoo, who by this time was lying with her head against the bosom of an old woman, looking as if she was already dead. Most of the women bowed towards her in homage. One of them, as if she was speaking up for the weakest of them who could not speak at all, said to Nhy Canatoo:

'Dear Lady, you are like the rose-garlands on our heads; we will embark with you, as though we were your slaves, for the sad harbour of death; we console ourselves with your presence and shall take leave less sorrowfully of this troublesome flesh to go to meet the true, all-powerful Judge, before whom we shall cry out for justice for you and perpetual vengeance for this unwarranted crime!'

Nhy Canatoo, gazing towards them with her face like a death-mask, replied in so faint a voice that you could hardly hear her:

'*Hikay hokan finarato quiay vanzilau maforem hotapir* – don't leave me, dear sisters, but help me to carry these children.'

Then she turned and laid her head again in the old woman's bosom without speaking another word.

Then the Ministers of the Arm of Wrath (as the executioners are called) started to carry out the sentences on these poor women. Soon every single one of them was hanging upside down, tied by the feet, seven women to each gallows. Their heads cracked loudly on the ground and in less than an hour every last one of them had choked on her own blood. Such was the painful death they all met.

When that was finished the stewards on horses pushed all the people back from the scaffolds. The crowd was so large that nobody could have made their way through it.

Then Nhy Canatoo was brought to the gallows with her four little children by the women who had been supporting her. The Rolim of Mounay, who was considered to be a holy man by these people, said a few words of encouragement to her and she asked for a little water to drink. This was brought to her straightaway. She took some water in her mouth and then shared it out among her children, whom she was holding in her arms. She kissed them again and again and said to them, weeping sorely:

'O my children, my dear little children, you are born again now in the innermost part of my soul! Ah, if I was able to redeem your lives by enduring death a thousand times, how happy I would be! Believe me, if you could be spared, then, as surely as I see you now and all these people here see me at this sorrowful, frightening hour, I could accept death from the hand of this insignificant enemy as gladly as if I were in the presence of Almighty God in the peace of his celestial home!'

She looked at the executioner, who had already tied the hands of two of her children, and said to him:

'I beg you, my friend, not to be so pitiless as to make me see the death of my own children, because you would be committing a grave sin. Give death to me first and I will plead with God on your behalf to have mercy on your soul!'

She took her little children in her arms again and smothered their faces with kisses as if she was saying goodbye to them. Then she breathed her last on the bosom of the old woman without stirring again.

The executioner moved quickly and hung Nhy Canatoo from the gallows in the same way as all the other women, and then did the same to her little children, hanging two on either side of their wretched mother.

The sight of this cruel and pitiful scene provoked such a tumult of cries and shouts in the crowd gathered there that the very earth trembled beneath our feet; then a riot broke out among the soldiers in the camp itself. It was so wild and uncontrollable that Tabin Shwe-ti had to take refuge in his own stockade, guarded by six thousand Burmese cavalry and thirty thousand footsoldiers. Even so he was still very fearful of what might happen but there was nothing he could do to restore order until night fell and things calmed down. This happened because six hundred thousand of the seven hundred thousand men in the camp were from Pegu, and Nhy Canatoo had been a daughter of the King of Pegu. However, until this execution Tabin Shwe-ti had had them so browbeaten with ill-treatment that they hadn't dared raise their eyes from the ground.

Such was the vile and degrading death of Nhy Canatoo, the daughter of the King of Pegu, wife of Saw Binnya, Viceroy of Martaban, and a princess in her own right with an income of three contos of gold.

That same night her wretched husband was thrown into the sea with a boulder tied around his neck, along with fifty or sixty of his subjects, including some nobles with incomes of thirty or forty thousand cruzados, and some of the fathers, husbands and brothers of the one hundred and forty innocent women who had suffered such cruel and humiliating deaths. Among these women were three of Nhy Canatoo's ladies-in-waiting whom the Burmese king had once ordered to be made ready for marriage to him – but in those days neither they nor their parents would entertain the prospect. Such changes do time and fortune bring.

☐The chapters that follow in Pinto's narrative – not translated in this abridged version – deal mainly with Pinto's complicated adventures in Siam, Burma and the surrounding kingdoms during 1546 and '47. These chapters are summarized below.

After the sack of Martaban, the Burmese king attacked Prome, the second great city of Talaing. The queen was the daughter of the Shan King in Ava and she put up a fierce resistance to the invader. Her troops fought as *amoks* (men possessed by fury) but in the end the city was lost. On 23rd August 1545, the Burmese king entered the city and called the queen, who was a handsome woman, to his presence. He had her stripped naked and flogged, before she was done to death by torture. In the past he had been one of her suitors and had been turned down. This was his revenge for the humiliation he had suffered.

On hearing the news, the queen's brother left Ava with an army to assist in the defence of Meletay. He wreaked havoc on the enemy, but had to retreat before the Burmese superiority in numbers. The fortress of Meletay fell to the Burmese. The King of Ava now prepared a huge army to recover his daughter's lost kingdom and sought new alliances. The Burmese king, in fear of a coalition against him, sent an ambassador, with Pinto and a Portuguese bodyguard, to the city of Timplan, capital of the empire of Calaminhan, with the intention of gaining military support. According to Pinto, 'Calaminhan' means 'lord of the world'; the country he describes under his name has been identified as the Shan/Laotian States.

Pinto gives a long account of the temples in Calaminhan. He describes the pagoda of Tinagogo and the Hindu festival of Juggernaut, in which many pilgrims threw themselves beneath the wheels of the huge Juggernaut car, to be crushed to death. He describes the reception given the ambassador at the court of Calaminhan. Pinto traced some survivals of the Christian religion brought to these lands by the Apostle Thomas.

The Burmese ambassador and his retinue returned to the city of Pegu, where the Burmese king was residing with all his court. The king was overjoyed with the letter from the Calaminhan accepting his treaty of friendship. His joy, however, was tempered by the news of the death of the rolim, or Arch-abbot, of Mounay. The Burmese king swore then he would change his sinful ways. He went to the funeral, saw to the installation of the new rolim and demonstrated his respect for the Church.

On his return to Pegu, the former ambassador was ordered to attack a village in the jungle, taking Pinto and the other men in his bodyguard with him. On the way they ran into a strong force of Talaings and were routed. Pinto and his companions escaped through the jungle, were sheltered by a hermit, found a canoe and reached Bassein. From there they sailed to Goa, where Pinto leaned that his patron Pêro de Faria was living in the city, as his appointment as captain of Malacca had ended in 1543.

Faria entrusted Pinto with a new commission. He was to sail to Java and there load a cargo of pepper for China. Pinto left Goa for Malacca and after a short stay there he sailed on to Bantam, capital of Sunda. Sunda was a feudal kingdom that owed allegiance to the Emperor of Damak, who ruled over the great island. The emperor was at war with one of his lords, the Hindu-Buddhist Pasuruan. Damak was a Muslim and wanted to impose his religion all over the island. The King of Sunda was a vassal of the Damak and was asked to bring his forces to support the emperor. Pinto was invited to join the king and so, reluctantly, become involved in the war.

The Emperor of Damak held council in a tent to discuss the strategy of the siege. His mouth was dry and he asked his page to give him some leaves of betel to chew. The page, a boy about thirteen years of age, did not hear what the emperor said, the first or the second time. The emperor asked him again, and the page arrived carrying the betel in a gold box. The emperor asked the boy whether he was deaf, and touched him gently on the head. For a Javanese a touch on the head was the greatest dishonour. The boy cried out and, mortally offended, drew his ceremonial sword and killed the emperor.

The country was in disarray following the emperor's death. The King of Sunda embarked his army, and Pinto left with him for Bantam where his ship was already loaded with pepper. He sailed for China, avoided Japanese pirates, but was shipwrecked in the South China Sea. He was left drifting with his companions on a raft. One of the Negro servants died and, as they were starving, they ate his corpse. Rescued by a passing ship, Pinto was taken to Bantam, where two Portuguese merchants helped him by lending him some money and taking him to Siam.

In the capital of Siam, Ayuthia, Pinto was buying merchandise for his trade expedition when a revolt in the north of the country forced the King of Siam to mobilize his people, including foreigners. Pinto was involved in this campaign, which took him away from the capital for a few months.

When the victorious king returned he was the victim of a palace conspiracy. The principal queen had committed adultery with one of the lords at the court and was with child by him. On his return, she gave the king a magnificent reception and poisoned his food. In less than a week he was dead and their young son was crowned. As the boy was too young to rule, the principal queen became the regent. By a succession of palace intrigues, she and her lover usurped the throne and had all the lords of the council put to death. This last act of cruelty so incensed the people and the aristocracy that two lords killed the evil couple at a royal banquet. A brother of the poisoned king was chosen as the new ruler of Siam, being crowned at the beginning of 1547.

The new king had been an abbot for thirty years and had to leave his monastery to take up his royal duties. He had no experience of war. And this was the moment the King of Burma, Tabin Shwe-ti chose to attack Siam in order to get the White Elephant, which would give him supreme power over all Buddhists. The Burmese mustered a large force, in which a Portuguese adventurer, Diogo Soares de Melo, commanded Tabin Shwe-ti's personal bodyguard of some five hundred

Portuguese mercenaries. The Burmese invaded Siam and laid siege to Ayuthia, but the city resisted vigorously. Tabin Shwe-ti was planning a final assault on the city when he received the news that the 'xemindó', Smim Htaw, a son of the former King of Pegu, had roused the Talaings against the Burmese. Alarmed by the news, Tabin Shwe-ti left in haste and returned to Burma, where he defeated the xemindó, who succeeded in escaping the battle-field alive.

The Burmese king had begun his reprisals on those who had rebelled against him, when he was informed that Marta-ban was in revolt and had espoused the cause of the xemindó. Tabin Shwe-ti issued orders to all the lords of the kingdom to come to his aid. Meanwhile he was informed that the Xemin of Satão, the governor of Sittang and a Talaing nobleman, had given his support to the xemindó, sending him secretly a large amount of gold. Perturbed, the king asked the xemin to come to his presence. Anticipating the reason for his being summoned, the xemin feigned illness and prepared a plot against the Burmese. With the help of his relatives and supporters, he moved in secret and great haste to the pagoda where the king was staying. By good luck they found him engaged in responding to a call of nature. They killed him and moved swiftly away, but were intercepted by the Burmese guards, who had been alerted to the assassination, and a vicious fight took place. The xemin won and he soon had the support of many people who had hated Tabin Shwe-ti. Such was the number of people in his favour that the xemin declared himself king, taking the title of Smim Saw Htut.

Many Burmese soldiers were killed in the fight with the xemin's forces, among them eighty of the Portuguese body-guard under the command of Diogo Soares. Diogo Soares was forced to surrender, and to save his life and that of his men he swore to serve the Xemin of Sittang from then onwards.

However, during the now-assassinated Tabin Shwe-ti's reign, in 1546, Diego Soares (who had been not only Captain-General of the Bodyguard but 'the King's Brother', Governor of the kingdom of Pegu and one of the richest men in the realm), accompanied by a train of soldiers and riding his elephant, had happened to pass the house of a wealthy Hindu merchant. Hearing the sounds of music, he enquired what was going on. When he was told it was a wedding, he decided to congratulate the merchant, who came to the door, deeply flattered by the presence of such a grandee. The merchant called his daughter, whose marriage ceremony it was, and asked her to give Diogo Soares a ring she was wearing. This she did with grace, kneeling in courtly fashion.

The girl was extremely pretty; and Diogo Soares was used

to taking any woman he fancied. He pulled her by the hair and wanted to take her with him. Her father begged him to leave the girl and offered him everything he had, even offering personally to be a slave to him if he would let her go. Soares ordered one of his mercenaries to kill the father and the poor man took to his heels. The bridegroom rushed forward and was immediately cut down, as were his kinsmen. In the midst of such a tragedy, the girl managed to strangle herself with a sash she was wearing. Diogo Soares did not show any regret at what he had done, only expressing his disappointment at being unable to possess such a beauty.

After this 'black and abominable action', as Pinto says, the girl's father never left his house. He knew that, as long as Tabin Shwe-ti was king, he would never have justice. But after the assassination of Tabin Shwe-ti, he decided to go into the open and by telling the crowds in the square his personal tragedy he aroused them to such a frenzy that they went up with him to the royal palace clamouring for justice.

The new king, Smim Saw Htut, was alarmed, thinking this was a mutiny. But when he was informed about the nature of the crowd's demand, after some hesitation, he ordered his sergeant to hand over Diogo Soares to the crowd. When the sergeant arrived, Soares knew that this was God's punishment for his sins. After some resistance, he left, showing deep repentance and devotion, kissing the ground and asking the mercy of God. He was delivered to the mob who stoned him to death.

Smim Saw Htut now reigned as the undisputed king of both Sittang and of the kingdom of Pegu. At the end of four months of his rule, he began to distribute favours and honours to whom he liked. This lavish and arbitrary behaviour caused scandal among the people and dissatisfaction grew. Smim Saw Htut's increasingly arbitrary rule drove the people to support the xemindó, who ousted his rival and was crowned in his place as the King of Pegu.

The xemindó was a good ruler, pacified the country and brought justice to the Talaings. But Chaumigrem, or Bayn Naung, the brother-in-law of the Burmese king, who had been slain by the Xemin of Sittang, invaded the Talaing territory and defeated the xemindó in a pitched battle. At the time Pinto was living in Pegu, engaged in lucrative business, and he and the other Portuguese living in the city feared that Chaumigrem might sack the place. It was a very delicate moment. But it turned out that the new ruler wanted to live in Pegu. At his request, the Portuguese inside the city acted as arbitrators and negotiated with the authorities the safety of the place and its inhabitants. The entry of the Burmese king was a magnificent spectacle of oriental pomp and splendour.

The xemindó had fled the battle-field to the Arakanese frontier where he hid. But his identity was discovered and he was captured and brought to Chaumigrem. Pinto describes in great detail the scenes of humiliation to which he was subjected by the new ruler. The latter was cruel in his dealing with his opponent. He called the xemindó's daughter to see her father's humiliation; he prostrate on the ground, was speechless with anguish for the misfortune he had brought upon her. At this sight, some of the Tailaing lords present wept. Their compassion for the victim enraged the Burmese. He ordered the lords to be executed immediately, as well as the xemindó's daughter.

In a final act of humiliation, the xemindó was dragged through the city. Pinto, who never conceals his compatriots' misdeeds, tells us of a nasty incident which happened when the defeated xemindó passed a group of Portuguese merchants assembled in a body under their leader Captain Gonçalo Pacheco. One of them, who had some grievances against the xemindó, shouted his pleasure at seeing him in that miserable state. Captain Pacheco was shocked and told the man to shut his mouth, which he promptly did: the xemindó praised the God of the Christians as a true one. He mounted the scaffold and was beheaded. Funeral ceremonies followed with the purpose of conveying to the Talaings the idea that the spirit of the dead xemindó accepted the legitimacy of the new ruler, for the powerful xemindó had been the venerated King of Pegu for two and a half years.

Following the execution of the xemindó, Pinto departed with Captain Gonçalo Pacheco and the other Portuguese from the city of Pegu. All 160 of them were allowed to leave with their property and all the gifts the Burmese king had made them. Pinto and twenty-six companions went to Malacca; the others went in different directions, wherever they thought they could best make their fortunes.

After staying one month in Malacca, Pinto embarked on his second visit to Japan and put up at the port of Fucheo in the kingdom of Arima. There, a love story led to a political drama. One of the king's vassals wanted to marry his daughter to a prince of Arima who was living in the Daimyo of Bungo's court, but the daughter was in love with another young man, who eloped with her, taking her to the safety of a convent. When her father knew of her escape, he tried to avenge his honour and created such an affray looking for her that the king and his men came to be involved in the fight that followed. The king and the queen were killed by the men of the enraged vassal. These deaths were avenged by the prince, the king's son.

With the city devastated at the end of the revolt, Pinto moved on to another port, Yamagawa, where he sold his merchandise at a handsome profit. Before leaving he took on board a Japanese fugitive – a young man who converted later to Christianity, being baptized under the name of Paul of the Holy Faith.

The Portuguese now sailed to Malacca and there, in 1547, Fernão Mendes Pinto met Father Francis Xavier, who had already gained the reputation of a saint. Xavier was very interested in the young Japanese fugitive and took him in his care. From this young man, and from Pinto, Xavier sought information about Japan.

Pinto describes the great deeds of Xavier in Malacca. On 9th October 1547, an armada of the King of Achin set fire to Portuguese ships in the harbour. The captain of the fortress, Simão de Melo, had an insufficient number of soldiers to protect the town, for many Portuguese had become buccaneers or were engaged in private business. When seven Malays with their noses and ears cut off were sent to him with a threatening message from the Achin, he begged Xavier for advice. Xavier urged that the population should repair the foists they had in the harbour, and fight the Achin. This they agreed to do, but when one of the foists put to sea and sank, no one else wanted to sail on them, taking the sinking as an omen of God. Xavier was called upon again. He told the people that two galleys would come to their rescue. No one believed the priest and there was nearly a mutiny until Xavier came to see them again, quietened their spirits, and infused them with fresh courage.

Later on that very afternoon, watchers spotted two ships out at sea. Xavier, fearing they might not put in to Malacca, went on a boat to meet them. The galleys belonged to Diogo Soares, a Galician (the same who committed the abominable action previously described, for which he was finally killed by the mob in Pegu). He had no intention of calling at Malacca for he did not want to pay any dues to the customs, so Xavier negotiated with him an exemption from payment if he agreed to fight the Achinese armada. So Diogo Soares came to Malacca to discuss the strategy of an attack.

On 25th October 1547 the Portuguese fleet, under the command of the admiral, Dom Francisco de Eça, sailed off to look for the Achin. On reaching the coast of Kedah, as they were entering the Perlis River, the Portuguese got the news that the Achinese were building a fortress on the coast and were lying there in wait for ships sailing from Bengal to Malacca. The admiral was overjoyed at the news, having already spent five weeks looking for the enemy. In the battle that took place in Perlis River, ther first good shot was fired by Diogo Soares, who sank the flagship of the Achinese armada. This brought so many vessels to her rescue that they all became entangled with each other, offering an easy target for the Portuguese gunners.

In Malacca, after so many weeks without any news, people had begun to wonder whether their fleet had been defeated. Fr. Francis preached twice a week at the main church and prayed every day for the success of the arms of Portugal. One day he said to the congregation with a cheerful expression on his face that victory had been granted to the Portuguese. The congregation was surprised, happy but still apprehensive. Six days later a ship arrived bringing the news of the victory in the Perlis River. This was known among the people as Xavier's 'miracle of the Achin'.□

208 : *Fr Francis Xavier sails to Japan. The progress of his mission there.*

THROUGH THIS GLORIOUS VICTORY OVER THE ACHINS, GOD HAD brought renown to his blessed servant, Fr Francis Xavier, both for the way he had initially inspired the fleet and then, later, for his premonition of our fleet's victory; thus the Lord brought confusion and then repentance to those cynics through whom the fiend had worked so hard to discredit Fr Francis. He left Malacca for India in December, 1547, to organize his mission to Japan. He brought with him the Japanese convert, Hanjiru, who later took the name of Paul of the Holy Faith.

However, Fr Francis wasn't able to make the voyage to Japan the following year as he had planned, mainly because of his responsibilities as Director-General of the Society of Jesus in the Far East but also on account of the death of the Viceroy of the Portuguese Far East, Dom João de Castro, in Goa in June, 1548. Garcia de Sá succeeded João de Castro and it was he who finally arranged Fr Francis' departure in April 1549. He gave Fr Francis a letter for Dom Pedro da Silva, the commander in Malacca, directing him to arrange transport to wherever God should lead his blessed priest.

Fr Francis arrived in Malacca on the last day of May, 1549. He was held up in Malacca for a few days by delays in the preparation of his ship, a small junk owned by a Chinese; but everything was

226

finally ready for the voyage to Japan at sunset on the feast of St John, June 23rd, 1549.

The next morning they hoisted sail and set out for Japan. The voyage was difficult enough, but I'll excuse myself from describing it in detail because it doesn't seem necessary, nor will I do more than touch briefly on what is most important to my purposes, given the severe limits imposed by my feeble wit.

On August 15th, the feast of Our Lady's Assumption, Fr Francis reached the port of Kagoshima in Japan. This was the home of Paul of the Holy Faith, and Francis was warmly welcomed by the local people and – more importantly – by the local daimyo who received him with more celebration than anyone else and honoured him as a special guest. It was obvious just how pleased the daimyo was with the good intentions and purposes that had brought Fr Francis to his domain – indeed, for the whole year that Fr Francis was there the daimyo always showed him great favour, much to the annoyance of the 'bonzes', the Japanese priests.

These bonzes frequently took the daimyo aside and reproached him for the considerable licence he allowed Fr Francis to preach a religion that was so at odds with their own. One day the daimyo was so irritated by their complaints that he said to them:

'If his preaching contradicts yours, then argue it out with him yourselves! But leave me to judge who can, or cannot, preach because I will not have your foul tempers scandalizing him: he is a foreigner who has placed his trust in me!'

This outburst only added to the bonzes' annoyance.

Fr Francis' plan had always been to spread the knowledge of the holy name of Christ among the highest nobility first, because it seemed to him the quickest way to make converts among the ordinary people, and he now decided to spend some time in Hirado, a hundred leagues further north, and he duly headed north as soon as the opportunity arose.

The eight hundred souls that Fr Francis had won for Christ by his preaching in Kagoshima were left in the care of Paul of the Holy Faith. Paul persevered in their Christian instruction for another five months until he was driven out by the bonzes. He escaped on board a ship to China, where he was later killed by thieves on the rampage in Ning-po.

These eight hundred converts in Kagoshima were thus left without a priest or any Christian to guide them – but Our Lord granted it to them to preserve what they knew of the faith from the Christian doctrine that Fr Francis had written down for them; and in the seven years they were left unattended by any Catholic priest not one of them reneged on the faith they had received from Fr Francis.

Little more than twenty days after Fr Francis arrived in Hirado, it seemed wise to him to sound out the nobility, to see which region would be most suitable for his plans. He was accompanied by two Castilians: Fr Cosme de Torres had come from Panama to the Moluccas in 1544 as a soldier aboard a fleet sent by the Viceroy of New Spain. Fr Francis had met him in Goa and cajoled and guided him into the Society of Jesus and then taken him as a companion on his travels. His other companion was a lay brother called Juan Fernandez, a very modest and upright man from the city of Cordoba.

Fr Francis now left Fr Cosme in Hirado and travelled with Juan Fernandez to the city of Kyoto which is the most easterly point on the whole island of Japan. Fr Francis had been informed that Kyoto was the residence of the Kubumkama, the supreme bonze in all Japan. Three other dignitaries who called themselves daimyos also lived there, each of whom was responsible for a distinct area of administration: justice, war, and the general welfare of the kingdom.

The journey to Kyoto was very difficult indeed on account of the severe mountainous terrain they had to cross, made all the more difficult because they were travelling in winter, in a latitude of 40° where the cold, the wind and the rain are almost too much for anybody to endure – and yet Fr Francis lacked even the essentials of proper food and clothing. At several places along the road there were toll-gates where foreigners were not allowed to pass without paying a fee. Fr Francis had no money at all, of course, so he got through by acting as footman to noblemen whom he would approach along the road. In order to pass through the gate unquestioned Fr Francis had to keep up with the pace of the nobleman's horse.

Fr Francis eventually reached this notable city of Kyoto, the metropolis of the whole kingdom of Japan, but he didn't get to see the Kubumkama, who wanted a fee of a hundred thousand caixas (that's six hundred cruzados) before he would grant an audience. At times like this, Fr Francis could not hide his disappointment at not having the money necessary to achieve something he so keenly desired.

So all his labours in Kyoto bore no fruit, not only because of the wars and rivalries that were rife in Japan at the time (and seem to be the normal state of affairs there) but also on account of other difficulties and obstacles that are too numerous to mention: from all of which my readers can clearly understand how seriously the enemy of the Cross regarded the plan that this servant of God had in mind for Japan.

Fr Francis saw the poor harvest for his labours in Kyoto and, so as not to waste his time completely, he moved on to Amagasaki, a city eighteen leagues away, and from there he returned by sea to Hirado. He spent a few days there with Fr Cosme, but he didn't use the time to rest himself after his recent labours; rather he was making plans to submit himself to even greater hardships.

After these three days in Hirado Fr Francis went to Yamaguchi, where he converted more than three thousand people in little more than a year. Then, on September 1st, 1551, he heard reports that a Portuguese carrack had arrived in Bungo, sixty leagues away. He sent a convert by the name of Matheus overland to Bungo with a letter for the captain and the merchants on the carrack. The letter read as follows:

'May the love and grace of Our Lord Jesus Christ, through the mercy of God Almighty, dwell continually in your souls. Amen.

'The merchants here in Yamaguchi inform me that a Portuguese ship has arrived safely in Bungo. However, the reports aren't as reliable as I would wish them to be, so I have decided to find out for certain and send this Christian convert on my behalf. I earnestly beg you to tell him your port of origin, where you have just come from, and when you intend to return to China.

'If God Our Lord is thus served, I want to get back to India this year if at all possible. Give Matheus your names and the name of your ship and her captain, and all the news about the situation in Malacca. And don't forget to withdraw yourselves from your business for a little time to make use of the opportunity to examine your consciences: that is the commodity in which profit is more certain than all the silk in China, no matter how many times you may double your outlay on it.

'I am determined, if it so pleases Our Lord and God, to join you there shortly after Matheus returns to me.

'May Jesus Christ, for pity's sake, keep us all in His hands and preserve us in this life to enjoy the grace of his holy service. Amen. From the city of Yamaguchi, September 1st, 1551. Your brother in Christ, Francis.'

This Matheus received a warm welcome from us and the captain and half-a-dozen merchants quickly wrote a reply to Francis, giving him all the news from India and Malacca, and told him we intended leaving for China in a month. Three carracks in China were due to sail for Goa in January, and one of these was captained by Diogo Pereira, an old friend of Fr Francis, with whom he would feel very much at his ease on the voyage to India.

Matheus left for Yamaguchi again as soon as he had our reply for Fr Francis. He was well pleased with everything he had been given and the good treatment he had received while he stayed with us. It took him five days to reach Yamaguchi and Fr Francis was waiting eagerly for him to hear about the carrack and to read the letters we had sent. Three days later Fr Francis set out for Funai, the capital of Bungo, where our carrack was anchored. Our captain was Duarte da Gama and there were thirty Portuguese traders on board, myself among them.

One Saturday, three Japanese Christians who had been travelling with Fr Francis, came to our ship and told Duarte da Gama that the blessed priest had stopped two leagues away at a place called Pinlashu; he had pains in his head and his feet were swollen up after the sixty league walk from Yamaguchi. Da Gama realized that if Fr Francis was ill he would need a few days to recuperate before he could finish the journey; or else we could arrange a mount for him, but whether he would accept it was another matter.

209 : *Fr Francis reaches the river Finji where our carrack is anchored. He meets the Daimyo of Bungo.*

WHEN DUARTE DA GAMA HEARD FROM THE JAPANESE CHRISTIANS that Fr Francis was lying sick in the village of Pinlashu, he immediately sent word to the Portuguese, who had gone ashore to sell their goods in Funai, which was a league from where the ship was anchored. We all returned to the ship in great concern and discussed among ourselves what we should do. It was decided that we should go to Pinlashu ourselves and bring Fr Francis back with us.

We set out for Pinlashu shortly afterwards but we hadn't gone more than a quarter of a league along the road when we met Fr Francis walking towards us, accompanied by two Japanese Christians. These converts were important noblemen who had been converted more than a month earlier and because they had become Christians the Daimyo of Yamaguchi had confiscated the equivalent of three thousand cruzados in rents and kind from them.

We were all dressed in our finest clothes and riding good horses, so we were confused and embarrassed when we saw how Fr Francis was dressed. He was carrying a bundle on his shoulders that held everything he needed to say mass. He was so weak that the two Japanese took it in turns to help him carry the bundle. You can be sure that the sight of him upset and shamed us, but he wouldn't accept a ride on anyone's horse, so we had to dismount and walk along with him although he wouldn't hear tell of that either, which greatly impressed the two converts.

When we reached the Finji river, where the carrack was anchored, Fr Francis was welcomed with an overwhelming display of joy. Every gun on the ship fired four rounds in a salute – sixty-four rounds from bases, falconets and camels, never mind all the rest – and the shots reverberating around the mountains surrounding the river made an enormous amount of noise.

The Daimyo of Bungo was in Funai at this time but when he heard the thundering guns he was so alarmed and taken by surprise that he supposed we had been attacked by a pirate fleet that had been reported to be in the area. He immediately sent one of his courtiers down to the port to find out what was happening.

When this courtier arrived he gave Duarte da Gama a letter from the daimyo and some appropriate tokens of friendship. Duarte da Gama replied with due courtesy and explained that we were celebrating the safe arrival of a priest we considered to be a saintly man, a man for whom the King of Portugal himself had the greatest respect.

The courtier was so amazed by what he had seen and heard that he turned to Duarte da Gama and said:

'I'm not at all sure what I'm going to tell the daimyo! Our bonzes have told him that this man isn't a saint at all, as you claim. They say they have seen him at different times talking to demons with whom he has dealings and that he uses sorcery to work miracles to trick the ignorant and the gullible. They also say he is not just poor, but so poor that even the lice crawling all over his body are so sickened that they will not taste his flesh!

'Well, I'm afraid that from now on the bonzes will have lost all credibility with the daimyo! He will never want to see or hear them again because the man for whom you do so much and honour with such celebrations as this – well, we have to believe that he is what you claim him to be and not what the bonzes have tried to persuade the daimyo that he is!'

We continued to correct what the bonzes had said about Fr Francis and confirmed to the courtier what he had already grasped for himself. We told him everything we knew about Fr Francis, all of which left him utterly amazed. He left shortly afterwards and when he arrived back in Funai he told the daimyo about everything he had seen:

'My Lord, the guns were being fired to celebrate the arrival of Fr Francis Xavier, which has made the Portuguese happier than if their carrack had its holds full of silver! It seems obvious to me that what the bonzes have said about this Fr Francis is a lie. Believe me, my Lord, he is a man of such serious intent that anyone who saw him could have nothing but the greatest respect for him.'

The daimyo replied:

'In that case they have done well to honour him, and you have done well to make that judgement about him.'

The daimyo immediately arranged for a young nobleman, his cousin, to go and meet Fr Francis and bring him a letter, which read as follows:

'To the Father bonze from Tenjiku-jiu: may your welcome visit to my country be as pleasing to your God as the praise he receives from his saints in heaven! I was informed of your arrival from Yamaguchi by Kamsiu Nafama, whom I sent to your ship earlier. Your arrival here makes me so happy, as any of my people will tell you, that I now beg you with all my heart – since

God does not deem me worthy enough to be able to command you – I now beg you to satisfy the desire of this soul that loves you and come before morning to knock on the door of the house where I will be waiting for you; or else command me to importune you not by resorting to shouting but by prostrating myself before your God – the God whom I confess to be the God above all other Gods that live in the heavens, the best of the best – and begging Him that through your gentle instruction He should show to the haughty of the world just how much the poverty of your holy life pleases him, so that the blind children of our own flesh should not delude themselves with the false promises of the world. Send me word about your health so that I can sleep content through the night until the cocks awaken me at dawn to tell me that you are coming along the road.'

The daimyo's cousin had come in a 'funce', a boat with oars the size of a large galliot; he was accompanied by thirty noblemen's sons and a very old man by the name of Pumindono, the illegitimate half-brother of the daimyo of Minato, who acted as his guardian. The boy took his leave of Fr Francis and the rest of the Portuguese gathered there and, when he was ready to go aboard the funce again, our carrack fired a salute of fifteen cannon for him. This made the young lad feel very pleased and proud with himself. He looked at Pumindono and said:

'The God these people worship must be great indeed, and his secrets hidden far from us, because He permits a man as poor as this to command the obedience of rich merchant carracks like this; and the loud blasts of their guns show that God is well pleased with merchandise that is so humble and so despised by the world that it seems a grave sin even to think about worldly goods!'

The old man agreed:

'Yes, how good it would be to have this poverty, that is so pleasing to the God he serves, to bargain with in the hereafter because he will finish up with far more riches than the rich of this world, even though our bonzes have brazenly preached the opposite to anyone who would listen to them!'

When the daimyo's cousin returned to Funai he went straight to see the daimyo. He had been greatly moved by the great honour and respect shown to Fr Francis and he told the daimyo:

'Your Excellency must not treat this man the way the bonzes

want you to – believe me, to do that would be a great sin! Nor should Your Excellency have the idea that the man is a beggar, because the ship's captain and all the Portuguese traders assured me that if Fr Francis asked them to give him the ship and all its cargo, they would gladly hand it over to him there and then, with no questions asked!'

The daimyo said:

'What you tell me is confusing, but what the bonzes told me is even more so. However, I promise you that from now on I will judge them on their merits, not just on who they are.'

As soon as it was daybreak the following morning, Duarte da Gama held a meeting with the merchants and all the other Portuguese on the carrack. He wanted to discuss how best to handle this first meeting between Fr Francis and the Daimyo of Bungo. We all agreed that for the honour of God Fr Francis should attend with as much pomp as possible, which would make the bonzes look like liars for what they had said about his poverty. It was obvious that people would draw conclusions from his appearance, so it was essential, especially among people who had no knowledge of God, for Fr Francis to make the right impression.

Fr Francis himself didn't share this viewpoint but after they had given him their reasons he was more or less forced to give in to the opinion of the others.

Once this was settled, everybody quickly got themselves dressed in the finest clothes they were able to find and we set out for Funai in the sloop and two 'manchuas' with canopies and fluttering silken flags; we played fanfares of trumpets and fifes one after the other in turns, which was such a novelty that it caused a great deal of excitement among the people on the shore and such a large crowd had gathered by the time we reached the quayside that there wasn't even room for us to get out of our boats.

Then the 'kamsiu', the captain of the daimyo's bodyguard, arrived at the quays. The daimyo had sent him with a sedan chair for Fr Francis to use but he didn't want to use the chair while the rest of us were left on foot, so he walked from the quay to the daimyo's palace accompanied by a large crowd of courtiers and all thirty Portuguese from the carrack, as well as all our Chinese sailors who were very well turned out as well.

Fr Francis was wearing a sleeveless cassock of black camlet under a white surplice, a stole of green velvet embroidered with lace and he had a golden chain around his neck. Duarte da Gama carried a cane in his hand like a chief steward, and five of the richest, highest ranking and most respected Portuguese carried various bits and pieces in their hands as if they were Fr Francis' servants: one of them carried a book in a white satin bag; another carried a pair of black velvet slippers that had belonged to somebody on the ship; a third man carried a walking stick with a golden tip; the fourth held an altarpiece of Our Lady wrapped in scarlet damask; and the fifth man carried a small parasol to shield Fr Francis from the sun.

So in this procession, surrounded by all this pomp and ceremony, we passed through the nine principal streets of Funai, watched by so many people that from the pavements up to the roof-tops was packed full of them.

210 : *The honour accorded to Fr Francis by the Daimyo of Bungo at their first meeting.*

OUR PROCESSION REACHED THE OUTER COURTYARD OF THE daimyo's palace where we were met by Finjandono, the captain of the palace guard, with six hundred archers, lancers and swordsmen, who were all very well turned-out and looked as if they belonged to some great king.

We passed this guard of honour and went into a very long verandah. Here the five men carrying the various objects I described earlier knelt down and offered them to Fr Francis. The courtiers who saw this were so surprised that they said to one another:

'Our bonzes will hang themselves! We'll see no more of them anyway because this man isn't what they said he was like at all – this man has been sent by God to confound the jealous!'

We walked along this verandah until we came to a large building where there was a large crowd of courtiers wearing satin and damask robes of many different colours and swords decorated with gold. A boy of six or seven years old, who was holding the hand of an old man, came up to Fr Francis and said to him:

'May your welcome arrival in the house of my lord, the

235

daimyo, be as pleasing to the both of you as the rains that God sends from the heavens when our rice fields cry out for them!

'Enter in safety and enter in joy! Because I assure you, by the truths of our religion, that all good people here wish you nothing but good fortune, while evil men are saddened by your arrival as if it were a dark and stormy night!'

The boy listened in silence while Fr Francis delivered his reply in similar language; then he spoke again:

'Your destiny must be great indeed, because you came from the ends of the earth to be derided in strange lands as a beggar; and how great beyond any comparions must be the generosity of the God who welcomes the confused opinions of this world, a generosity to which our bonzes are complete strangers, affirming on oath in public that neither women nor poor people can be saved by any means at all.'

Fr Francis said:

'The Lord, who lives and reigns in the highest heavens, has permitted the mists to be lifted from your eyes and now you recognise the errors of your blindness; and when God gives you this vision, He also gives you the grace to renounce the false paths you followed.'

Fr Francis and the boy continued this weighty discussion – the rest of us, of course, were all astounded to hear one who seemed so young speaking like that – as we walked on and entered another building where there was a large gathering of children, the young sons of the lords of Bungo. When they saw Fr Francis come in they all stood up and paid their respects to him by kneeling down and bowing their foreheads to the floor three times; among the Japanese this is the greatest sign of respect for someone, offered, for example, by a son to his father, or a vassal to his daimyo or his master. Then two of the boys, who seemed to be speaking on behalf of all the others, said to Fr. Francis:

'Holy father and bonze, may your happy arrival be as pleasing to the daimyo, our lord, as the smile of the little baby for its mother while sucking at her breast! We swear to you by the hair on our heads that the very walls you see here cried out for us to celebrate your arrival and so glorify the God about whom you told so many marvellous things in Yamaguchi.'

Then they all took a few steps towards Fr Francis as if they wanted to accompany him, but the young boy who was leading Fr Francis by the hand nodded to them to sit down again. We started walking again and went down a very long verandah that ran alongside some orange-groves and eventually came to another building, as large as the first two. Here we were met by Fasharandono, the daimyo's brother, who later became the Daimyo of Yamaguchi. Fr Francis made a deep bow to him and Fasharandono returned the courtesy, saying to him:

'I assure you, Reverend Father, that this is a day of great joy for this household, a day when my master, the daimyo, will be richer than if he had all the treasure in China! May your arrival here be for his enjoyment and your honour, and everything you strive for to attain your desires.'

The boy who had been accompanying Fr Francis left him in the care of Fasharandono and took a few steps backwards, which was another show of courtesy that impressed us a great deal.

We walked on and went into yet another building where there was a large number of noblemen who also gave Fr Francis an honourable welcome. He stood there talking with them for a while until a messenger came out from another building and told us that we should go in. We went into the building, accompanied by most of the Japanese lords, and found ourselves in a luxurious hall where the Daimyo of Bungo was seated on a dais.

As soon as the daimyo saw Fr Francis he got up and took six or seven steps towards him. Fr Francis was preparing to kneel and bow at the daimyo's feet but the daimyo wouldn't allow it. He embraced Fr Francis instead and then knelt and bowed his head to the floor three times himself (which, as I've already said, is the courtesy between son and father, or vassal and master). This deference on the part of the daimyo greatly astonished all the lords who were there and saw it – although no-one was anywhere near as surprised as we Portuguese.

The daimyo took Fr Francis' hand and Fasharandono, who had accompanied Fr Francis thus far, stepped back a few paces. Then the daimyo sat down on his throne again with Fr. Francis directly beside him; Fasharandono stood a few steps away from them while the rest of the Portuguese and all the Japanese lords stood in front of the dais.

The daimyo and Fr Francis started by exchanging compliments. The daimyo showed himself to be very well disposed towards our priest, who replied with such agreeable courtesies of his own that the daimyo looked at his brother and then at his courtiers and called out in a voice loud enough for everyone to hear:

'Who can ask God where this will lead? Or ask why He has permitted us to be so blind, or granted this man so much daring?

'On the one hand, we can see now for ourselves that what people have said about this man is true and that he justifies what he says with arguments that brook no contradiction, that appeal so much to all natural reason that whoever considers this marvel fairly will be amazed and will not deny it, but rather, if he has good judgement, will confess it to be true.

'On the other hand, we see our own bonzes so ill at ease with our religion and so contradictory in what they preach that they say one thing today and another tomorrow, so that any man of sound intellect is utterly confused by their teachings that raise doubts about salvation itself!'

One of these bonzes was there in the hall when the daimyo said this. He was annoyed by the daimyo's words and said to him:

'This isn't a matter that Your Excellency can resolve readily because Your Excellency never studied in the monastery at Fian-jima. But if you have any doubts you can ask me and I will explain things to you. Then you will see the full truth of what we preach and how well spent is whatever we are given!'

The daimyo replied:

'Well then, if you know it, tell me and I will be silent.'

So now the man put forward his defence of the bonzes:

'Your Excellency, there can't be any doubt whatsoever about the sanctity of the bonzes because they have lived their whole lives as religious, which is pleasing to God, and spend the most part of every night praying for the deceased. They follow a vow of perpetual chastity and they don't eat fresh fish; they look after the sick and teach children the rules of good living; they make peace between warring daimyos so that the ordinary people are able to live in peace; they issue bills of exchange for heaven so that the dead can enjoy a lot of their wealth and property there; and at night they sustain with their alms the weeping souls who have begged them for guidance in the afflictions and trials they suffer by virtue of being poor; they have degrees from the

238

seminaries of Bandou, confirmed by the Kubumkama of Kyoto; but above all else they are great friends of the sun, the stars, and the saints in heaven and are able to talk to them every night, and very often hold them in their arms!'

The bonze carried on like this, making all sorts of ridiculous claims, speaking at times with such anger in his voice that on no less than four occasions he called the daimyo a *fukido-hosa* which means 'a blind sinner'. The daimyo was so annoyed by the bonze's attitude, and so affronted by the way he had been spoken to, that he looked over at his brother two or three times and nodded to him to get the bonze to be quiet.

Fasharandono acted at once. He made the bonze stand up and the daimyo said to him:

'I have heard the proof and justification of the bonzes' sanctity that you wanted to give. I don't wish to deny it but I must also confess that the arrogance of your unbridled language has so scandalized me that I dare to swear on my own soul's salvation that hell has a greater hold on you than heaven does!'

The bonze replied:

'The time will come when I will not want to make use of men, and neither you nor any of the other rulers in Japan will be worthy enough so much as to touch me!'

The daimyo smiled at the bonze's arrogance and looked over at Fr Francis as if to say, what do you make of all this? Fr Francis wanted to calm things down and said:

'Your Excellency should leave these arguments to another day when the bonze is not so exhausted.'

The daimyo replied:

'You're right. I'm wrong for listening to him.'

He said to the bonze:

'You can leave me now but when you speak about God, don't use God to justify yourself. That is a grave sin. Instead, you should work patiently, for the love of God, to rid yourself of that foul temper and then we will listen to you.'

The bonze turned round like a man who had just been insulted and called out to everyone present:

'*Yakatawa passirim fijiancor passinawa* – let the fires of heaven roast a daimyo who speaks like that!'

Then he jumped up and, without pausing to take his leave, he went off snorting out of the door, leaving everyone else in the

239

hall to laugh and make jokes about him – all of which softened the daimyo's anger and before too long he was laughing as heartily as anybody else.

By now it was almost time to eat. Food was brought in and the daimyo asked Fr Francis if he wanted to eat dinner with him. Fr Francis made excuses three times over, saying that he wasn't hungry. The daimyo said to him:

'I know very well that you shouldn't feel hungry and you say you don't feel the need to eat, but I also understand that you already know (if you are Japanese like us) that this offer from a daimyo is the strongest token of love that he can give someone. Now, because I hold you in such high esteem, I am greatly honoured to invite you to eat with me.'

Fr Francis made as if to kiss the sword in the daimyo's belt, which is a way of expressing profound thanks among the Japanese, and he said:

'May the Lord, Our God, out of respect for whom you do this for me, send you so much grace from his home in heaven that you will be made worthy to profess his religion as one of his true servants, so that at the end of your days you will merit salvation.'

The daimyo replied:

'I'll grant you what you ask me, provided that you and I are left together to discuss these matters that I talked about with the bonze.'

Then, with a broad smile lighting up his face, the daimyo offered Fr Francis the plate of rice that was sitting in front of him, asking him again if he wanted to eat – and this time Fr Francis took something.

The sight of this made us all fall to our knees in thanks for the great honour that the daimyo had paid to Fr Francis in public, regardless of whether the slighted bonzes heard about it through gossip and tittle-tattle.

☐The Japanese bonzes resented the growing influence of Francis Xavier over the daimyo and began to rouse the people in protest against him. Pinto and his companions began to wonder if they should leave, taking Francis Xavier with them. Xavier visited the daimyo frequently and had persuaded him to give up a young boy he loved very much. Xavier not only denounced pederasty as a sin; he also condemned the right the mother had in Japanese law to kill her unwanted child. The daimyo decided that the chief theologian, the bonze Fucarandono, should hold a debate on matters of faith and morals with Xavier at the court. For this reason, Xavier and the Portuguese decided to delay their departure from Funai for a few more days.

In his theological disputations with the bonzes, Xavier refuted the idea that the world had no beginning and no end, upholding the view that it had been created by God. He repudiated the Buddhist practice of issuing 'letters of exchange for heaven' – the *cochumiacos*. These were bought for money from the bonzes, the purchasers being told they would be rewarded tenfold with riches in the other life. 'Our good deeds in the world,' said Xavier, 'are what is rewarded in heaven by salvation.' He objected to the exclusion from salvation not only of the poor (unable to afford *cochumiacos*) but also of women, supposed to have more sins than men. 'Jesus Christ,' said Xavier, 'died on the Cross to redeem all sinners who have been baptized'; the idea of exclusion was abhorrent to the Christian mind.

The Christians were accused by the bonzes of giving indecent names to God – such as *diusa*, which in the Japanese language means 'lie' – and to the saints, as when they said in the litany, 'Sancte Petre ora pro nobis' – the word *santi* being obscene in Japanese. Xavier explained that their objection to these words derived from mere linguistic misunderstandings: the word for God was 'Deus'; and in the litany, in view of the confusion, he proposed to replace 'Sancte Petre' by 'Beate Petre'. These answers, and the previous arguments provided by Xavier, pleased the daimyo, who treated him with great respect when the time came for Xavier, and the Portuguese, to leave.☐

214 : *Sailing from Japan to China we run into a fierce storm. The miracle of the sloop.*

THE NEXT MORNING, AFTER WE HAD ALL BID FAREWELL TO THE Daimyo of Bungo, with all the compliments and courtesies that always attend such occasions, we returned to our ship and set sail from Funai.

We followed a course in sight of land until we came to the island of Meleitor which belongs to the Daimyo of Minaku. From there we headed out into the open sea, running ahead of winds veering towards monsoons. We kept to our course for another seven days, when the wind, at the conjunction of the new moon, blew up from the south, threatening us with rainstorms and all the signs of winter. Indeed it grew so rough that we were forced to turn about to nor'nor'east, sailing through seas that had never before been crossed by the seamen of any nation.

We didn't know where we were going and we were completely at the mercy of fortune and such a wild, tumultuous storm as men have never imagined. It lasted for five days and in all that time we never once saw the sun, so the pilot wasn't able to calculate our position exactly in degrees or minutes, only to hazard a guess. On the basis of that we went to seek shelter among the islands of Papua, Celebes or Mindanao, some six hundred leagues from our estimated position.

Early on the second evening of the storm the sea grew so rough with such mountainous waves that our carrack wasn't able to make any headway through them at all. The officers agreed that the poop and the fo'c'sle should be levelled to the decks so that the vessel would be more manoeuvrable and respond better to the helm. Every single man on board got down to work and this was done as quickly as was humanly possible.

The next task was to secure the sloop to the carrack. With a great deal of difficulty the sloop was brought alongside and then fitted with moorings of two new hempen ropes. It was pitch black and very stormy when this was finished and it wasn't safe to bring the men who had been working on the sloop back on board the carrack, so these fifteen men – five Portuguese and ten slaves and Chinese sailors – had to spend the whole of the night on the sloop.

The blessed Fr Francis was with us day and night throughout all this trouble, sometimes doing his share of hard work like every other man on board, at other times inspiring and consoling us in such a way that, apart from God Himself, he was the one who most gave us heart and encouraged us not to be so overwhelmed by our difficulties that we simply gave ourselves over to our fate – which some people would have been prepared to do if Fr Francis had not been there.

It was almost midnight when we heard the shouting from the sloop: the fifteen men were calling on God to have mercy on their souls. Everyone on board rushed to the side to find out what was happening. We saw the sloop being swept away towards the horizon: the moorings that had held the sloop fast to the carrack had been broken.

Our captain was stunned by this disaster. He didn't stop to think about what he was doing but ordered the carrack to follow the sloop, thinking that he would be able to save it – but the carrack itself was in difficulty and only responded slowly to the rudder, due to its lack of sail. We ended up stranded, broadside on between the huge waves. The mountainous seas crashed down on us and so much water swept down over the topdeck that the ship almost foundered. Everyone on board called out with all their might, calling on the Mother of God to save us.

Fr Francis responded quickly to this. When the wave struck the ship he was in the captain's cabin, kneeling in prayer at a sea-chest. When he realized what was happening to the carrack and saw all of us thrown one on top of the other against the sides of the ship he raised his hands to heaven and called out in a loud voice:

'O Jesus Christ, love of my soul, save us now, Lord, for the sake of the five wounds you suffered for us on the wood of the true Cross!'

And at that very moment as he prayed the carrack miraculously regained the peaks of the waves and then responded very quickly to a bonnet that had been fixed to the bottom of the foresail, swinging round so that it righted itself and, thanks be to God, was soon being steered from the helm again.

The sloop however, had disappeared without trace. We all wept over the loss and prayed for the souls of the men who had been on board her.

We spent the rest of the night running like this before the storm with more than enough difficulty. At daybreak there was no trace at all of the sloop to be seen from the crow's nest atop the mainmast. There was nothing to see but the tops of the tall waves breaking into white flowers.

After little more than half an hour of daylight Fr Francis, who had been resting in the captain's cabin, came up onto the poop-deck where the master of the ship and the pilot and six or seven other Portuguese were standing. He bid them all good morning with a joyful, tranquil look on his face and then asked if there was any sign of the sloop. When he heard there was no trace of it he asked the ship's master if he wanted to send someone up to the crow's nest to keep a watch for the sloop. One of the men who was standing there butted in:

'We'll see it when we're drowned ourselves!'

This upset Fr Francis and he said to the old man, whose name was Pêro Velho:

'Brother Pêro, how little faith you have! But why? Do you think, perhaps, that some things are impossible for Our Lord and Our God? You see, I place all my trust in Him and in the Most Blessed Virgin Mary, his mother, and I have promised her that I will say three masses for her Son in her blessed Chapel of the Mount in Malacca if he permits those souls in the sloop to be spared.'

Pêro Velho was shamed by these words and didn't speak again.

Then the ship's master, the better to satisfy Fr Francis, climbed the mast along with another sailor. They kept a watch from the crow's nest for almost half an hour but they had to tell Fr Francis again – as far as the eye could see, there was nothing at all to be seen. Fr Francis said to them:

'Well, you can come down now. There's nothing more to be done.'

Then he called me over to him on the poopdeck. Everyone thought he was looking very downcast. He wanted me to arrange a drink of warm water for him because he had an upset stomach – but I, for my sins, wasn't able to help him because the stove had been lost the day before when everything on the top deck had been thrown overboard.

Then Fr Francis complained that he was feeling very giddy and losing his balance from time to time. I said to him:

'Father, you shouldn't keep going on like this. You haven't slept for three nights now!'

And probably he hadn't so much as eaten a bite either, which is what one of Duarte da Gama's servants told me. Fr Francis said:

'Believe me, I'm suffering these pains because of those men lost in the sloop. I know how wretched they must be feeling and since we lost the sloop I have never stopped weeping for my nephew, Afonso Calvo, who was one of the men on board the sloop.'

I noticed him yawn repeatedly so I said to him:

'Father, go and lie down for a little while in my cabin and you might be able to rest a little.'

He accepted the offer, telling me it was made out of my love for God, and he asked me to leave my Chinese slave outside his closed door, to be there if he was needed. This would have been around six or seven o'clock in the morning, and he stayed there in the cabin all day long until the sun began to go down. At that time I called to my Chinese slave, who was still waiting at the door, to bring me a jar of water. I asked him if Fr Francis was still asleep. He said:

'He never slept at all! He's been in there on his knees all day long, praying and weeping!'

I told him to go back and sit outside the door again and to help Fr Francis if he called for someone to come.

Fr Francis was withdrawn in prayer like this until the sun was well down the sky; then he left the cabin and went above to the poopdeck where all the Portuguese were gathered, sitting on the deck because of the violent heaving and rolling of the ship. He greeted us all and then asked the pilot if there was any sign of the sloop yet. The pilot told him:

'It's just not possible for them to have survived in seas like this; and even if we suppose that God has worked a miracle and spared them, we must be more than fifty leagues away from them by now.'

Fr Francis replied:

'It does indeed look that way to our common sense but it would make me happy – and it's not costing us anything to do – if, for the love of God, you would go aloft yourself, or else send one of the sailors, to keep a lookout for the sloop. Then, at least, it won't be something we have neglected to do.'

The pilot said he would gladly go to the crow's nest himself. He and the ship's master went aloft but it was more to keep Fr Francis happy than in the hope of sighting the lost sloop.

They stayed up aloft for a long time before shouting down to the deck that there was still no sign of the sloop – or anything else for that matter. It was plain for all to see how much this upset Fr Francis. He rested his head on a rigging-block and remained like that for a little while, panting like someone who was ready to start weeping. Suddenly he opened his mouth and took a deep breath like a man overcoming his sadness, then raised his hands to heaven with tears in his eyes and said:

'My Lord Jesus Christ, my true God and Master! I beg you, by the pains of your sacred passion and death on the Cross, to have mercy on us and save the souls of the faithful aboard that sloop!'

That said, he rested his head on the rigging-block again and remained there as if he was sleeping. After no more than the time it takes to say two or three credos a cabin-boy who was sitting in the rigging started shouting:

'It's a miracle! There's the sloop! A miracle!'

The shouting made everyone rush over to the port side where the boy was standing – and there we could see the sloop, about the length of a musket-shot away from us.

We were all so astonished by such an unexpected and unlikely event that we broke down weeping like children, so that no-one on board could hear themselves speak because of all the sighing and sobbing. The next thing was that everybody rushed over and threw themselves at Fr Francis' feet – but he would have none of it and went below to the captain's cabin again, locking himself in so that no-one could talk to him.

Our companions in the sloop were very soon back on board the carrack and welcomed with such relief and joy as my readers can readily imagine, so I'll refrain from describing all the details of their return because it was an occasion more to be simply remembered than written about.

The half hour or so before night fell was spent welcoming our friends back aboard. Fr Francis meanwhile sent a slave to bring the pilot down to see him. He told the pilot that he should give praises to God because the recovery of the sloop was all God's work. Then he told him to get on and make the carrack ready because the respite from the storm would not last very long.

We all set to work with a vengeance, and with great devotion we also gave thanks to the Lord, just as Fr Francis had told us. And then, thanks be to God, before the main yard had been hoisted and the sails broken out, the storm died down all of a sudden and we were able to follow our proper course, running ahead of strong northerly winds that were as good as a monsoon for us – so everybody was happy and in high spirits. This 'miracle of the sloop', which I have described, happened on December 17th, 1551.

215 : *Fr Francis sets out for China. His death.*

WE FINALLY SAILED AWAY FROM THE PLACE WHERE WE HAD NEARLY been destroyed by the storm and had then been granted that miraculous favour through the mercy of the Lord Our God and the prayers of this blessed priest. Thirteen days later, thanks be to God, we reached the coast of China and dropped anchor off Sanchuan, where at that time the Portuguese had a trading post.

It was late in the season when we arrived at Sanchuan and there was only one carrack lying in the roadstead, captained by Diogo Pereira, and he had his main yard-arm hoisted, ready to leave for Malacca the next day.

Fr Francis transferred to Pereira's ship because Duarte da Gama, with whom he had sailed from Japan, was taking his ship to winter in Siam: the bow was lying ripped open from the battering it had received during the great storm and in Siam the ship could be repaired and fitted out again with everything it needed.

Diogo Pereira was a great friend of Fr Francis and on the voyage back to Malacca the priest gave him an account of the progress of his evangelization in Japan and explained just how important it was to him to try to enter China in order to spread the Word and make known the law of Our Lord Jesus Christ to the pagans there, and thereby win the debate he had had with the bonzes in Yamaguchi. For when the bonzes had found themselves shamed in their religious discussions and arguments with Fr Francis, they had told him at the last that the doctrines they held and preached had come to Japan from China, and had been held to be sound by every generation for the last six hundred years, so they would not contradict them on any account until they heard that Fr Francis had won over the Chinese, using the very same arguments that he had offered to them to prove that his religion was the true one, and that what he had to preach deserved to be listened to.

Such was the test proposed to this blessed servant of God, who, out of the high regard he had for his honour and his faith, decided not to leave the challenge unheeded. Fr Francis could win his argument with the bonzes in Japan and at the same time preach the Word of God to the bonzes in China. He had set out for India planning to explain all this to the viceroy and to ask him

247

for whatever help he could give to put this plan into effect.

Fr Francis outlined his plan to Diogo Pereira and the most experienced men aboard the carrack and asked them what they thought of it. These were men with a great deal of knowledge about China, and they told him:

'Father, you have absolutely no chance of being allowed into China to preach the Gospel. The only way you could get into China legally would be if the viceroy in Goa sent an embassy there on behalf of our master, the king, acting with the highest authority and bearing very expensive gifts to offer the Emperor of China as a token of our friendship, employing all the eloquence and courtesy that they are used to. However, such an embassy would require a great deal of finance and some very expensive gifts, so it's doubtful if the viceroy would want to do it.'

Fr Francis was obviously upset by this answer but he knew it was true. He also considered the difficulties for his plans that could be thrown up by the weather and the general problems facing the Portuguese colonies.

He discussed this mission many times during the voyage to Malacca. Diogo Pereira, for the sake of God's name and his own friendship with Francis, offered the use of his ship for the mission; he also offered to pay out of his own pocket to get Fr Francis into China and do everything else necessary, as the need arose, for the mission to succeed.

Fr Francis accepted his offer and promised Pereira that he would receive full satisfaction for his expenses from our master, the king. This plan of action was agreed before they reached Malacca, and Fr Francis sailed on to Goa immediately from there. Diogo Pereira himself remained in Malacca, preparing to sail to Sunda for a cargo of pepper, but he sent his agent, Francisco de Caminha, along with Fr Francis, with thirty thousand cruzados' worth of musk and silk to buy everything in Goa that was needed for the expedition to China.

When Fr Francis arrived in Goa he told Viceroy Dom Afonso de Noronha what he was determined to do; the viceroy lavishly praised such a holy and worthwhile undertaking and offered to help Fr Francis in whatever way he could. He gave Fr Francis an official directive for Diogo Pereira to go on this holy journey as ambassador to the Emperor of China. Fr Francis was happy enough with this response from the viceroy and he concluded all the necessary arrangements as quickly as he was able.

When Fr Francis returned to Malacca he gave the letter of appointment to Dom Alvaro de Athaide, the commander there, but Dom Alvaro didn't want to pay it any heed because at the time he had a serious disagreement with Diogo Pereira, who had refused him a loan of ten thousand cruzados. Fr Francis laboured with all his powers and goodness to heal the rift between these two men but he never succeeded – the dispute was rooted in hate and greed and the devil himself had put a match to the tinder.

Fr Francis negotiated with Dom Alvaro for twenty-six days but in all that time the commander never conceded anything to the priest nor gave permission for Diogo Pereira to set out for China with Fr Francis, as had been laid out in the orders from Goa.

An enormous amount of money had already been spent, but Dom Alvaro deliberately misinterpreted the viceroy's directions. He would say sarcastically that the Diogo Pereira mentioned by the viceroy was a nobleman back in Portugal, not the one waiting to sail with Fr Francis – claiming that until a little while ago this Diogo Pereira had been a manservant to Dom Gonzalo Coutinho and wasn't qualified to go as an ambassador to such a great ruler as the Emperor of China.

Some honourable men in Malacca saw the whole affair was going from bad to worse, with the commander making no attempt to justify himself or pay any heed to what was being said to him. Moved by their zeal for the honour of God these men met together one morning and went to see Dom Alvaro. They said to him:

'Dom Alvaro, we have come here today to beg you to stop acting in a way that is so detrimental to the honour of God, because such behaviour will merit no mercy in the next life.

'We also urge you to listen to what the people here in Malacca are demanding of you as with one voice – that you should help a man as holy as Fr Francis to preach the word of God to the Chinese pagans, because this is a man that Our Lord wants to use to open up a door for his Gospel so that many, many souls may be saved.'

Dom Alvaro replied as follows:

'I'm a bit too old for you to be giving me advice. If the priest wants to do God's work, let him go to Brazil or Africa where there are just as many pagans as there are in China. I'm telling you now, on my solemn oath, that so long as I am in command in Malacca Diogo Pereira will not be going to China, not as a merchant and certainly not as an ambassador. As for God, I will render an account of my actions when he asks me for it.

'Diogo Pereira wants to make this journey to China under the protection of the priest in order to make a hundred thousand cruzados for himself – but it's a mission that should have been given to me on account of the services rendered to the Crown by my father, Vasco da Gama, rather than to one of Dom Gonzalo Coutinho's valets, whom the priest supports in this evil undertaking with no justification at all!'

And with that Dom Alvaro dismissed the men.

When the Inspector of Trade, the Crown Agent and the port customs officials heard how outrageously Dom Alvaro had treated these merchants, they went to see him one morning as representatives of the Crown's interests. They said to him:

'Dom Alvaro, there is a regulation in the port of Malacca that has been issued and endorsed by past governors. The regulation in question specifically states that under no circumstances whatever are ships to be hindered from leaving the port if they have undertaken to pay the appropriate duties on their return to Malacca.

'Now, Diogo Pereira has given us a written undertaking, which we have with us here if you wish to see it, that he will contribute thirty thousand cruzados towards the maintenance of Malacca's defences when he returns from China, by way of taxes and duties on his ships and cargo. Indeed, he has already paid a half of this, with other merchants standing surety for the remainder until he returns.

'So we ask you now to allow Pereira's ship to sail because if you hinder it without good reason – as you have been doing – we will lodge a complaint on behalf of the Crown about your conduct as commander of the colony.'

Dom Alvaro's reply this time was as follows:

'If Diogo Pereira has indeed pledged thirty thousand cruzados to the Crown, then I'll make a pledge as well – to give the lot of you thirty thousand belts around your heads with this club here!'

As he spoke he rushed over to an alcove to lift the club while the officials made themselves scarce as fast as they could.

And that's how Fr Francis spent twenty-six days after his return to Malacca, unable to do anything at all to soften the foul temper of Dom Alvaro, who spoke rudely to the blessed priest for no reason at all and treated him in a manner utterly at odds with Fr Francis' authority and intelligence.

Fr Francis was deeply annoyed and saddened by all this, and affronted by Dom Alvaro's insults, but he suffered it all with a great deal of forebearance. No-one heard him say a single word about the matter other than to raise his eyes towards heaven and exclaim:

'Praised be the Lord Jesus Christ!'

He would say this with such passion, and often with tears flooding his eyes, that the words seemed to be pouring out of his very soul; and people openly remarked around the town that if Fr Francis was looking for martyrdom (as everyone presumed he was) then his troubles at the hands of Dom Alvaro were martyrdom enough.

Indeed, let me say that, when I think about what I saw with my own eyes, the great honours accorded to this priest by a pagan like the Daimyo of Bungo, simply because we told him that Fr Francis was a man who preached the word of God, and compare that with the treatment he later received in Malacca, then I am left speechless in amazement, as I believe any Christian who had witnessed both scenes would be.

However, in spite of all this, Fr Francis finally set out for China, but in very different circumstances to those which he had planned.

He sailed in Diogo Pereira's carrack but Pereira himself remained behind in Malacca. The ship's provisions and cargo were supplied entirely by Dom Alvaro and his followers and the captain was personally chosen by Dom Alvaro. Fr Francis himself was isolated, without any authority at all, dependant on the quartermaster's charity. He had nothing with him other than the cassock he stood in.

However, Fr Francis' intention had always been to suffer among the infidels for the profession of his faith, so for his part he couldn't raise any obstacles to the voyage, which is why he embarked for China at that time, regardless of the circumstances, when the opportunity presented itself.

When the ship was ready to set sail the quartermaster sent his young nephew at two o'clock in the morning to tell Francis, who was at the chapel of Our Lady of The Mount, to come down and get aboard the manchua that would bring him out to where the carrack was anchored.

When Fr Francis received the message, he quickly left the church, leading the quartermaster's nephew by the hand, along with two of his followers who were to accompany him down to the quay; one of the two was Fr João Soares, who later returned to Portugal, to the town of Covilhã, When he saw Fr Francis stepping aboard the manchua full of sadness and melancholy, he said:

'Reverend Father, now that you are setting out on such a long journey, you should speak to Dom Alvaro, if only to silence your followers who say that you have been deeply hurt by all that has happened.'

Fr Francis, who was standing there with one foot on the manchua, ready to go aboard, replied:

'Brother João, God saw fit to make me such that if I feel deeply hurt by what has happened it is because of what has been done to the honour of God, and that is a just response and no sign of imperfection.

'As for speaking to Dom Alvaro, as you ask me to, it's too late now, nor will he and I ever meet again in this life; however, we will meet again in the valley of Jehosaphat on the day when God's awesome majesty is revealed and Jesus Christ, the Son of God and the Lord of all, will come to judge the living and the dead, myself and Dom Alvaro among them.

'He will have to give his reasons then for hindering me from going to the infidels to preach the Word of Christ, the Son of God nailed on the Cross to save sinners; yet I assure you, here and now, that before very long, as the start of his punishment for that sin, Dom Alvaro's reputation, wealth and very life will be sorely troubled. As for the rest, may the Lord our God have mercy on his soul!'

Fr Francis looked over at the main door of the chapel in front of him and knelt down, then raised his hands like a man praying and said, although he was weeping so sorely that his tears choked his words:

'O Jesus Christ, my God, love of my soul, I beg you, by the pain of your most holy passion and death, to consider what you continually offer on our behalf to the Eternal Father when you show your precious wounds to Him; remember what those wounds have earned for us and grant salvation to Dom Alvaro's soul, so that by following the path of your mercy he may be pardoned by you.'

Then he lay face down on the ground for a little while, lying there as if he couldn't hear a sound; then he stood up, took off his shoes and beat them on a stone, as if he was shaking the dust off them.

Fr Francis boarded the manchua and bid farewell to his two companions, weeping so much that Fr João Soares, who was weeping as well, said to him:

'Is this separation to be forever? Why are you leaving us when you see us so disconsolate? For myself, I just hope in the Lord Our God that I will see you in Malacca again very soon and we will be able to spend some time together at our leisure!'

Francis said:

'Thus it will be if it so pleases His divine mercy!'

With that the manchua pulled away from the quay, and at first light the carrack set sail from Malacca.

Twenty-three days later the ship dropped anchor off the island of San-chuan, where at that time the Portuguese traded with the Chinese from the city of Canton, twenty-six leagues away.

The ship had been anchored there for a few days and everything had been going smoothly: the merchants were attending to their business and the trading was going well. As for Fr Francis, if he couldn't carry out the whole of his plan he at least wanted to carry out some small part of it, so he approached a well-respected Chinese merchant asking him to take him with him when he returned to Canton. Some of the Portuguese raised objections to this because they saw the unreasonable state of mind Francis was in and that he lacked anything that would give an appearance of authority to what he had to say.

However, when they had discussed all the pros and cons of the matter an arrangement was made with the merchant: Fr Francis would pay him two hundred taels (which is three hundred cruzados) and he would bring Fr Francis into Canton. Fr Francis would be blindfolded so that if he was discovered to be a foreigner, as it was certain he would be, and he was tortured to make him confess who had brought him into Canton, he wouldn't be able to say who had brought him there. We were afraid that if Fr Francis was discovered the Chinese courts would have his head chopped off; but he accepted all these arrangements and had no fears whatever about what lay ahead, nor did the trials that everybody portrayed for him deter him for a moment. By now it was understood how keen he was to suffer martyrdom for the sake of the Lord Our God.

However that same God, whose secret ways no man can fathom, ordained that it was for the best that his servant should not enter China at this time. The reasons for this God alone knows but He diverted Francis in a way that seemed to be just, as all his workings are.

This Chinese merchant admitted that he was well satisfied with the payment for bringing Francis into Canton but his heart told him not to do it because it could cost him his own life and the lives of all his family. So Fr Francis was left aboard the ship, unable to do anything about this holy work that he was so eager to undertake.

Fr Francis had been in poor health already, suffering from fever and dysentery; now there was also melancholy, and this bitter disappointment and his bad health began to get the better of him. He got steadily worse until one day he collapsed onto his bed and suffered a severe loss of appetite which lasted for four-teen days; then he realized that he was fatally ill and asked to be taken ashore.

Fr Francis was brought ashore and put in an old hut made of branches covered with grass. He lay there for another seventeen days, badly lacking the necessities of proper medicines, food and shelter. Three men who were there at the time told me this neglect was due to some of the Portuguese who thought such neglect would win the favour of Dom Alvaro, who, they pre-sumed, wasn't worried about Fr Francis at all; but I think, besides, that the abandonment God permitted his blessed servant to suffer at this time was his means of revealing how similar was Fr Francis' life and death to those of other holy men and women that in faith we hold to be now reigning in heaven with God the Father.

After seventeen days, with his face and body racked and weakened by pain and distress, and knowing in his soul that the

254

hour of his death was near, Fr Francis bade farewell to everyone there with his eyes full of tears, assuring them that he was already on the road and begging them all to pray for his soul because he had great need of their prayers. Then he sent a slave, who had been looking after him, to close the door because the noise of all the people outside was disturbing him.

He lay there for another two days and by this time he wasn't fit to lift so much as a cup of water to his mouth. Late on the second day he took a crucifix in his hands and fixed his gaze on it; there wasn't a sound out of him except when, from time to time, he would sigh, 'Jesu, love of my soul,' although eventually he wasn't able to pronounce a single word.

Everyone who was there in the hut says they saw Fr Francis weeping openly with some sign of energy, always with his eyes fixed on the crucifix, until he finally gave up his soul to God at midnight on Saturday, December 2nd, 1552. His death was deeply mourned by every single person who was there.

216 : The burial of Fr Francis at San-chuan. His body is later brought to Malacca, and from there taken to Goa.

WE QUICKLY SET ABOUT ORGANIZING THE BURIAL OF THIS BLESSED body and everything necessary was done as well as was possible at the time, given the conditions at San-chuan.

On the Sunday evening, two hours after vespers, the body was taken to where a grave had been dug, little more than a stone's throw from the beach, and was duly buried there.

Everybody present was deeply moved, especially the more conscientious and God-fearing, although there were a few who didn't appear to share in the general sorrow; God alone knows if they were merely keeping their grief to themselves – He knows the truth about all things and will judge these people accordingly – but what is known to us all is that, fifteen days after the funeral, a man, whom I shall not name for the sake of his honour, sent a letter to Dom Alvaro in Malacca in which he noted dryly:

'Fr Francis died here on December 2nd but there were no miracles surrounding his death and he lies buried here on the beach at San-chuan along with all the others who have died while we have been here. When we sail for Malacca we will bring his body with us, if it is in a fit condition to be moved, so that the gossips in Malacca won't be able to say that we are any less Christian than themselves.'

Three months and five days after Fr Francis' death the carrack was lying with her yard-arm hoisted ready to sail. Some Portuguese went ashore and directed that the grave holding that holy body should be opened, so that the remains could be brought back to Malacca if at all possible.

When they opened the grave the body was lying there without any sign of corruption whatsoever: indeed there wasn't so much as a single mark or stain on either the shroud or the surplice the body had been dressed in – both of them were as clean, fresh and sweet-smelling as if they had just been washed.

This discovery amazed everyone and some were so stunned by what they had seen with their own eyes that they beat themselves repeatedly on the head in remorse for what they had said and done earlier. They cried out now with flooding tears:

'O how wretched are we who satisfied the devil by choosing to be his ministers and causing you so much trouble in Malacca, such a pure servant of God as we now see you to be and readily admit for all to hear! And how miserable are we who denied you alms so many times when we knew very well just how badly you lacked the necessities to sustain your holy life.

'Let the deceitful world hang itself! Let Malacca, with all its promises of wealth hang itself! At the last you alone are blessed who served God with such dedication – which, for our greater confusion, we are all now ashamed into proclaiming about you!'

And they continued talking like this with the tears pouring down their cheeks, tearing at their faces and lamenting their past wrong-doing, praying that Our Lord, through the pleas of his beloved servant Francis, might show mercy to them.

The holy body was put in a specially made casket and taken aboard the very same carrack in which Fr Francis had come to San-chuan. It was left in the pilot's cabin for the duration of the voyage back to Malacca.

At ten o'clock in the morning on the day after the ship arrived in Malacca the president and all the members of the Fraternity of Mercy, accompanied by the deputy bishop and all the clergy from the main church, not to mention all the other Portuguese in

Malacca – with the exception of Dom Alvaro de Athaide and his supporters – went down to bring the body ashore and escort it to the hermitage at the chapel of Our Lady of the Mount, which is where Fr Francis had always stayed in Malacca when he was alive; and, of course, it was from there that he had set out on his mission to China nine months and twenty-two days before.

The body was buried at the hermitage on March 17th amid scenes of great sorrow and emotion. It remained there for another nine months until December 11th, 1553, when it was again disinterred and placed in another casket, provided by Diogo Pereira, which was lined with damask and had a cover of brocade. The body was carried from Our Lady of the Mount, in a procession attended by most of the Portuguese nobility in Malacca, and put aboard a sloop, decorated with expensive rugs and a silken canopy, which brought the casket out to a ship belonging to one Lopo de Noronha, which was ready to sail to India.

Two members of the Society of Jesus escorted the body to Goa: one was Pêro de Alcaçova, the other was João de Tavora, who later taught in the Jesuit college at Évora.

On the voyage back to India, a distance of five hundred leagues from Malacca, some indisputable miracles were witnessed, as all the people on board the carrack later testified to the viceroy Dom Afonso de Noronha.

I won't bother to describe these miracles because they have already been widely reported and I don't want to waste time on things other people have already written about.

218 : *The reception accorded these holy remains in Goa.*

THE FOIST CARRYING THESE HOLY REMAINS FROM THE CARRACK to the city quays in Goa was received by Afonso de Noronha in his official capacity as viceroy, attended by footmen carrying silver maces. He was accompanied by all the Portuguese nobility from along the Indian coast and such a large crowd of ordinary people that four constables did well to clear a path for the coffin through the throng.

The cathedral chapter was there as well as the president and brothers of the Fraternity of Mercy, all wearing their finest vestments and carrying white candles and bearing a new coffin covered by a cloth of new brocade with fringes and trimmings of gold. However, it was finally decided to keep the remains in the coffin in which they had come from Malacca, rather than move them yet again.

Large numbers of priests and brothers from the Society of Jesus went aboard the foist when it had tied up at the quay and lifted the coffin which was lying on top of the awning amidships. Then a large group of orphan children from St Paul's College uncovered a crucifix and one of them began to chant the psalm, *Benedictus Dominus Deus Israel*. All the other children responded as one voice with such clarity and harmony and in such stirring piety that it made everybody's hair stand on end. The sighs and weeping were so widespread among that enormous gathering of Christians that the mere sight of the occasion would have been enough for any sinner to repent and change his ways.

All these people organized themselves into an orderly procession at the quay and then moved away, followed by the holy remains of Fr Francis. A large cloth of brocade had been placed over the top of the coffin and some people carried silver thuribles on either side of it, spreading the sweetest-smelling incense all around. The other casket, provided by the Fraternity of Mercy, was carried ahead of the procession towards the churchyard.

The burial in Goa of these holy remains that day was performed with so much ceremony and expense for the greater glory of God and His blessed servant, that the Hindu and even the Muslim inhabitants of Goa started putting their fingers in their mouths – which is a common gesture among them to express amazement.

When the procession entered the city gates it passed along the Rua Direita, the main street in Goa. For the occasion of the funeral the street was bedecked from top to bottom with very expensive rugs and silken cloth, all the windows were decorated and crowded with the nobility's wives and daughters, and below in the doorways there were all sorts of devices for spreading perfume and other sweet smells.

It was the same in all the other streets the procession passed through on its way to St Paul's College, and although the day was a Friday, a fast day, the college was ready to celebrate. All the altar-cloths were of brocade, all the candle-sticks and crucifixes were silver, and everything else had been prepared in a similar spirit.

When the procession arrived at the church the coffin was placed by the main altar beside the pulpit. Then a solemn Mass was celebrated: the priests wore vestments of brocade, there was a beautiful choir in attendance and all sorts of musical instruments, as befitted such a solemn occasion; however, there was no sermon, because it was getting late and the people were very eager to pay their respects to the holy body.

When the mass was finished, the coffin was opened for the people to see the body. They paid their respects with their eyes full of tears, but because there were so many people there and everybody was pushing forward to get a closer look at the body, the crush got to be so great that the railings inside the church, even though they were stout and well made, were forced out of the ground and smashed.

When the clergy saw that the commotion was getting worse and that they would have to do something about it, they closed the coffin and told the people they could see the body again at their leisure in the evening. Everybody left the church when they heard this but, on several occasions afterwards when the coffin was opened again, the crush of the crowd was still so great that women and children were shouting and panicking in fear of being trampled on and suffocated.

On the same day as the burial, António de Ferreira, a married soldier in Malacca, landed in Goa in the evening with some gifts of expensive cloth that had been sent by the Daimyo of Bungo to the viceroy. The gifts were accompanied by the following letter:

'To Afonso de Noronha, the Viceroy in Goa, the illustrious, powerful and wealthy master of the Indian coast, the amazing lion of the waves by virtue of his big ships and enormous guns:

'I Yakatawa, Daimyo of Bungo, Lord of Fakatawa, Yamaguchi and the land between the two seas, sovereign ruler of the small island kingdoms of Tosa, Shamanasheki and Miajima, wish to make it known to you that in the past I spoke with the Tenjiku-jiu Fr Francis about this new religion that he had been preaching to the people of Yamaguchi.

'I promised him in confidence that when he returned to Bungo I would receive from his hands the waters of holy baptism and a new, Christian name for myself, even though such an unusual step would shock my subjects and put me at loggerheads with them.

'He promised me in turn that, if God spared him, he would return to Japan quickly. Now, however, his absence has outlasted my hopes and I have sent this man to find out from Your Excellency and Fr Francis himself why his return has been delayed for so long.

'So I ask Your Excellency, whatever the circumstances may be, to beg him – since no worldly king can command him – to return quickly to Bungo with the first monsoon. His coming will do a great service to God and also renew my friendship with the great King of Portugal, so that our two lands may be united in love, and his subjects will be able to enter all the ports and rivers of Bungo exempt from duties and be able to drop anchor there as freely as if they were in Cochin or Goa.

'Your Excellency must advise me how best to serve your king in friendship, because I will act accordingly in the time it takes the sun to travel from morning to night.

'António de Ferreira will bring you some weapons that I used when I defeated the Lords of Fiunga and Shamanasheki. Wearing these arms, as on the day I fought with them, I promise obedience, through you as through an older brother, to that invincible king from the ends of the earth, the lord of the treasures of mighty Portugal.'

Don Afonso de Noronha read this letter and then gave it to Fr Belchior, General Superior of the Society of Jesus in the Far East, and said to him:

'Why don't you go to Japan as soon as you can? This mission would render a great service to God Almighty. You could take staff from St Paul's College with you.'

Fr Belchior thanked the viceroy profusely for the favour he was showing in proposing such a mission. He told the viceroy that since His Excellency had recommended and sanctioned it, he would start immediately to make arrangements to sail for Japan with the spring monsoons.

The viceroy praised Fr Belchior and thanked him for appreciating what a great service the mission would render to Our Lord and God.

219 : *The new mission sets sail for Japan. Delay in Malacca.*

FOURTEEN DAYS LATER, ON APRIL 16TH, 1554, FR BELCHIOR, GENERAL Superior of the Society of Jesus, left Goa aboard the carrack that was bringing Dom António de Noronha to take up his post as the new commander in Malacca in succession to Dom Alvaro de Athaide. Dom António was the son of the viceroy, Dom Afonso de Noronha, who had ordered Dom Alvaro to be arrested on charges of insubordination: during his time as commander in Malacca Dom Alvaro had ignored directives from the viceroy and committed other misdemeanours which I excuse myself from dealing with here because it would contribute nothing to my purpose.

The carrack reached Malacca on June 5th and Dom António was warmly welcomed and brought in a 'Te Deum' procession to the church of Our Lady of The Mount where mass was celebrated and a homily delivered.

When mass was over and the crowd came out of the church, which was around eleven o'clock, Gaspar Jorge, Chief Magistrate in the Far East, who was going to carry out the investigation into Dom Alvaro's conduct, ordered the alarm bells to be rung to gather everybody together. He announced to the crowd the brief he had been given by the viceroy and then produced a list of allegations and proceeded to question Dom Alvaro in detail about them. Two clerks kept a record of everything that was said and both records were then signed as being accurate by Dom Alvaro and the chief magistrate.

This all took a very long time but at the end of the cross-examination Dom Alvaro was stripped of his office, had all his property confiscated and was placed under arrest. The same was done to all the people who had supported Dom Alvaro when he imprisoned Gamboa, the Inspector of Merchandise, and when he disregarded his orders from the viceroy and all the other disgraceful things that he had done during his time in office.

These punishments were applied with such excessive rigour that most of the men involved fled to the neighbouring Moorish kingdoms – indeed so many of them fled that the Portuguese fort at Malacca was left undermanned and exposed, so that it could have been overrun and captured. However, Dom António, the new commander, handled the situation with great prudence: he granted a general pardon to everyone involved – with the exception of Dom Alvaro – although even so they only returned very reluctantly to Malacca.

These abuses, coupled with the crimes committed earlier by Dom Alvaro, had diminished the standing of Malacca. The council's authority was destroyed by the Chief Magistrate Gaspar Jorge's proclamations about its shameful conduct and some people were so startled and terrified by such goings-on that they abandoned their houses and merchandise and went to live among the Moors.

When this punishment was meted out to Dom Alvaro it was plain to see that Fr Francis' prediction had come true. He had told Fr João Soares that before too long Dom Alvaro would be brought low by troubles involving his honour, his wealth and his very life – now Dom Alvaro had lost his reputation and his property and it is well known that he died back in Portugal while he was free on bail in the course of facing charges brought against him by the crown prosecutors. The cause of his death was a large tumour that started on his neck and gradually ate away his insides, making the sight and the smell of him so unbearable that nobody could bring themselves to go near him.

I'll say no more about Dom Alvaro now other than that death came to him very quickly and that God alone understands the workings of His divine justice.

The trouble caused by Gaspar Jorge's excesses threw the whole of Malacca and the surrounding region into uproar – and it stopped Fr Belchior from sailing on to Japan that year, as he had planned. Instead, he was forced to stay over in Malacca for another ten months, until April, 1555.

All the while the chief magistrate, Gaspar Jorge, continued in his rigorous treatment of this one and that one, causing outrage throughout Malacca; besides all that, he was so sure of himself and the wide-ranging powers he had been given by the viceroy that he started to interfere in the business of Dom António, the new commander. Indeed, he usurped the commander's duties to such an extent that Dom António was commander in name only and little more than the overseer of the fort. This upset Dom António deeply but he endured the affront and hesitated to act.

The excesses and abuses of the chief magistrate involved a lot of disgraceful behaviour that I won't bother to discuss here because if I started I'd never get finished, but it lasted for more than four months until, one day, Dom António saw his opportunity finally to take the action it seems he had decided on much earlier. He had some hand-picked men seize Gaspar Jorge at the fort during a siesta and lock him up in a building.

The story goes that Gaspar Jorge was stripped naked, bound hand and foot with a rope, then whipped and tortured by having hot olive oil dripped down on to him until he was half-dead. Next they put chains on his feet, manacles on his hands and an iron collar round his neck and humiliated him by pulling out every single whisker on his face, besides committing many other cruelties against him, which was openly admitted at the time.

Such was the treatment that the miserable Gaspar Jorge – law graduate, Chief Magistrate of Portuguese Asia, Chief Benefactor of Orphan Children and the Deceased, Royal Inspector of Merchandise in Malacca and the Southern Region, to give him his official titles – such was the treatment he received from Dom António de Noronha, if all that is said about the affair is true.

When the monsoons came, Gaspar Jorge was sent back to Goa in irons to face serious charges. These were annulled by the court and instead a warrant was issued against Dom António himself. Dom Pedro de Mascarenhas, who at this time had succeeded Dom António's father as viceroy, ordered that Dom António be brought under arrest to Goa to answer allegations made by Gaspar Jorge and to explain his treatment of the chief magistrate.

Dom António promptly came to Goa, where the magistrates ordered him to answer the accusations against him within a period of three days. Dom António was by nature averse to all these duplicated and triplicated judicial procedures – he said Gaspar Jorge's lawyers were just using them to wear him down – and it seems that he didn't want to wait the full three days allowed by the court before answering the charges. However, within twenty-four hours Gaspar Jorge had gone where he would never bother anybody again – after he had been given a tasty bite at a banquet (according to the rumours). That put an end to the affair once and for all.

Dom António was cleared and freed to return to take up his command in Malacca again. He left Goa a month later but he hadn't been back in Malacca for more than two and a half months when he died of dysentery. And that was how all of unhappy Malacca's scandals and disturbances at that time were finally resolved.

When the monsoons started again Fr Belchior was able to continue his journey to Japan. He left Malacca on April 1st, 1555, aboard a Crown caravel that Dom António had provided for him, as directed by the viceroy.

□On their journey to Japan Fr Belchior and Pinto stopped at Patani to get provisions, avoiding with difficulty the ships of the King of Jantana who was raiding the coast with armed men. They visited the island of San-chuan off the Chinese coast, where Xavier had been buried, and there tended his tomb. On they sailed to the island of Lampakow. By then, however, the monsoon was over and the Portuguese vessels had been battered by heavy seas, so Pinto and Fr Belchior decided to stay on the island to await favourable winds.

At this point in the text, in a digression, Pinto gives a brief summary of the places where the Portuguese merchants had settlements before the Chinese gave them Macao in 1557. The islands of Ning-po and Lampakow and the port of Chincheo had small but flourishing Portuguese communities which had been destroyed because of the misdemeanour and the violences committed by some individual Portuguese. He tells us the incidents that led Ning-po to be razed to the ground by the Chinese in 1542. It was the greed and brutality of his compatriots that had caused such disasters.

During their stay in Lampakow, Fr Belchior and Pinto learned of an earthquake on the mainland and took this as a punishment inflicted by God on all sinners. The weather then relented, and the expedition to Japan continued.□

223 : *The mission arrives in Japan. I am sent ashore to meet the Daimyo of Bungo. The masque of the wooden hands.*

AS SOON AS A FAVOURABLE MONSOON ARRIVED WE SET SAIL FOR Japan, leaving Lampakow on May 7th, 1556, on board a carrack owned and captained by Dom Francisco Mascarenhas, nicknamed 'the Straw', who had been the senior officer in Lampakow that year.

We followed our course for fourteen days until we sighted the westernmost islands of Japan, lying in a latitude of 35° west-nor'-west of Tanegashima. Our pilot realized he had made a mistake and turned about and sailed south-east to round the point of Satamisaki, then followed the coast of Tanoura as far as the port of Hyuga. Here the compass showed the coast to be running northeast, and the currents were flowing to the north, so our pilot had lost his bearings altogether, but even when he discovered he had gone astray his sailor's pride would not allow him to admit it. Our intended destination was sixty leagues behind us and it was with more than enough trouble that we turned about into headwinds and finally made the port of Funai fifteen days later.

We were well and truly weary and both our lives and our merchandise had been put at risk because that whole coastal region was in revolt against our ally, the Daimyo of Bungo, and the people were staunch supporters of the religion that our priests had denounced there.

However, as I said, by the mercy of God we dropped anchor in the bay of Funai, which is the capital of Bungo and now the home of the largest and most vigorous Christian community in the whole of Japan.

It was agreed by most of the other Portuguese that I should be the one to go to the fort at Usuki where, we had been informed, the daimyo was staying. I had my fears about going ashore because of all the unrest in the country at the time; however, I was forced to give in because they were all such persuasive talkers.

I soon got myself ready and had four companions to go ashore with me. Dom Francisco de Mascarenhas gave me gifts worth five hundred cruzados for the daimyo and I then set out for the fort. I landed at the city quays and went straight to the house of the Kamsiu Andono, an admiral of the fleet and commander of the palace guard. He gave me a warm welcome which dispelled most of my fears.

I explained the purpose of our visit and asked him to arrange horses and an escort to bring me to see the daimyo. The kamsiu quickly got to work and provided me with far more men and horses than I had requested.

We set out from Funai and at nine o'clock the next morning we came to a place called Fingau, which is about a quarter of a league from the fort at Usuki. Through one of the Japanese escorts I told the oskim, the local commander, how I had got there and that I was part of an embassy from the Viceroy of the Portuguese Far East to the Daimyo of Bungo. I asked him to find out when the daimyo would want to meet me. The oskim replied straightaway through his son:

'Your arrival, and the arrival of all your companions, is most welcome. I have already sent a messenger to the daimyo who left with a large crowd of people for the island of Saiki yesterday to hunt and kill a gigantic fish, the likes of which we didn't know existed, which has come inshore from the middle of the ocean to feed on a huge shoal of little fish. Now they have it trapped in the bar-mouth and I'd say that the daimyo won't be back here today, unless he arrives after dark.

'Now, if I hear from the daimyo, I will send word to you straightaway. In the meantime I will arrange some good lodging where you can stay and relax and take it easy. You will be provided with everything you need because the King of Portugal himself should feel as much at home in Bungo as he would in his colonies of Malacca, Cochin and Goa!'

Then one of the kamsiu's men, who had been appointed for the task, brought us to a pagoda called Amidam-shu, where we were treated splendidly by the bonzes.

As soon as the daimyo received the news of my arrival he despatched three funces – which are small boats with sails and oars – from the island where they were hunting the great fish. On board one of the funces was one of the daimyo's ministers, one of his court favourites, called Oretandono, who came to the house where I was staying that afternoon.

After we had been introduced he told me why the daimyo had sent him and then took out a letter from inside his robe. He kissed the letter with all the ceremony and courtesy that these people habitually use and then handed it to me. The letter ran as follows:

'Sir, I have been informed of your safe arrival at Fingau but at the moment I am occupied with the sort of business I enjoy very much. However, let me assure you that I am so happy to hear of your arrival that if I had not already sworn to stay here until I have cornered and killed this enormous fish then I would go to meet you myself without delay.

'So now I beg you as a friend that, since I cannot go there to

266

meet you for the reasons I have mentioned, you should come here at once in the boats I have sent to bring you, because your arrival here, and the killing of this fish, will make my satisfaction complete.'

As soon as I had read the letter I set out with my companions, sailing in one funce with Oretandono while our slaves and the gifts for the daimyo came in the other two boats. These funces are very light and swift and in little more than an hour we had reached the island where the daimyo was hunting, which was two and a half leagues away from Fingau.

When we arrived there the daimyo and more than two hundred other men, armed with harpoons, were in sloops chasing a big whale that had followed an enormous shoal of fish into the shore. The whale was a novelty and a marvel to the Japanese, who had never seen the like of it before.

When the whale had finally been killed and dragged ashore the daimyo's pleasure was so great that all the local fishermen were freed from a tribute they had always had to pay to him and he also gave them titles of nobility; he increased the salaries of some of his favoured noblemen and he ordered the geishos, who are gentlemen-in-waiting, to be given one thousand taels of silver each (which is fifteen hundred cruzados).

So the daimyo received me with a broad smile on his face and then asked me detailed questions about all sorts of things. My answers to some of these questions were embroidered a little because I thought it was necessary for the sake of our reputation and to preserve the high esteem in which the Japanese had held Portugal up until then. At that time they thought the King of Portugal alone could truthfully call himself the King of the World, on account of his lands, his power and his treasure, which explains why our friendship was considered to be so important by the Daimyo of Bungo.

When the daimyo had finished with these questions he left this island of Saiki and returned to Usuki. He arrived there at one o'clock in the morning and was joyfully welcomed by his entire household with festivities and celebrations in the Japanese fashion, everyone congratulating him on such a glorious feat as the killing of that whale, attributing to him alone what other people had done – so my readers can see that this harmful vice of flattery is so natural a part of life in the palaces and courts of rulers that even among the pagan barbarians it has its due place.

The daimyo dismissed all his courtiers and attendants and dined in private with his wife and children; he didn't even want anyone there to wait on him because this banquet was laid on for him by his wife, but he did order all five of us Portuguese to be brought from the house of one of his treasurers where we were staying.

When we arrived the daimyo begged us, for the love we bore him, to eat in front of him using our hands, just as we did at home in our own country, because his wife would greatly enjoy seeing this. He ordered a meal to be prepared and platters of clean, well cooked delicacies were brought in by beautiful girls. We eagerly got stuck into everything they set before us but the comments and the teasing of the ladies-in-waiting and the mockery they made of us when they saw us eating with our hands were all far more enjoyable to the daimyo and his wife than any comedy that could have been performed for him. The Japanese use two small sticks to lift their food to their mouths and they regard it as the depth of piggery to eat with the hands as we do.

Then one of the daimyo's daughters, a beautiful girl of fourteen or fifteen, asked her mother's permission for six or seven of her friends to put on a little play about what they had just seen; her mother agreed after talking it over with the daimyo.

The girls went out into another room for a few minutes. In the meantime the ladies who remained enjoyed themselves immensely at our expense with all sorts of jokes and witticisms which shamed us all – especially my four companions, because all this was new to them and they didn't understand Japanese either, whereas I had seen one of these little plays performed during my first visit to Japan and had seen the way fun was made of the Portuguese in other places as well.

We were still sitting there feeling humiliated – although suffering it as best we could because we saw how much the daimyo and his wife were enjoying it – when the beautiful princess came back into the room dressed up to look the part of a Japanese merchant, with a sword embellished with gold stuck in her waistband. She knelt in front of her father with all due respect and said to him:

'O most powerful Daimyo and Lord, although this boldness of mine is deserving of a severe punishment for the way it closes the gap that God wants there to be between your greatness and my baseness, the necessity in which I find myself makes me ignore any restraints on my boldness.

'Lord, I am an old man now and have many children by my four wives. I am very poor indeed, but as a father I still desire to leave my children provided for. I asked my friends to help me and some of them gave me the money to invest in goods that, for my sins, I wasn't able to sell anywhere in Japan; so then I decided to exchange them for anything at all that I could get for them.

'I explained my situation to some of my friends in Kyoto, where I came from originally, and they assured me that you alone could help me in this.

'So I ask you now, Lord, to show respect for my white hairs and my old age, not forgetting all my children and my dire poverty, and I ask you to save me in my despair; to help me would be a great example of charity. You could also do a great favour to the Tenjiku-jius who have come in their great ship, because this merchandise of mine is something which would be more useful to them than to anyone else; it would help them with a great handicap under which they continually labour.'

While this speech was being delivered the daimyo and his wife could not contain their laughter at the sight of their beautiful young daughter done up as an old merchant, with so many white hairs, so many children and so much need.

When the daimyo was able to smother his laughter for a few moments he replied with all due solemnity:

'Bring your merchandise here to let me see it, and if it is the sort of thing the Tenjiku-jius could make use of I will ask them to buy it from you.'

His daughter gave a deep bow and then withdrew to the other room again. We were all so embarrassed by what we had seen so far and we didn't know what would be coming next!

We five Portuguese were the only men in the room besides the daimyo but there must have been more than sixty women there and they began to fidget, nudging each other with their elbows, and making a noise with their low, muffled laughter; however, this quietened down and the old merchant came back in to show some samples of his merchandise to the daimyo.

These samples were carried in by six beautiful young girls who were dressed in fine clothes as well, with golden swords and daggers stuck in their waistbands and serious expressions on

269

their faces. They were all daughters of leading courtiers that the daimyo's daughter had chosen herself to help her put on this entertainment for her mother and father. The six girls pretended to be the merchant's children and each one carried a parcel of green taffeta on her shoulders. They performed a delightful dance in the Japanese style accompanied by two harps and a mandolin and from time to time they sang verses like this in sweet voices that were a a delight to listen to:

'O powerful Lord of riches and might
for the sake of your name
keep our poverty in your sight!
We are wretches here
in a strange, strange land,
the people despise us
for our lack of a home;
despised and insulted
from morning 'til night!
For the sake of your name, Lord,
keep our poverty in your sight!'

They sang two or three more verses in this style – and in Japanese it seemed to be very well done – repeating at the end of each verse the refrain, 'For the sake of your name, keep our poverty in your sight!'

When the music and dancing was finished the girls knelt down in front of the daimyo and the old merchant, in another pleasant speech, thanked the daimyo for the favour he wanted to do them by letting them sell their goods.

Then the six girls unwrapped their parcels – and a great pile of wooden hands fell out onto the floor, just like the ones that are offered up to St Amaro here in Portugal!

The merchant remarked gracefully with well chosen words:

'Since nature subjects the Portuguese, for their sins, to such filthy wretchedness that their hands must forever be stinking of fish or meat or whatever else they eat with them, this consignment of wooden hands would be of great use to them because while their own hands are being washed, they will be able to eat with these wooden hands!'

The daimyo and his wife burst out laughing at this but when he saw how deeply ashamed we were he apologised:

'Please forgive us: my daughter saw how friendly I am with

you all and she did this just to amuse herself a little. You were only in it because you are like brothers to her.'

We replied:

'Your Excellency, the Lord our God will repay you for the honour and favour you have shown us by allowing us to be entertained by you here tonight, and we will make our great privilege known to the whole world for as long as we live.'

The daimyo and his wife and their daughter – still dressed in her merchant's clothes – thanked us for this sentiment in their usual elaborate, courteous fashion. Then the daughter herself said to us:

'If your God wishes to take me as his serving girl, I will put on better and more enjoyable plays than this one; but I'm sure that He won't forget about me anyway.'

When we heard this we all fell to our knees and kissed the hem of her kimono and told her:

'We place our hopes in God that one day you will become a Christian and then we may yet see you as the Queen of Portugal!'

And that set the girl and her mother off laughing uncontrollably again.

We took our leave of the daimyo then and went back to the house where we were staying. When it was morning the daimyo sent for us again and asked us in detail about the priests' mission, the viceroy's plans, his letter, our carrack and the goods we had brought with us to trade, and many other things that he wanted to know. The meeting lasted for more than four hours before he dismissed us, telling us that in six days' time he would be going to Funai and should bring the viceroy's letter to him there. He would also meet Fr Belchior and make arrangements about everything with us.

224 : The Daimyo of Bungo officially receives the embassy from the viceroy.

SIX DAYS LATER THE DAIMYO MOVED FROM THE FORT AT USUKI TO his palace at Funai accompanied by an enormous entourage including courtiers and a guard of six hundred foot-soldiers and two hundred horsemen in a magnificent display of majesty. When he arrived in Funai the people rejoiced and welcomed him with all sorts of festivities and costly entertainments peculiar to Japan, as the daimyo took up residence again in his imposing, sumptuous palace.

The next day he sent for me and told me to bring him the letter from the viceroy because he would deal with this first and then talk with Fr Belchior about the other matter.

I went straight back to my house to get everything ready and at two o'clock in the afternoon the 'kamsiu nafama', the military commander of Funai, and four leading courtiers with a large crowd of people in attendance arrived to escort me to the palace.

There were forty-one Portuguese in all and as we walked (which is the Japanese custom) to the palace with our escort we could see all the streets we passed along were clean and tidy but just so crowded that the 'noh-taranas', who are stewards with iron rods, had more than enough to do to clear a way through the crowd for us.

The gifts for the daimyo were carried by three Portuguese on horseback and a little way behind them came two beautiful caparisoned jennets carrying jousting weapons.

We entered the outer courtyard of the palace and found the daimyo seated there on a platform that had been built for such receptions. The entire court was in attendance and included ambassadors from Ryukyu, Cochin, the island of Tosa and Kyoto. Besides these, the enormous courtyard was taken up with more than a thousand musketeers and four hundred men on fine-looking, caparisoned horses, and then all the ordinary people who were far too numerous to count.

When our party reached the daimyo's platform we went through all the courtesies and ceremonies that are the usual formalities on such an occasion. Then I went up and offered him the letter from the viceroy. The daimyo stood up and took it from my hand, then sat down again and gave it to his 'kamsiu grito', who was like a secretary, who read the letter out in a voice loud enough for everybody to hear.

When the kamsiu grito had finished, the daimyo asked me a few questions about Europe, in the hearing of his courtiers and the other ambassadors, one of which was, just how many foot-soldiers and how many knights and cavalrymen could the King of Portugal put on to a battlefield?

I was afraid of lying to him and I confess I was too embarrassed to answer – but one of my companions who saw my embarassment took the matter in hand and told the daimyo that the King of Portugal could field somewhere between a hundred thousand and one hundred and twenty thousand men in all. This information astonished the daimyo immensely – and me even more so.

The daimyo appreciated the extravagant answer that this Portuguese had given him and he amused himself for more than half-an-hour putting questions to this man until the daimyo and everyone else present were so awed by the glories and grandeurs of Portugal that the daimyo declared:

'I swear by the laws of our faith that nothing would give me more pleasure than to meet the ruler of so great a kingdom full of these marvels that I've heard so much about, from the value of the king's treasure to the massive numbers of his ships on the sea. If I could meet such a king, I would die content!'

Before the daimyo took his leave of us he said to me:

'Whenever you are ready you can tell the priest to come and see me. He will find me here, ready to listen to him and anyone else he brings with him.

225 : *The daimyo's response to the embassy and to the Jesuit mission.*

WHEN I RETURNED TO THE HOUSE WHERE I WAS STAYING I GAVE AN account to Fr Belchior of the welcome I had received from the daimyo and everything else that had happened. I told him how eager the daimyo was to meet him and that I thought it would be a good idea – since the rest of the Portuguese were already gathered there, dressed for the occasion – to go to see the daimyo straight away. Fr Belchior and the other priests agreed with me, and he went to put on some robes and jewellery that would convey his standing and authority.

Fr Belchior left the church accompanied by our party of forty-one Portuguese. All of us were dressed in finery, with ruffs and thick golden chains across our breasts. There were also four little orphan boys from the Jesuit college in Goa, wearing cassocks and hats of white taffeta with crosses of red silk sewn on their chests. Brother João Fernandez was there to act as interpreter between Fr Belchior and the daimyo.

When we arrived in the outer courtyard of the palace, a handful of courtiers were waiting there for Fr Belchior. They welcomed him with a great show of courtesy and affection and then brought him to a room where the daimyo himself was waiting to meet him.

The daimyo's face was beaming with joy as he took Fr Belchior by the hand and said to him:

'Believe me, Father, that this day alone can I truly call my own on account of the great pleasure I have in seeing you standing here before me – it's as if I was looking again at blessed Father Francis himself, who was as dear to me as my own life.'

He led Fr Belchior away into another chamber that had been lavishly prepared and decorated and sat down with Fr Belchior beside him. He also made a great fuss of the four orphan boys who were a great novelty since no-one in Japan had ever seen any European children before.

Fr Belchior formally thanked the daimyo in the Japanese fashion (as he had been taught by Brother João Fernandez) for the great honour accorded to him, then they settled down to discuss the prime purpose of the visit, which was that the viceroy had sent Fr Belchior to serve the daimyo and to show him the one sure path to salvation.

The looks on his face and the nods of his head indicated that the daimyo was pleased to hear all this. Fr Belchior carried on with a pious speech in the manner of a sermon that had obviously been well-prepared, touching on everything that seemed appropriate in the circumstances. Then the daimyo replied:

'I don't know what words I should use to praise you, blessed Father. I have the greatest pleasure in seeing you here under my roof, and in everything that my ears have heard you speak about. However, I will make no decision just yet because of the unsettled situation here in Bungo that I'm sure you know about already; but I beg you sincerely, since it was God who brought you here, to rest yourself after the troubles you have endured for his sake.

'As regards the viceroy's reply to the letter I sent with António Ferreira, I won't go back on my offer. However, the time just isn't right at the moment because I am very much afraid that if my subjects saw any sign of a change in me at all, they would think that the warnings of the bonzes were accurate. Indeed, I am sure that the priests who have been here for a while already have made you aware of how much risk I am in here. In earlier upheavals I have lived with as much danger as any man has ever had to live with, and it was necessary for me to preserve my own life one morning by killing the thirteen leading noblemen in Bungo, along with sixteen thousand of their allies and followers, and almost as many again either escaped and fled into exile or else were banished by me. But if, at some future hour, God should give me what my soul has asked of him, then it would not involve very much for me to agree to what the viceroy has suggested in this letter.'

Fr Belchior replied:

'I am very pleased to hear your good intentions, but you should remember that life is not the gift of men, since all men are mortal, and if you should happen to die, God forbid, before you could put your intentions into effect – what will happen to your soul then?'

The daimyo smiled and said:

'God knows!'

Fr Belchior saw that, for the time being, the daimyo was not going to give him any better answer than soothing words and laudable sentiments with no intention of making a definite decision about this matter that was so important to Fr Belchior; so he played along and started talking about something else altogether that he knew the daimyo would enjoy talking about.

They spent a large part of the night talking about life in Portugal and the world in general, which were topics that fascinated the daimyo. Finally, the daimyo dismissed Fr Belchior with some well-chosen words, holding out the hope of his becoming a Christian sometime in the future, the reason for the delay being clear to everyone at the time.

The next evening, two hours after Vespers, Fr Belchior met the daimyo again, but apart from the warm welcome the daimyo gave him, as he always did, their talk never touched again on the matter of the mission. Instead, the daimyo left Funai and returned to the fort at Usuki, leaving a message for the priest that begged him to come to the palace again a few days later because the daimyo did so much enjoy talking with Fr Belchior about the majesty of God and the perfection of his holy law.

After two and a half months of this, during which the daimyo offered nothing more than a few vague promises about the mission, accompanied at times by a few blatant excuses, Fr Belchior was so dissatisfied that he decided it would be best to return to India, to fulfil his duties as Provincial General, and for other reasons as well. One of these reasons was a letter that one Guilherme Pereira brought to him from Malacca. The letter told him that one of his brothers, João Nunes, had left Portugal as the Papal appointee to the Patriarchate of Ethiopia. This gave Fr Belchior a jolt, because it occurred to him then that by going with his brother to Ethiopia he might reap a much better harvest than in Japan, where he was already disillusioned about the time and the effort he had wasted.

However, these worthy plans never bore fruit either, because at that time Ethiopia was ruled by the King of Zeila with the backing of the Turks, and the Prester John himself had retreated with a small band of followers to the mountains of Tigremahon, where he died of poisoning at the hands of the Moors. He was succeeded as ruler of the little part of the empire that remained intact by his eldest son, David, who appointed a man from Alexandria as his Patriarch. This man had been David's teacher but he was a schismatic and so hardened in the error of his ways that he openly preached that only those who followed the Coptic rite were true Christians, and not those who accepted the authority of the Pope.

So the five years of the governorships at Goa of Francisco Barreto and Dom Constantino de Braganza passed by and none of these plans had been put into effect, and the two Belchior brothers and priests had both died, one in Goa and the other in Cochin, without contributing anything more to the salvation of the Abyssinians – nor will it ever be achieved, I believe, unless Our Lord miraculously intervenes, because of Ethiopia's evil neighbours, the Turks, who control the Straits of Mecca.

When I saw the outcome of Fr Belchior's negotiations in Funai and saw that he was ready to return to the carrack for good, I went to Usuki to see the daimyo to ask him for his official reply to the viceroy's letter.

His reply was ready and he gave it to me straight away along with gifts for the viceroy that included some expensive weapons, two gold swords and one hundred fans from Ryukyu. The letter to the viceroy was as follows:

'My honourable Lord Viceroy, seated on the throne of those

276

who dispense justice through the authority of a royal sceptre, I, Yaretandono, Daimyo of Bungo, wish to make known to you that your ambassador, Fernão Mendes Pinto, came to me in the city of Funai with a letter from your lordship, and a gift of weapons and other items that pleased me very much and will be of use to me. I value the gifts very highly because they have come from the land of Tenjiku-jiu at the ends of the world where, through the authority of enormous fleets and vast armies of men from many different nations, the Crowned Lion of mighty Portugal rules, whose servant and vassal I pledge myself to be from this day onwards with all the loyalty of a friendship as sweet and true as the singing of a mermaid in a storm at sea.

'So I ask you as a favour that for as long as the sun keeps the purpose and path that God has set for it and the seas rise and fall on the sands of the beach, for just as long you will remember this homage that I send back with your ambassador to your King, my elder brother, out of respect for whom my obedience is unswerving, as I trust it always will be, and that these weapons I have sent him will be taken as a sign and a token of my pledge, as they would be between rulers in Japan.

'Issued from the fort at Usuki, on the ninth mamoco of the third moon in the thirty seventh year of my life.'

I returned with the letter and the gifts to the carrack which was anchored two leagues away in the port of Saiki. Fr Belchior was already on board, along with everyone else involved with the mission, and we set sail for Goa the following morning, 14th November 1556.

226 : *From India back to Portugal. My homecoming.*

WE SET SAIL FROM THE PORT OF SAIKI AHEAD OF NORTHERLY monsoons and reached Lampakow on the fourth of December, where we found six Portuguese carracks under the command of a merchant by the name of Francisco Martins, the agent for Francisco Barreto who was the successor to Dom Pedro de Mascarenhas as Governor of the Portuguese Colonies in the Far East.

By now the monsoon season was almost over, so our captain, Dom Francisco Mascarenhas, didn't stop over in Lampakow any longer than was necessary to take on provisions for the voyage back to India. We left Lampakow on the day after Christmas, 1556, and reached Goa on the sixteenth of February.

I immediately went to Francisco Barreto and informed him about the letter I had brought him from the Daimyo of Bungo. He told me to bring it to him the next day and when I returned I brought him the weapons and all the other gifts the daimyo had sent with me as well as the letter.

Barreto spent a long time reading and studying the letter, then he said to me:

'Believe me, in all honesty, these gifts you have brought give me more pleasure than the governorship itself! With these gifts and this letter from the Daimyo of Bungo I hope so to win the favour of our master, the king, that apart from the favour of God himself they should be enough to keep me out of the dungeons in Lisbon castle, where most of the other Governors of the Far East have had to pay for their sins on their return to Portugal!'

To show his satisfaction with my work and some appreciation of the expense I had incurred to my own pocket, Barreto offered me all sorts of gifts and money which I didn't want to accept then – but I gave him a detailed account, including named eye-witnesses, of how many times I had been taken prisoner and had my goods stolen while in the service of the king. At the time it seemed to me that such an authenticated account would be enough to guarantee that when I got back to Portugal I would not be denied what I reckoned was owed to me for my loyal service.

Barreto told me to write a full inventory of all that I had spent or lost; he appended it to my written evidence and then wrote a letter on my behalf to the king.

I was very pleased, reckoning that I would be more than recompensed for my services, and I was confident in my hopes and in the transparent justice that I considered to be on my side. I set sail for Portugal, so proud and pleased with all my pieces of paper that I thought they were the most valuable things I owned. I had convinced myself that the favours due to me wouldn't be delayed at all and that I would scarcely need even to ask for them.

I arrived safely in Lisbon, thanks be to God, on the 22nd of September, 1558, during the regency of Her Highness Queen Catherine, blessed be her memory. I brought her the letter from

Francisco Barreto and told her myself all the benefits to God and the Portuguese Crown that I thought would come of my mission to Japan.

The queen sent me to the official who deals with such claims. He had encouraging words and promises of satisfaction for me, which at the time I took to be pledges. He held on to my miserable pile of papers for four and a half years, at the end of which I had nothing to show for it but all the bother and nuisance I had experienced in acquiring the papers. Indeed, I'm tempted to say that this fruitless waiting was harder to bear than all the poverty, shipwreck and misery I had endured earlier in my life.

When I saw that all my past hardships and service were of as little benefit to me as my present petitioning, I decided to retire with the small amount I had brought back from the Far East, the little I had finally saved for myself from the midst of so much misfortune and hardship, all that was left to me of the wealth I had spent in the service of this country. Everything else I decided to leave to the workings of divine justice.

I acted quickly on my decision. What annoyed me was that I hadn't taken the step much sooner and thereby saved a good portion of my money from being wasted.

And that was the end of my twenty-one years in the service of my country. I had been captured twenty-one times and thirteen times sold as a slave, a victim of all the unfortunate circumstances that I have described at length in this account of my far-reaching travels.

But whatever the outcome has been, I still understand that being left without the rewards I strived for through so many hardships and so much service, that lack of reward has been ordained by divine providence as punishment for my sins, rather than being due to neglect on the part of anyone who has the responsibility of satisfying people like myself.

Let me say that I have always noticed in all the kings and queens of Portugal a pious, grateful zeal and a generous, magnanimous desire to reward not just the people who serve them well but even those who don't serve them at all. They are like a pure stream that quenches the thirst, although at times that stream flows along channels that do not distribute the water as well as they should do.

So my readers can clearly understand that if I (and others as neglected as myself) am left unrewarded for all the services I have rendered the Crown, then the blame lies with the channels and not with the stream itself; or rather, it is the working of divine justice, which cannot err and which orders all things for the best and as most befits us.

For all of which I give thanks continually to the King of Heaven who chose to work his holy will through me in this way – and I don't bother complaining about earthly kings, because I know I don't deserve any better on account of all my great sins.